The Open University

Faculty of
HEALTH
&
SOCIAL
CARE

K100

Understanding Health and
Social Care

Block 1
Who Cares?

The Open University, Walton Hall, Milton Keynes MK7 6AA

First published 1998. Second edition 1999. Third edition 2003.
Fourth edition 2005.

Designed, edited and typeset by The Open University

Printed in the United Kingdom by The Charlesworth Group, Wakefield

ISBN 0 7492 1337 X

For information on Open University courses and study packs write to the Information Assistant, School of Health and Social Care, The Open University, Walton Hall, Milton Keynes MK7 6YY, phone 01908 653743, or visit www.open.ac.uk/shsw

4.1

26998B/k100b1u1i4.1

K100 Course Team

Original production team

Andrew Northedge (Chair)
Jan Walmsley (Deputy Chair)
Margaret Allott
Tanya Hames (Course Secretary)
Joanna Bornat
Hilary Brown
Celia Davies
Roger Gomm
Sheila Peace
Martin Robb
Deborah Cooper (VQ Centre)

Jill Alger, Julie Fletcher (Editors); Janis Gilbert (Graphic Artist); Hannah Brunt, Rob Williams (Designers); Paul Smith (Librarian); Deborah Bywater (Project Control Assistant); Ann Carter (Print Buying Controller); Pam Berry (Text Processing Services); Mike Levers (Photographer); Vic Lockwood, Alison Tucker, Kathy Wilson (BBC Producers); Maggie Guillon (Cartoonist)

Staff tutors

Lindsay Brigham
Anne Fletcher
Carole Ulanowsky

External assessor

Professor Lesley Doyal, University of Bristol

This is the K100 core course team. Many other people also contributed to making the course and their names are given in the Introduction and Study Guide.

Revision team

Andrew Northedge (Chair)
Corinne Pennifold
Christine Wild (Course Team Assistant)
James Blewett
Joanna Bornat
Hilary Brown
Sue Cusworth
Celia Davies
Marion Dunlop
Pam Foley
Tom Heller
Vijay Patel
Sheila Peace
Lucy Rai
Marion Reichart
Angela Russell
Geraldine Lee-Treweek
Danielle Turney
Jan Walmsley
Jo Warner

Hannah Brunt (Designer); Deborah Bywater (Project Control);
Maggie Guillon (Cartoonist); Sarah Hack (Graphic Artist); Sharon
Kennedy (Compositor); Julie Fletcher and Denise Lulham (Editors)

External reviewers

Professor Gordon Grant, University of Sheffield; Mary McColgan,
University of Ulster; Nigel Porter, University of Portsmouth

External assessor

Professor Gordon Grant, University of Sheffield

Critical readers

Fiona Harkes; Sylvia Caveney; Gillian Thompson; Katy Sainsbury;
Eunice Lumsden; Lynne Fisher; Margaret Brown; Paula Faller

Contents

Study skills by Andrew Northedge

Introduction

Welcome to Block 1 of Understanding Health and Social Care. This block, entitled 'Who Cares?', introduces you to a range of people who *do* care and people who are cared for. By the time you have completed it we expect you to have an idea of the range of activities that go on under the name of care, and the sorts of people care concerns. We also hope that you will understand some debates about who should provide health and social care, how it should be organised, controlled and paid for, and that you will have an insight into the complexity of care and care relationships. You should be better equipped not only to understand health and social care, but also to improve your ability to do some practical things associated with care – for example, to develop approaches which respect the dignity of people who need care, to make use of a range of sources of help and information, and to develop effective working relationships.

Unit 1
Caring: A Family Affair?

Prepared for the course team by Jan Walmsley and Andrew Northedge
Updated by the authors with advice from Jo Warner

While you are working on Unit 1, you will need:

- Course Reader
- Offprints Book
- *The Good Study Guide*
- Audio Cassette 1, side 1
- Care Systems and Structures
- Wallchart

Contents

Introduction

Dream parents

Mummy would love me, daddy would too,
We'd go out on picnics or off to the zoo,
We would play in the park and feed the birds,
Listen to their songs and imagine their words.
My life would be full of joy and laughter,
All because they cared, my mother and father,
Never would I feel all cold and alone,
Knowing that I could always go home.
They would teach me to care and always to share,
And never to forget that they will always be there.
Love is eternal, it's my life long dream
Thank you for this, you're my king and my queen.

(Anastasia Lee-Harmony, 1996)

It may seem odd to start a course on Understanding Health and Social Care with a poem, but it's there as a reminder that ideas about care have deep emotional roots, and that those deep emotional roots are closely associated with ideas about families and what they should be like. In fact, the reality of Anastasia Lee-Harmony's own experience of family care is very different from that offered by the idealised 'dream parents' in the poem. We shall return to examine the ideal and the reality of family care later in Unit 1.

We all have some personal knowledge of care. Much of that knowledge comes from experience in families. Babies do not survive unless someone gives them at least a minimum of care. Most people also know what it is like to care for others – as a parent, a son or daughter, a brother or sister, a partner. Being cared for, or giving care, is as near as you can come to finding a universal experience. For almost everyone their first experience of being cared for is in the family, as an infant in the arms of a mother or a mother substitute. Families are the starting point for care. You might even go as far as to say that families exist *in order to* provide care. And many ideas about what care is or should be come from experiences of families, or beliefs about what families ought to be and how they should behave. Lee-Harmony's poem is an example.

In the main, society is organised as if the need for care is exceptional, exclusive to the very young, the very old, and adults who are ill or have a mental or physical impairment. Care is needed when we cannot function in daily life without the practical help of others. Babies need the fairly constant attention of an adult until they learn to eat, move around independently, follow 'rules' of day-to-day behaviour. At the other end of life also, as people cope with declining health, limited physical mobility and sometimes degeneration of mental capacities, help with daily living is needed. Most adults, however, are usually seen to need 'care' only if they are unusual in some way – if they experience illness, disease, or physical or mental impairments.

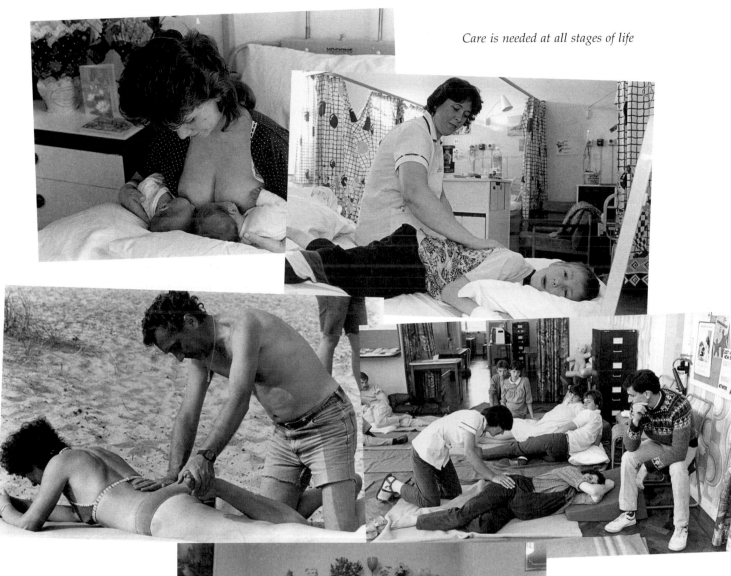

Care is needed at all stages of life

Yet most people, at all stages of life, need some kind of care – emotional support, advice, having their washing done, their food shopped for and cooked, their feet massaged, their bath run. This need for care is not usually met by any kind of specialist services. It is supplied by family, friends, lovers, workmates, neighbours. Take health care, for example. We usually think of health care as being supplied by paid professionals – doctors, nurses, chemists and the like. But in a book about women, health and the family, Hilary Graham argues that:

> For most of us it is families who meet our health needs in childhood; for warmth and shelter, for love and comfort. Families, too, serve as our first and most significant health teachers. In adulthood, most people create new families (often more than one) to support them 'in sickness and in health'. In old age, it is our family again who cares most and does most for us.
>
> (Graham, 1984, p. 17)

This first unit in Understanding Health and Social Care takes care in the family as its starting point because the overwhelming majority of care, including health care, is supplied in families, much of it in private, much of it unnoticed and unremarked upon. However, in the world of health and social care, that kind of care – all the work behind the scenes entailed in bringing up healthy children or maintaining adults – is not of interest until something goes wrong: the baby 'fails to thrive', the young child has 'special needs', the teenager becomes a drug addict, the parent 'can't cope'. So, although all the private activity is immensely important, it is not our main focus. Our focus is on those occasions when that privately supplied care is not enough, when the private care world of the family meets the public world of official statistics, care agencies and paid workers. The effect is to make 'care', that everyday word, into an official term, and to make the people who deliver that care in families into semi-official beings – 'informal carers'.

The idea that families do and should provide care sounds straightforward. But behind this apparently simple idea there are a number of unstated questions and some quite contentious political issues. Here are some of the questions we will be addressing in Unit 1.

Core questions

• Who are the carers within families?

• What do we mean by the word 'care'?

• What demands do care relationships place on people and when should the state play a part?

• How do families and caring fit together?

We approach these questions through a case study. The course contains a lot of case studies as they are a way of focusing on situations in detail. Many of the case studies, like the one in this unit, are about people's lives. Some case studies later in the course are also about organisations, for example Lennox Castle Hospital in Block 4.

Section 1
Who are informal carers?

Who are informal carers?

Section 1 explores what is meant by the term 'informal carer'. 'Informal carer' is an official term that is used when the private world of the family meets the public world of formalised care provision. To distinguish the care work that is done in families from the work done by paid workers – social workers, nurses, care assistants and the like – whose job is also related to care, the term 'informal carer' has been coined. But how do we actually know when someone is an informal carer, as opposed to being a mother, a daughter, a father or a son?

We approach this question through the first case study of the course, the Durrants.

1.1   Introducing the Durrants

> ### The Arthur and Lynne case study
>
> Unit 1 focuses on a single case study, about Arthur and Lynne Durrant. This enables us to explore some broad questions about care, carers and caring which might be quite boring and divorced from real life if they were presented in the abstract – as official statistics, extracts from White Papers or legislation.
>
> The case study is not 'typical'. In fact, it presents a fairly unusual situation, one which you might not recognise from your own experience. It was chosen *because* it is unusual. It raises important questions in a particularly challenging way – questions about who carries responsibility for caring for whom, why they carry that responsibility, the impact caring has on their lives, the support they get, and the support they might need.
>
> I use the case study to pose questions and test ideas which otherwise might be difficult to focus on. When you think about a practical situation in all its complexity questions acquire a sharper edge. If you work in a hospital, say, or with children, do not be put off by the differences. Think instead about the similarities – how you would answer the questions the unit explores in relation to Lynne and Arthur in a situation with which you are familiar.

The story is presented on Audio Cassette 1, side 1. It is based on a real-life incident, narrated during two long interviews about her life by the woman we have called Lynne Durrant. But it is not real life, because it has been dramatised to ensure no one can recognise the people or the places named, and some details have been changed. The drama introduces Lynne Durrant, a single woman in her forties, who lives with Arthur, her father. Arthur is insulin-dependent. He also depends on others to meet many of his physical needs. As a child Lynne was certified as being a 'mental defective' in the language of the time, and excluded from school on those grounds. Although she now has a job, she is still known to social services as a person with a learning disability. Lynne and Arthur live in a high-rise flat on a large estate built by the local authority in the 1960s. The estate is still largely in public ownership, known locally as council housing.

Activity 1   **Getting to know the case study**

Allow about 45 minutes for this activity

This activity is designed to get you familiar with the Durrants' case study. It is in two parts.

(a)   Read Chapter 4 in the Reader entitled 'Caring in families: a case study'. This tells you the basic story derived from research interviews with Lynne and Rita, her disability employment worker, whom she chose to have present at the interviews.

(b)   Play part 1 of Audio Cassette 1, side 1. Listen to it all through once. Make sure you have a broad idea of what's going on.

When you have done both, jot down some ideas about how the Durrant family compares with the family conjured up in the poem, 'Dream parents'.

Comment   The Durrant family is a long way from the idealised family in the 'Dream parents' poem. This points to the sheer diversity of families. I noted in particular that there is no mother in the Durrant family, nor are there any young children.

1.2 What is an informal carer?

Lynne is a daughter and a sister. Is she also an informal carer?

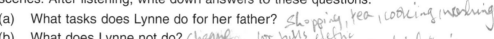

When the private world of family meets the public world of formalised care provision

Activity 2   **What Lynne does and does not do**

Allow about 15 minutes   Play the beginning of Audio Cassette 1 again, and listen to the first two scenes. After listening, write down answers to these questions:

(a)   What tasks does Lynne do for her father?   *Shopping, tea, cooking, washing*

(b)   What does Lynne not do?   *Cheque for bills electric*

(c)   How are the things she does not do different from those she does?   *Practical things done by her father*

(d)   Is Lynne rewarded for what she does for Arthur?   *bath Arthur*

Comment   (a)   I noted that Lynne mentions shopping, preparing and heating his meals, doing his washing. She pays the rent.

(b)   She does not wash him, assist him in going to the toilet, dress him or give him his injections.

(c)   I thought that washing, toileting and dressing are tasks which demand considerable physical closeness and touching. This she avoids. Giving him his medication also requires a degree of physical closeness, perhaps, but its main difference from the tasks Lynne does lies in the level of responsibility implied. If she got the medication wrong consistently, her father's condition might get worse, and that would have serious consequences. So the things she does not do differ from those she does in two ways:

• she does not do things which demand a lot of touching, physical closeness

• she does not do things which carry a high level of responsibility.

(d)   Lynne is not rewarded in any conventional sense. She is not paid. It is possible she gets some kind of emotional reward, although that is not immediately obvious.

Why does Lynne draw the line where she does? As far as physical closeness goes, if Lynne were to dress or wash Arthur it would be deviating from the normal rules which govern social behaviour. It is not common for women to touch men unless they are in a fairly intimate relationship – partners, lovers, mothers with young sons. To start taking her father to the toilet would mean breaking an unwritten social rule about how adults behave towards one another, specifically how adult daughters behave with their fathers. She would see his genitals, possibly have to wipe his bottom. When it comes to administering medication, we heard it is the community nurse's responsibility. The nurse might well be held responsible if anything went wrong.

So these are tasks Lynne does or does not do for Arthur. Is this what we mean by care? It is a long way from the sort of care the poem refers to. It is not care in the sense of an all-enveloping love and protection. But it is done without payment, and it involves doing things for a family member which need doing. In fact it is much more like the sort of caring assumed in policy documents and in research studies on health and social care.

In the box below is a list that two researchers drew up from census data of the sorts of task done by informal carers in the home.

What informal carers do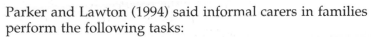

Parker and Lawton (1994) said informal carers in families perform the following tasks:

- personal services, like washing someone, or taking them to the toilet

- physical labour, like changing bedclothes, doing laundry, moving people who cannot move without assistance

- paperwork, like paying bills, writing letters

- practical assistance, like fetching prescriptions, shopping

- keeping people company

- taking people out

- giving medicine

- keeping people occupied.

So is Lynne what we might describe as an 'informal carer'? She does not call herself one, but nowadays we have government policy and legislation about carers. Is she the sort of person they mean? This is the subject of your next activity.

Activity 3   **Is Lynne a carer?**

Allow about 5 minutes   Compare the tasks Lynne does for Arthur with the list in the box. How many of them does she do? Which does she not do?

Comment   Lynne's contribution to her father's welfare includes physical labour, paying bills and practical assistance.

She does not do what Parker and Lawton term personal services, and expresses distaste at the prospect of even touching him. She does not give him medicine.

As far as we know she does not take him out, or keep him occupied, but she does keep him company to a limited extent, just by being around at times.

If she did not do any of these things, someone else would have to do them – possibly a paid carer. In these terms, Lynne probably is a carer although, as I noted earlier, she does not call herself one, and neither do other people in the drama. Arthur certainly does not see her as his carer. To him, she is his mentally handicapped daughter.

A definition of an informal carer

Are we any nearer to a definition of an informal carer which goes beyond the case study? Well, three points stand out so far. An informal carer:

1   performs certain services for someone else with whom they already have a relationship

2   is not paid a wage for those services

3   is responsible for the welfare of someone who needs extra help with daily living, because they are ill or otherwise disabled.

I can therefore put forward a definition of an informal carer as: *a person who takes unpaid responsibility for the physical and/or mental well-being of someone who cannot perform the tasks of daily living unaided, because of illness or disability.*

1.3 Defining terms

Why are we spending so much time and energy on asking whether Lynne is a carer? Does it matter? It would matter if Lynne wanted to apply for financial or practical support as a carer. It matters to budget holders to know how many people qualify, because carers are eligible for financial assistance. It would also matter to organisations which campaign for the needs of carers – organisations like the Carers National Association, Mencap, Age Concern or MIND. It would matter to a social worker making an assessment of the Durrants' situation.

A National Strategy for Carers

In 1999 the UK Department of Health published its National Strategy for Carers which recognised that 'Carers play a vital role – looking after those who are sick, disabled, vulnerable or frail. The government believes that caring is something which people do with pride. We value the work that carers do. So we are giving new support to carers. Carers care for those in need of care. We now need to care about the carers.' (Department of Health, 2000, p.11)

The Strategy has three elements:

*   Information, including a new charter laying down what help and support carers can expect.

*   Support – carers need to be involved in planning and providing services, and should be consulted.

*   Care – carers should have their own health needs met, should be able to expect services to help them care, and should be able to take a break.

The Strategy covers all four countries of the UK.

 (www.doh.gov.uk/carers.htm, accessed 15 May 2002)

Nowadays the internet is a major study resource. When you see this icon in the margin, it signals a website you might like to look up. Whether you do is entirely your choice. You can get along fine with K100 by simply sticking to the printed texts. These website links are there just in case you want to follow up a particular interest in a topic.

If we are to understand society we need to be as clear as we can be about the meaning of the words we use. When discussing something as complex and controversial as society and social policy, there are very few words whose definition is universally agreed. People alter definitions to develop new arguments. Although we are never likely to come to a watertight definition of any word – as the philosopher said, 'I know what a mountain is, but that doesn't mean I can define it' – understanding the different meanings words carry is something that merits attention.

My definition of an informal carer sounds fairly straightforward, but there are problems. Here I will consider four complications:

1   interdependence

2   duration and frequency

3   labelling

4   networks.

After considering these in turn, I will return to the definition and try it out in a different context.

Interdependence

The definition suggests that it is a simple matter to recognise the carer in a given situation. In some, perhaps most, care relationships this is true. However, the case of the Durrant family is complicated. Both Arthur and Lynne are included in categories often seen as needing the services of a carer – Lynne has a learning disability, Arthur's health is impaired by illness. But both have a claim to be seen as carers, too.

Activity 4   **Is Arthur a carer too?**

Allow about 5 minutes   What does Arthur do for Lynne? Does he do any of the things listed in the 'What informal carers do' box?

Comment   Arthur reminds Lynne that the rent is due, and writes out the cheque.

He gives her practical assistance. He manages her money. He gives her a shopping list and the cash to pay for the shopping.

He keeps her company – even though she says she doesn't want it! And he keeps her occupied, although in ways she resents.

The fact that Lynne believes she could very well do without Arthur's help does not change the fact that Arthur is also a carer in some of the ways identified in the 'What informal carers do' box. Indeed, he would probably recognise himself as a carer more readily than he would recognise Lynne.

On the basis of this example, it is possible to say that sometimes there is *interdependence* or reciprocity. People depend on one another, rather than one person always giving and the other always receiving care.

Duration and frequency

The second complication associated with identifying carers is related to how much caring they do and how often they do it. This aspect came to the fore when carers were first identified in the 1985 General Household Survey, an annual statistical survey carried out by the Office of

Population, Censuses and Surveys in the UK (Green, 1988). From answers to a question in the survey which asked if respondents took on 'extra responsibilities' for someone who was 'sick, handicapped or elderly', it emerged that there were over six million carers in the UK. This figure was estimated at 5.7 million in 2000 (Department of Health, 2000). In a UK population of 55 million people, that amounts to around one person in every 10.

With the Welfare State pronounced dead, TERESA HUNTER looks at the plight of a forgotten army

Sacrifice of the relatives left to cope as best they can

Stop for a moment and think of 20 people that you know of all ages. Are two of them informal carers?

This estimate has been modified by refining the category of carer to mean a person who *both* is the main carer *and* also spends 20 hours a week or more on caring. It is calculated that there were approximately 1.5 million people in this category in 1995 (Bytheway and Johnson, 1997).

Adding this requirement to the definition makes it easier to target services and support, but excludes many people who, like Lynne, do work of considerable importance but do not get recognition. Indeed, the Carers National Association, the main group campaigning for the needs of carers, resists this narrower definition, and still quotes the figure of seven million in its publicity and press releases.

Labelling

The term 'informal carer' is a label. It was coined to describe people who take on unpaid responsibility for the welfare of another person. It is a term which has meaning only when the public world of care provision comes into contact with the private world of the family where caring is a day-to-day, unremarked-upon activity, like reminding a young child to clean her teeth. Labelling yourself as an informal carer requires a major shift in the way you see yourself, a shift neither Arthur nor Lynne has made.

This is your first chance to use the K100 wallchart. Look at 1987 on the wallchart. Highlight 'Carers National Association' and write 'U1:19' next to it.

Activity 5   **Are you an informal carer?**

Allow about 5 minutes   Have you ever had 'extra responsibilities' for someone who cannot perform the tasks of daily living unaided, because of illness or disability? If so, did you call yourself an informal carer?

Comment   There is no way of knowing what your answer was. Perhaps you already
           saw yourself as a carer. Possibly you are now more likely to identify
           yourself as a carer than before you began to study this unit!

'Carer' is a word coined by professionals. It is a term that many
ordinary people who fit the definition, like Lynne, do not apply to
themselves. As Jill Pitkeathly, Director of the Carers National
Association, put it:

> *Most of Great Britain's six million carers do not know that they are carers
> – 'I'm not a carer, I'm a wife, a mother, a son'.*

> *(Pitkeathly, quoted in Burke and Signo, 1996, p. 24)*

It is sometimes quite hard to draw the line between what someone does
as a member of a family and what constitutes being a carer. The task of
recognising family carers has become more important as the importance
of the job they do has been recognised. Carers are entitled to have their
needs taken into account when decisions are made about what sort of
extra help families need in caring for someone who is disabled or frail
(see Section 3). Once they are identified, carers can be asked to take
responsibility for someone who needs care. Carers can claim certain
benefits like invalid care allowance, too. But to label yourself an
informal carer means taking on a new identity.

Networks

The fourth complication of my definition of a carer was networks. The
drive to recognise someone as an informal carer or main carer risks
leaving out of the picture other people who play an important part in
sustaining someone, but who are not the main carer. In Lynne's case, for
example, we heard that her boyfriend, Eddie, was an important figure.
If her needs for care were under the spotlight, would Eddie figure? He
probably does not count as a main carer, but without him her quality of
life would be impoverished.

So, although my definition may be helpful in pointing at what we are
talking about, it is a very general definition, and risks over-simplifying
what might be an extremely complex set of relationships: it may include
a lot of people in the category 'informal carer' who may prefer not to be
labelled in that way, and exclude others.

To explore these limitations further, I shall apply the definition to
another care situation.

1.4 Young carers

Who is left out of the definition of informal carer? At first sight, taking
account of the four complications noted above means that no one is left
out. The definition can embrace anyone who is taking unpaid
responsibility for the welfare of another person. Where do children and
young people come into this? Maybe in answering Activity 5 you
considered whether parenting young children makes you a carer.
Looking after young children is not usually seen as making someone a
carer. It is seen as mainly the private responsibility of families unless
social services or other agencies have cause for concern, or families
themselves ask for help. The public world which finds it necessary to
identify informal carers does not concern itself with healthy children,
although the parents of sick or disabled children do count. Informal
carers are recognised when someone of any age has exceptional needs
for care.

Now consider this scenario.

Katrina

Katrina's situation was reported in the weekly magazine *Community Care*. Katrina is 15 years old. She lives with her single mother and her younger brother and sister. Katrina's mother has agoraphobia – she is frightened to go out of the house, and subject to panic attacks. Much of the responsibility of care falls on Katrina – managing her mother's condition, taking her younger siblings to school and to evening activities, doing shopping and housework. She started to miss school because she had too much to do at home; then, she says, 'I missed so much I did not see any point in going back'. Katrina does not resent her responsibilities. She is proud of them, and the important contribution she makes. But, she says, it leads to friction: 'I often have arguments with my mum, usually over little things. I tell her I can't be an adult in the house, then be treated like a kid when I go out.'

(Adapted from Bond, 1995, p. 22)

Activity 6	**Is Katrina an informal carer?**
Allow about 5 minutes	Try out our definition of informal carer on Katrina. Is she an informal carer?

Comment   Katrina seems to deserve the title 'informal carer'. She is taking responsibility not only for her mother, but also for her younger siblings. She is not paid. And her mother is ill.

Katrina is by no means unique. In 2000 it was estimated that there were between 20,000 and 50,000 children who were carers (Department of Health, 2000), and the National Strategy for Carers made the needs of young carers a particular focus.

Yet for many years children and young people were omitted from considerations about informal carers. They did not figure in statistics, they were overlooked, unnoticed – and therefore unsupported. We will be examining why young carers (as carers under the age of 16 are called) became visible in the 1980s and 1990s later in the course. What we focus on here is some of the complexities of naming young carers, using the four complications of the definition identified earlier:

1   interdependence
2   duration and frequency
3   labelling
4   networks.

Interdependence

Although Katrina's mother depends on Katrina for some of her own needs and the needs of the younger children, she also cares for Katrina in that she is legally and financially responsible for her. She is also able to give love, advice and support. So it is a two-way relationship. Nevertheless, young carers challenge prevailing ideas about what children or young people do in families. There is apparently a 'role reversal' – as Katrina put it so neatly, her mum expected her to be an adult in the privacy of their own home, but a child in public. You might recognise parallels with Lynne Durrant here. Part of Lynne's frustration was that Arthur treated her as a child, while accepting and expecting an adult's contribution to his care and to the household finances.

As you saw in the case of the Durrants, both parties gave care as well as received it. In families with young carers, this is also likely to be the case.

Duration and frequency

We do not know if Katrina's caring responsibilities took up more than 20 hours per week. In a sense, though, whether they did or not is immaterial. What is important is that her schooling was adversely affected. We can speculate that, even if caring accounted for less than 20 hours per week, the emotional impact of being a young carer overflowed into a far larger proportion of her life.

Labelling

Official language about informal carers is at variance with the way we normally talk about family life. How many children or young people who care – for parents or other relatives – would spontaneously label themselves a 'young carer'? How many parents would describe their son or daughter in this way? How many people who frame census questions would have thought of including a question to find out, until 'young carer' became a category like 'disability' or 'age' that census takers consider important?

Labelling a child or a young person as a carer has an impact not only on their own identity, but also on that of the person they care for. Statistically speaking, this is usually a lone parent because otherwise a partner is likely to be the informal carer. But how does it feel as a parent to be designated as needing care from your child? Some disability activists argue that it is demeaning to disabled parents to be singled out in this way (Keith and Morris, 1994), and that it distorts the focus: support should be offered to the parent to function as a parent, not to the young person to function better as a young carer.

A particular issue when it comes to recognising young carers is fear – fear on the part of the adult that their child will be taken away so that they can enjoy a 'normal' childhood elsewhere, fear on the child's part that the relative they care for will be transferred to a home or a hospital. Despite the pressures young carers have to cope with, most seem to prefer that to the loss of their family. Indeed some, like Katrina, feel proud of what they do.

For all these reasons labelling a child as a young carer may be at variance with the way the family wants to present itself to the outside world.

Networks

The way Katrina's story is presented leaves out others who may be involved with the family. This is because the story was part of a campaign by *Community Care* magazine to highlight the plight of young carers. It made sense to emphasise Katrina's role and omit information which might detract from the impact of a single-issue campaign.

The discovery of young carers is an interesting example of what happens when the official spotlight is turned on a particular group in society. There have always been children and young people taking responsibility for other members of their families. Charles Dickens' novel *Little Dorrit*, written in 1855, was about what we might nowadays call a young carer. But once it becomes recognised that these are not just isolated examples and that young carers are a sizeable minority, pressure builds up to provide support for them. Katrina, for example, was put in touch with a new service for young carers set up by her local authority, a service that would have been unheard of only ten years earlier.

The purpose of this section was to explore how informal carers are defined, and the topic of young carers was introduced to illustrate the complexity of defining them. I therefore won't digress any further into discussion of how young carers get support. The important point is that using labels like 'informal' or 'young carers' changes the way we look at the world. Twenty years ago Katrina would have been seen as an aberration, a phenomenon which went against the grain. Now she is a young carer. Naming her as such opens the way to thinking about how she and others like her can get support. But it also closes off options. Seeing her as only a young carer, and her family only in that light, can also blinker us to the complexity and individuality of their situation.

1.5 Informal carers: summing up

Section 1 has explored what is meant by the term 'informal carer'. I have developed a definition of an informal carer and examined it in the context of two rather unusual family situations, the Durrants' and Katrina's. I have also noted some of the complications that trying to define and identify informal carers gives rise to.

I have not yet begun to address the difficult question of what label to give the people on the receiving end of care, people like Arthur or Katrina's mother. That is discussed in Section 2, and, as you will see, finding the right word for these people can be even more controversial than finding the right word for people who deliver care in families.

In the end, are definitions useful? The answer is, yes, they do have some uses. If you are not labelled as being in a category that is eligible for services, then you will not be provided with anything. Being called a young carer or an informal carer opens doors to resources of various kinds. But it can also distort a very complicated picture of relationships within families. So any definition needs to be used with caution. And, as the position of the Carers National Association shows (Section 1.3), claiming the right to impose your own definition is a part of public life. There will always be competing definitions of terms like informal carer, as long as they are in the public arena.

1.6 Introducing key points and study skills

At various places in each unit there will be key points boxes where we sum up the main ideas introduced so far. The first key points box follows. You can use it now to check that you have grasped the main ideas, and later, when you come to revise, the key points will remind you of the content.

Key points

- An informal carer is defined as a person who, without payment, does some tasks for someone (or some people) who are unable to do them for themselves.

- Informal carers care for people whose needs for help in daily living are seen to be greater than normal.

- Being a carer involves doing things for others on a regular basis. It can be a 24-hour commitment or it can be less intense.

- It is important to be able to identify carers if help and support are to be offered to them.

- Identifying carers can be difficult: many people who care for relatives do not see themselves as carers, and in some relationships identifying the carer is complicated because there is interdependence.

You will also find study skills boxes like the one below scattered throughout the course.

Study skills: Introduction to K100 study skills strand

You have just finished the first section of the first unit of K100. How do you feel about it? I hope it has been interesting and not difficult so far.

You are at the start of what should be a very stimulating nine months of study. But it's not likely to be all plain sailing. A lot of people find independent study through the OU an excellent way to learn – yet it takes a certain ability to plan sensibly, to find a way past obstacles, and to keep your spirits up when things aren't going as well as you had hoped. So that you can keep on top of your studies and get the most out of the course, we aim to help you develop a range of useful skills and strategies.

In the study skills boxes we shall:

- offer ideas and tips for the tasks you are currently working on

- suggest activities to help you experiment with different study techniques

- encourage you to think back over the studying you have just been doing in order to draw out general lessons for your future studies

- point you towards sections of the Set Book, *The Good Study Guide*, which are relevant to the issues you are exploring.

If you follow these guidelines, by the end of the course you will have read most of *The Good Study Guide*. But don't feel you have to wait for instructions: just dip into the book whenever you want guidance. It is designed to be read in that way. Use the index at the back to find whatever you are looking for. The combination of the study skills boxes and *The Good Study Guide* will give you a thorough introduction to all the skills you need for success on this and any future courses you may take.

Sometimes you may feel that stopping to read about study skills disrupts the flow of your studies. (Perhaps you feel that now.) However, you make more progress with your skills, and it is more interesting, if you work on them while you are in the middle of studying. In the long run it will save you time. It will also make your studies much more satisfying if you have a clear idea of what you are doing and a range of well-developed skills to draw on.

 Make a start now by turning to *The Good Study Guide* and reading Section 4 of Chapter 1 (pp. 14–18) on 'The challenge of studying'. (It should take about 10 minutes.)

Section 2
Care: a loaded word

'Care' is a loaded word. Care is not just about tender loving feelings, it is about work as well. Being seen as someone who needs care says something about a person – their competence, their position in society, their status. This section explores those meanings.

2.1 What do we mean by the word 'care'?

In the poem which opened the unit, care is a warm 'feel good' word, associated with what happens in nice families. But in the discussion of what a carer is in Section 1, it seemed that doing care was also hard work for Lynne and Katrina. Care is a familiar word, yet it isn't a word Lynne used about the work she does in the household. In fact, the only time the word passes her lips is when she mentions 'the home cares'. On the other hand, the paid staff in the drama refer to 'care packages', 'community care', 'care skills' and 'care needs'. 'Care' is a word that they use frequently.

So care has a variety of meanings. It is a technical term when used by professionals, and it denotes some kind of work. When it is used by ordinary people like Anastasia Lee-Harmony, it has something to do with love, emotion and protection. What *do* we mean when we use the word 'care'? This is the subject of the next activity, which involves doing some very basic research.

Activity 7   **What does 'care' mean?**

Allow about 30 minutes   At some point during this study week do some research about what care means. Ask as many people as possible to give you an instant one-word or one-phrase answer to the question, 'What do you understand by the word "care"?' After you have done this, add your own one-word or one-phrase answers.

If you cannot do this, look in newspapers or magazines, listen to the radio or watch TV, and make a list of ideas associated with care that you find.

Comment   I asked a range of people. These are some of the ideas they came up with:

loving	making a cake
cuddling	changing nappies
making phone calls	changing soiled bedding
healing	looking after people
doing things for other people	taking pains for
feeding someone	bothering about
cooking for my family	avoiding anger
affection	protection

To try to make sense of the jumble of ideas associated with care it is helpful to use some broader concepts. You have already encountered the idea that care is doing something for someone. We'll call this 'care work'. In this category we could put the following words from our list.

> **Care work**
>
> Doing things for other people; feeding someone; changing nappies; changing soiled bedding; looking after people.

These are like the tasks in the 'What informal carers do' box (Section 1). They fit one definition, drawn up to describe the sort of care nurses do: 'Doing for the patient [tasks] which if they were physically or mentally fit they would be able to do for themselves' (Henderson, 1960, p. 3).

Some of the other ideas could be described as expressions of love or affection.

> **Care – love or affection**
>
> Loving; cuddling; making phone calls; taking pains for; bothering about; protection.

But some things seem to come into both categories. 'Making a cake' for example, is both a task and, often, a way of expressing affection, as is 'cooking for my family'. In these cases, love or affection is expressed through doing something. This might also be true of 'healing' and 'protection'.

Broadly then, 'care' might mean both work and love. We can draw a distinction between:

- **work**: 'caring for' someone – undertaking the physical or 'tending' tasks they might need

and

- **love**: 'caring about' them – feeling affection, liking, love, wanting to protect.

Sometimes the two go together – people often express affection through doing things for other people.

Activity 8   **Categorising 'care'**

Allow about 5 minutes   Try putting the list of words and phrases you came up with into the two categories. Note any that do not seem to fit, and any that fit into both 'work' and 'love' boxes. As you work through the rest of Section 2, you may find that you can see where the strays go.

Comment   To return to the case study, does Lynne care for Arthur? She doesn't seem to care *about* her father much, does she? Although she is a daughter, and therefore might be expected to feel, at least, affection for her father, she appears to actively dislike and fear him. There are no expressions of affection or love, no cakes. Care as work – or care *for* him – is a different matter. To the extent that she performs some care work in the household, we might argue that Lynne is a carer, but not a very affectionate one!

Study skills: Studying actively

You have come across several activities now. How are you
approaching them? Do you stop to think and make notes? Do you
spend the amount of time suggested? Or are you tempted to skip
straight to the discussion after the activities?

As an adult student you are free to approach all parts of K100 as
you think best. In fact, to do well, it is important that you achieve a
sense of control over your own patterns of study. You need to be
able to think strategically and make your own choices about how
much time to give to the various elements of the course. But so
that you can allocate your time wisely, we should explain the
purpose of the activities.

The point of studying is to learn new ideas. That takes more than
just reading. It requires you to think for yourself as you go along.
Yet in your drive to get to the end of each week's study it is easy to
let the words of the course simply 'wash over you'. The activities
are there to engage your thoughts – to help you make connections
between your existing knowledge and experience and what you
are reading about.

To make proper use of the activities you need to have a pen and
notepad with you when you study. Writing down a few thoughts
of your own is the essence. It turns study from a mainly passive
process of 'soaking up' to an active process of 'making sense'. The
activities are very varied and some are quite challenging. But even
if you can't get fully to grips with some, just get *something* jotted
down before looking at our comments after the activity. Then you
can compare your own thoughts with our notes. Often our notes
will look quite different from yours. That doesn't matter. It is the
effort of concentration in jotting down your own notes – and the
stimulus to your thinking when you compare them with ours –
which help lodge new ideas in your head.

Your notes from activities can be a very useful resource when you
are writing assignments or revising for the exam. It's a good idea
to keep them all together in a folder. The activities are numbered,
which should help you keep your folder in order.

We give a rough time guide for each activity. It's up to you
whether you spend more or less time. But be wary of spending a
lot longer, or you may get thrown off schedule with your studies.

2.2 Care labels

Why is it important to explore the way language is used? Two reasons
were suggested in Section 1. Definitions are important so that services
and support can be targeted to where they are most needed. And words
carry several meanings. One course tester included as an example in her
answers to the activity about what care means:

> *'In care' means stigma for children and young people.*

This did not fit either of the definitions – care is work or care is love. So,
where does it fit? Being 'in care' is often assumed to be linked to being
from a 'problem family' or being a 'problem child'. So, although
intervention by services to rescue the child is meant to be a good thing,

children who have been in care often feel they have been given a label which says to the outside world 'this child does not come from a good home, this child is probably odd'. It can carry a negative message about them, in other words a stigma. If you know someone has been 'in care', you might be curious to know more or you might be prejudiced against them. In some circumstances, therefore, care can be a label just like the term 'carer'.

Take the case of Lynne Durrant. Lynne was labelled as someone in need of care. As a child, at the age of eight in 1956, she was certified as a 'mental defective'. This meant that two doctors were prepared to sign a form to say she was ineducable, unable to benefit from schooling, and therefore should be excluded from school. She went instead to an occupation centre run by the local authority for children who had been labelled as 'mentally defective'. The label defined Lynne as a particular sort of person, someone in need of care because it was thought that she would never be able to fend for herself as an independent adult. That label shaped Lynne's life to a great extent. She was excluded from school, never learnt to read or write, and got no educational qualifications. Little was expected of her. She did not try to get a job when she left the occupation centre. Instead she went to an adult training centre, another local authority service for people who had been labelled mental defective. Lynne's label defined her as eligible for special care provision. It both opened doors (to a sheltered life in the

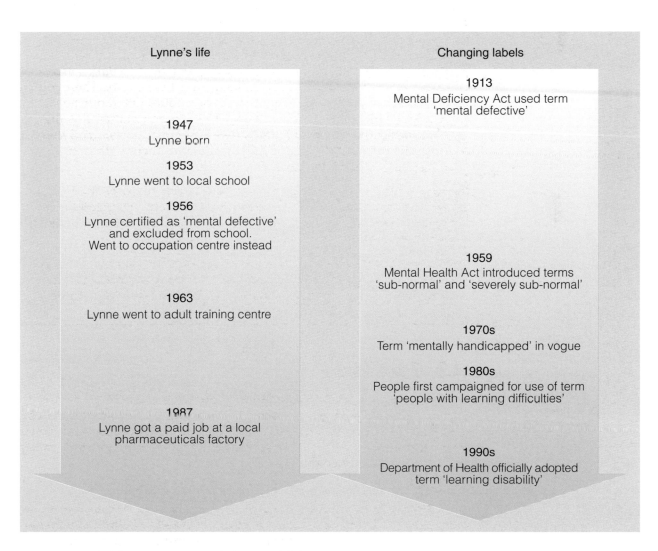

Lynne's life	Changing labels
	1913 Mental Deficiency Act used term 'mental defective'
1947 Lynne born	
1953 Lynne went to local school	
1956 Lynne certified as 'mental defective' and excluded from school. Went to occupation centre instead	
	1959 Mental Health Act introduced terms 'sub-normal' and 'severely sub-normal'
1963 Lynne went to adult training centre	
	1970s Term 'mentally handicapped' in vogue
	1980s People first campaigned for use of term 'people with learning difficulties'
1987 Lynne got a paid job at a local pharmaceuticals factory	
	1990s Department of Health officially adopted term 'learning disability'

Lynne Durrant's life – main events and changing labels

adult training centre and to certain financial benefits) and closed them (no job, no home of her own, no mature, long-term sexual relationship). Like 'carer', 'mental defective' was not a label Lynne applied to herself.

Times changed, and along with them the label that was applied to Lynne. She went through periods of being labelled 'sub-normal', then 'mentally handicapped', and finally, when I met her in 1992, she was introduced to me as 'a woman with learning disabilities'. In 35 years the official label applied to Lynne, and people like her, had changed at least four times, and that leaves aside the unofficial labels she was given by others – unflattering names like 'dumbo', 'spastic', 'mental', 'thicko'. However, it wasn't just a matter of the label changing. Life changed for Lynne, too. At the time you met her in the drama she had left the training centre and had a paid job alongside people who were not labelled. Although she still aspired to a home of her own, she had escaped at least some of the negative expectations that her label carried. In fact, she had acquired a new label – 'worker' – one which she *was* prepared to own.

Words and images

Words like 'mental defective' are also linked with images. Together, the words and the images make a powerful impact.

Activity 9   **Words and images**

Allow about 10 minutes   Look at the photographs of 'mental defectives' printed on this page. They are taken from a standard textbook entitled *Mental Deficiency* published in 1947 (Tredgold, 1947). What sort of 'care' do you think these people require?

Quadriplegic idiot

A group of Mongols

Epileptic ament with mania

Photographs of 'mental defectives' in a 1947 textbook

Comment   I found these images conjured up several types of care needs for me.

The first photograph is apparently taken in a hospital. The subject is naked, contorted and helpless. The photo suggests that he needs medical care to remedy the effects of the quadriplegia, and probably a good deal of looking after as he is apparently helpless.

The children in the second photograph (bottom left) are also in some kind of institution. They are wearing uniforms. At first sight I thought they were probably orphans, and would benefit from loving care in a family or family type environment, but the caption labels them as 'Mongols', not ordinary children.

The man in the third photograph is labelled as an 'epileptic ament'. He may be a nice chap, but he looks decidedly alarming, and the label is, to a contemporary reader, both mystifying and alienating. Maybe he needs a form of care which would stop him coming into contact with the public?

Together, the term 'mental defective' and the images appear to stress difference. The message is that these people are abnormal, not like us.

Of course, you would want to know more about all these individuals before making any pronouncements. But the point of the activity is to show that knowledge that they are mental defectives, combined with the images, tends to lead to a particular set of assumptions about who they are and what sort of care they might need.

Nowadays, as explained earlier, the term 'person with learning disabilities' has largely superseded the earlier labels – mental defectives, mentally handicapped, sub-normal. Along with the changing names come changing ideas about the care needs of people so labelled.

The photographs below conjure up very different images.

Sara

Shirley

Sara is a woman with learning disabilities but, unlike the people in the previous set of photographs, she is portrayed as active and competent, doing the ironing.

Although she is obviously disabled, Shirley is in her own home, an ordinary house, not an institution. She has aids to help her with daily living – a wheelchair and a communication device on the arm of the wheelchair. Probably she will need some special support, especially if the built environment is not wheelchair-accessible. But she looks far from being someone who needs either medical care or looking after.

The message from these words and images taken together emphasises what these people have in common with other people, what is shared, not what is different.

The photographs show contrasting images of people who are categorised as being in need of care.

- The mental defective label is linked to a highly medicalised form of care. These people, the photographs tell us, are very different from normal human beings. They need specialised medical treatment.
- The learning disability label linked with the more positive images presented here is associated with a rather different type of care – care as a helping hand with life, for people who are not so very different from the rest of humanity.

The changing images of people with learning disabilities shown in the photographs are not conclusive proof that changing labels brings changed realities for people like Lynne. But they do suggest that language both shapes attitudes and reflects changes in attitude.

Activity 10   **Changing labels**

Allow about 10 minutes   Another group of people whose labels have changed over the past century is people who experience mental illness. Make a list of labels for them that you can remember and then consider what the name changes say about them.

Comment   The broad range of terms has changed from 'lunatic' in nineteenth-century legislation through 'insane' or 'mad' to 'mentally ill' to 'people with mental illness' or 'people with mental health problems'. Particular medical conditions also give rise to labels – a 'schizophrenic', a 'manic depressive', a 'psychopath'. What is noticeable is that the range of terms moves from 'lunatic' which completely defines a person according to their mental state, rather like 'mental defective', to labels which put 'people' first and the condition second – like 'people with learning disabilities' or 'people with mental health problems'. The message is that they are not only 'a problem', they are also people. It is considered more humane to make the label secondary to what the person has in common with the rest of humanity.

labels change over time

Highlight 'Survivors Speak Out 1986' and write 'U1:32'.   Some people who have experienced care in mental health services go further than this. Survivors Speak Out is an organisation composed of 'users' of mental health services. They argue for the term 'survivor' because it switches the location of the problem from the person to the operation of the health and social care system itself.

Words can carry very different messages, and that is why the question of what people are called is often the subject of heated debate.

Ever-changing labels

By the time this course is a few years old, there will undoubtedly be new labels for people with learning disabilities and mental health problems, and other groups who are seen to need care. This is because new labels which are intended to de-stigmatise get contaminated by some of the negative attitudes attached to the condition they are describing. Thus 'sub-normal', introduced to replace 'mental defective' in the Mental Health Act 1959, is now seen as a term of abuse. At the time, however, it was seen as a way of emphasising a change in official policy away from segregated hospital care to care in the community. Even as we write, we are aware of controversy about the labels used to describe people with learning disabilities. People First, an organisation representing people with learning disabilities, prefers 'people with learning difficulties'. Rescare, an organisation representing parents who want to retain hospital care, prefers to use the term 'mentally handicapped', because they believe the terms 'learning disability' or 'learning difficulties' understate the very real needs for care and protection their sons and daughters have.

There will probably never be an end to this contest about the right terms to use. What is important is to be aware of the ideas they carry with them.

2.3 Care: a contested word

You have seen that the words used to label people who are seen as needing care can stigmatise them. By picking them out as unlike 'normal' people, people who do *not* need care, they can feel belittled, de-humanised and deprived of respect. But it is not just the labels like 'mentally handicapped', 'lunatic' or 'mentally ill' that are at issue. 'Care' as a word is itself under attack:

> *The terminology used in this area is important because it colours non disabled people's attitudes to disabled people and their needs ... 'Care' is being rejected by growing numbers of disabled people because it ... relates their needs to a society which treats them with compassion rather than to a society which respects their civil rights.*

(Kestenbaum, 1996, p. 6)

In other words, some disabled people are arguing that to be seen as a person in need of care is demeaning. It suggests dependence rather than interdependence, inequality rather than equality, charity not rights. They are saying that ideas about disabled people being citizens with basic rights, rather than pitiful objects of charity, need to be reflected in the language we use.

'Care' is a word that is not going to be abandoned overnight because some disabled people dislike it. It is enshrined in legislation, such as the National Health Service and Community Care Act 1990, the Carers (Recognition and Services) Act 1995, and in high profile government policy like the National Strategy for Carers. It is a word we will be coming back to time and again in the course. And it is hard to think of another word which does not have problems of its own. But it is important to remember, as you meet the term, that care is a word that carries a lot of meanings, and that for some people those meanings are negative.

Care: a cautious definition

We do need a definition of care for this course, just as we needed a definition of informal carer. So we propose that in the context of health and social care we define care as:

> *something that is needed when people cannot function in daily life without the practical help of others.*

But, as I have shown, care is a loaded word. It is both a word used by ordinary people to mean love, tenderness and protection, and a word used by professionals to mean a range of tasks concerned with supporting people who cannot function without the help of others. It is associated both with medical care and with support to people in living normal lives. And it is, to some people, a term which, when applied to them, is belittling and demeaning. It is a word we have to use, for lack of good alternatives. But it is a word to use with care!

Key points

- Care is both love and work – caring about and caring for. Sometimes the two go together, but this is not always the case.

- Labelling people as being in categories who need care is a way of targeting benefits and support: it can also lead to restricted opportunities and negative attitudes.

- Changing labels can help to change attitudes; and changing attitudes give rise to changes in language.

- For the purpose of K100 we have defined care as 'something that is needed when people cannot function in daily life without the practical help of others'. But this definition is not accepted by everyone.

Study skills: Time management

You have now completed two of the five sections of Unit 1. How are you doing for time? How long have you spent so far? Has it been one session of study, or several? What times of the day seem to work best for you? Will you be able to fit the rest of the unit in this week? Will you still have time for the short practice essay (TMA 07) in the Assignment Booklet (about 1 to 2 hours)?

These are challenging questions. Almost everyone finds time management difficult, especially when taking on something new. To get some ideas on fitting K100 into your week, have a look at *The Good Study Guide*, Section 2.3 of Chapter 2. Read pages 33 to 40. Then try setting yourself a target time for finishing Section 3 of this unit. Look in the unit contents list to see how many pages it is. Guess how many minutes you take per page, and see how close you are.

Section 3
Stresses and strains

Section 3 is about the stresses and strains of long-term family care relationships, what influences the nature of those relationships, and how the strains can be alleviated.

3.1 Caring: the human experience

What does caring actually mean for the people involved, the informal carers discussed in Section 1? There are some extremely graphic accounts of being a carer by those in the front line. Here are two of them.

Activity 11

Allow about 20 minutes

Accounts by daughters who care

Read the two extracts below. Both are by daughters caring for their infirm mothers and both appear in a book entitled *Caring*. Note down what they tell you about the experience of being an informal carer in a long-term relationship. Look for ideas which are common to both accounts, as well as differences.

The first extract is by Lilian McSweeney:

> *Anything I need to do for myself is done between calling in on mother ... summer or winter my last call is around 10 pm to check she hasn't fallen while using the toilet. When I say my day normally starts at 8 am, that wasn't so when she was bed-bound and incontinent. Then my day started at 5.30 am and I was there all day until midnight. Lifting and changing mother is extremely painful for me. I suffer with cervical spondylitis and I am advised not to lift or carry.*

> *My social life is practically non-existent. I know that life is passing me by and I cannot get a grip on it ... When I look to the future I quell the panic within. I am resigned to the fact that there is no way out. One day the caring will cease; the rigid routine will stop. What then? Will it be too late to build anything at all for myself? Will I be capable and able? If not, then who will care for the carer?*

> *(McSweeney, in Briggs and Oliver, 1985, pp. 103–104)*

The next extract is written by Val Hollinghurst. A fuller account appears in the Reader. She describes caring for her mother after she had a stroke:

> *One of the hardest problems I have found in caring for my mother has been in coming to terms with the tangled web of emotions: love, which naturally grows when you tend someone in need, mixed in with fear, resentment and guilt. Exhaustion and isolation made it difficult in the first stages to get anything in proportion or to make efforts to improve things.*

> *My family have learned from experience that I am a rotten nurse; but I am a good teacher, so why not try to teach my mother to care for herself. People do it for brain damaged babies, so it should be easier for an adult who only has to re-learn. The months of endless patient repetition that followed were exhausting ... But it was worth all the tears and anguish because as she learned to do more and more for herself, so her dignity as a human being returned. I can*

*think of nothing more important than human dignity. You hear of someone who does everything for their disabled relative and society praises them, rightly if they have reached the stage where any movement or decision is impossible, but most people can learn to do **something** for themselves and it would be cruel not to allow them to take choices even if that does involve risks. Life is a risky business after all ...*

The first time I plucked up courage to leave my mother at lunchtime, I stupidly left her a Thermos flask of hot food – not the most sensible thing for someone who could only use one hand. Yet when I rushed back, instead of disaster I was met by a triumphant mother who had gone out alone for the first time and got help from a neighbour. She wasn't going to miss her lunch! My mother's confidence grew from that day, and we both learnt from my mistake. We were becoming people in our own right instead of prisoners locked together in mutual dependency and resentment.

(Hollinghurst, in Briggs and Oliver, 1985, pp. 17–18; also in the Reader)

Comment

Here are some common features:

Caring is hard work. Both extracts say that caring is hard work. Lilian McSweeney emphasises the sheer physical strain involved in caring for her mother. Val Hollinghurst mentions exhaustion twice.

Caring restricts the lives of carers. Lilian McSweeney says 'my social life is practically non-existent'; she writes of 'life passing me by'; even when the caring stops there is nothing to look forward to. Val Hollinghurst's account is less graphic on this subject, but in describing the time when she left her mother she tells us that it was the first time she had done so. Her mother's welfare was uppermost in her mind, even when she was away from her.

Caring is emotionally intense. Lilian McSweeney speaks of quelling the panic within. Val Hollinghurst mentions 'the tangled web of emotions', singling out love, fear, resentment and guilt for special mention.

Caring requires skill. Lilian McSweeney learnt how to do new tasks such as lifting, while Val Hollinghurst transferred her existing skills as a teacher to a new situation.

Duty and commitment. Both daughters seem to take it for granted that caring for their mothers is something they just do. Neither feels it necessary to explain why they had this heavy responsibility for the well-being of another person. Because they are daughters, and because their mothers need care, they take it for granted that readers will understand that they are acting out of a sense of duty and commitment.

However:

The experience of caring varies from person to person. The messages from the two extracts are different. Lilian McSweeney emphasises the burdens of being a carer. Val Hollinghurst's account is as much about love and respect as it is about the hard work involved. What is most striking to me is that Val retained respect for her mother. She says the forced intimacy made love grow, and she appears to have gained genuine satisfaction from watching her mother regain dignity and a capacity for independence, and to know she has contributed to that.

Care is, as I said in Section 2, about work and love. The extracts show this mixture. It is important to recognise that caring is emotionally and physically taxing. It is equally important to hold on to the idea that caring is not just about burdens and sacrifice, it is also about love and respect. And some people actually enjoy it and find it rewarding. It is quite easy to lose sight of that while recognising the work care entails.

3.2 The knife incident

You have read about the strains of being a carer for two highly able-sounding women. So how does Lynne Durrant cope with the pressure? Not very well, it seems.

Activity 12

Allow about 20 minutes

The knife incident

Listen again to the last three scenes of the drama. Using what you have learnt about the strains of being a carer, write some notes on why you think Lynne brandished a knife at her father.

Comment

The knife incident happened on a Saturday night while Lynne was peeling the potatoes for the following week. She complained of being tired. We heard that the relationship with Arthur was strained and tense.

Arthur had been at home all day, alone as usual. He was quite probably frustrated with the limitations of his life. He couldn't even choose what to eat. At the time of the incident he was trying to get Lynne to say where she was going on Sunday. He seemed to be lonely and fed up.

The spark was when Lynne asked Arthur for spending money and refused to tell him why she wanted it. Perhaps it had something to do with her plans for Sunday.

Here are some of the ingredients of a long-term caring relationship that I noted from the two carers' accounts – physical exhaustion, restriction, emotional intensity. But Lynne lacked the teaching skills of Val Hollinghurst, and the existing relationship between her and Arthur exacerbated the situation. Not only was Lynne expected to bear the responsibility for her father's welfare, she was not even allowed the autonomy adulthood usually brings, like access to the money she had earned. No wonder her feelings boiled over.

In an ordinary family, this incident might have been a private affair. No harm actually befell Arthur, after all. As it is, the Durrants' family affairs are not a private matter; professionals are involved. Arthur told the home carer, and she told the social worker. You heard right at the end of the drama how Dev Sharma's efforts to at least talk to Lynne were thwarted by Arthur's taking his words and recycling them back to Lynne as if Dev Sharma were on his side in the argument, not a neutral person in a position to arbitrate. It was all made worse by Lynne's racist attitude to Dev, an issue we come back to in Unit 4

The knife incident reveals some of the difficulties of responding positively to a breakdown of long-term care relationships, particularly when those involved do not fall into neat categories recognised by care providers.

We don't know what the professionals actually did in response to this incident. But we can speculate on what might be done to help. This is what we look at next.

3.3 Supporting informal carers

Jane Lewis and Barbara Meredith (1988) did an in-depth research study of care relationships in families where they interviewed daughters who were caring for their mothers. They found that there were certain factors which made the caring task more or less difficult for the daughters:

1   relationships – especially the relationship they had with their mothers before they became carers

2   support – the amount and nature of support they received

3   choice – the amount of choice about becoming the carer.

Lewis and Meredith did not talk to the mothers – their interest was in what it is like for 'daughters who care', which is the title of the book they published from their research. However, these factors apply to people who are cared for as well as people who care. I shall explore these ideas in relation to both Arthur and Lynne.

Relationships

The existing relationship between mother and daughter was found by Lewis and Meredith to be a good predictor of how well people coped when one became a carer for the other.

Of course, in the case of the Durrants we are dealing with a father/daughter rather than a mother/daughter relationship. But it is worth considering the existing relationship between them. Arthur treated Lynne as if she were a child, or at best an adolescent. He controlled her money, he told her what to buy when she went shopping, he demanded that she tell him her whereabouts at all times, and he dismissed her expressed wishes to have a home of her own as 'nonsense'.

Could any of the paid workers involved have changed this? Dev tried but was thwarted by Arthur. However, if he could persevere and find a way for Arthur to relate to Lynne as an adult, it might help.

Support

Support is another key to workable care relationships. Where do carers get support? And what sort of support works?

To explore this issue I will again use the Durrants' situation. It is helpful here to distinguish between formal support, the kind provided by paid workers, and informal support, coming from friends and relations.

Formal support. Lynne has little direct support from the paid carers. She doesn't feel involved in their work and meets them rarely. So, although there is care for her father in essential tasks, there is little support from the staff for her. Even the social worker seems to Lynne to be on Arthur's side. He was caught up in the conflict between Lynne and Arthur and, because Arthur spoke to him first, apparently threatened her with being 'put away'. Rita is the only one who takes an interest in her, lends a helping hand, talks things through.

Informal support. Lynne is supported by her job. It gives her a routine, people to talk to, wages. In this respect, she is better off than Lilian McSweeney, who felt the future held nothing for her even when she stopped being a carer. Eddie is another important support. He takes Lynne for a meal; he helps to do the shopping; he is company for her. Perhaps in Lynne's eyes he is the most important support, albeit untrained and unpaid.

We need also to consider support for Arthur. There seems to be no one for him to talk to. Everyone does things for him, no one has the time or inclination to spend time with him. He appears to have no friends, no contact with neighbours, no hobbies except watching TV, nothing to do.

If support is what makes a family care relationship work, then the Durrants do not score very highly.

Activity 13   **Support for the Durrants**

Allow about 10 minutes   Jot down any ideas you can think of which might improve the support for the Durrants.

Comment   For Arthur, I thought of: a place in a day centre; a befriender from a voluntary organisation to talk to him and take him out; a holiday away from it all; talking books or newspapers; contact with his old workplace so that he can renew old acquaintanceships.

For Lynne, I wondered about: a holiday, possibly with Eddie; a designated social worker – not the same one as Arthur has; time on her own at home if Arthur has other places to go; training for staff to take her into account. Perhaps the ideal would be a home of her own, near Arthur and her job, where she could carry on supporting him in a less intensive situation.

One of the K100 course testers suggested simply asking them.

A day centre for Arthur?

In fact, the law now recognises that carers may have needs of their own which are not the same as those of the people they care for (see the box overleaf).

Carers (Recognition and Services) Act 1995

In 1995 the needs of informal carers were officially recognised for the first time in law through the Carers (Recognition and Services) Act. The Act lays down that carers are entitled to have their own needs assessed separately from those of the person they care for. The cartoon below is how a Carers National Association leaflet described the Act for carers.

Social workers have to take into account what carers say when deciding what help to offer – but taking into account is not the same as having a legal obligation to provide. (See Care Systems and Structures, Figure 2.)

Subsequently the National Strategy for Carers (1999) gave the needs of carers an even higher profile. Carers are still often isolated and disadvantaged, but their contribution has been acknowledged more fully than it was in the past.

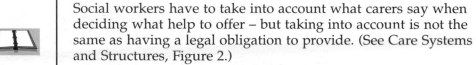

You are a carer if you care for a relative, friend or neighbour.

Social services will need to come round and see what your circumstances are and decide whether you can get help from the council. This is called a **needs assessment**.

The new Carers Act means that social services have to take into account what you say when they are deciding what help to offer you.

A new Act, called the Carers Act, can help you. Social services departments may be able to arrange for services such as meals on wheels, help in the home or a break for you both.

You can ask for your own assessment under the Carers Act when your relative is being assessed. If the situation has changed recently and you need more help in order to cope, ask for a re-assessment.

Social services may be able to offer you a break from your caring duties such as day/night sitting services or respite care in a residential home.

Carers National Association publicity leaflet about Carers (Recognition and Services) Act 1995

Some of these solutions might help both Lynne and Arthur by giving them a break from one another. Most are fairly inexpensive and might arise from a separate carer's assessment under the Carers (Recognition and Services) Act – if Lynne were seen as an informal carer.

Choice

What about choice? Neither Lynne nor Arthur actively chose to be in this situation. They slipped into it, as their circumstances altered. Why then did they find themselves in this unwanted position? Here are some explanations.

The job of caring traditionally fell on a single woman living at home with her parents

A single woman at home. Lynne was the one left at home when everyone else had left. Her mother had died. Her sister had married and was living in distant Yorkshire. Traditionally, say Lewis and Meredith, the job of caring for an elderly relative fell on an unmarried daughter. Lynne had no other caring obligations for husband or children. Lewis and Meredith say, 'Inevitably, women who always lived with their mothers "drifted" into caring for them, whereas those who had moved away from home to work or marry were usually faced with a conscious decision about caring' (1988, p. 23). Of course, this is not true in all cultures. In Asian families, it is often the *daughter-in-law* who takes on caring responsibilities.

Caring is women's work. Lynne is a woman. Women care for others. For a long time in the study of caring in families it was thought that most unpaid caring fell on female relatives (Equal Opportunities Commission, 1980, 1982; MacRae, 1995). In the light of more detailed examination of the General Household Survey data (see Section 1), doubt has been cast on this assertion. Men are particularly likely to care for their wives (Fisher, 1994). But, as you will find as you work through this course, there are very few facts about social life that are not disputed. It is still the case that, where a young person becomes a carer for an older relative, women are more likely to be in the role than men. These expectations of women relatives are reinforced by the opinions of friends, neighbours and others. Rita's speech about the importance of Lynne's paying back what her father had given her when she was little put these ideas neatly. If there had been no woman to care, Arthur might have been offered other choices.

> **Men carers: facts and figures**
>
> There is a wealth of information about how many carers there are, who they care for, and their circumstances and needs – the product of many research studies and statistical surveys carried out since around 1980. However, because it is hard to define carers (as discussed in Section 1) the facts and figures do not always add up. Here are some figures, to be treated with caution.

In 2000 there were estimated to be approximately 5.7 million carers in the UK (National Strategy for Carers, 2000). Of these, 2.4 million, or 42 per cent, were men.

The major contribution of male carers is care of their wives. Several research studies show that about 50 per cent of older people with significant impairments are cared for by their spouses, and these are divided roughly equally between men and women (quoted in Fisher, 1994).

It is also worth noting here that older people do not only receive care – they are also major givers of care. Twenty seven per cent of Britain's carers are over 65 (National Strategy for Carers, 2000).

Poverty and economic dependence. We know that money was a big issue in the Durrant family. It was Lynne's request for 'pocket money' that triggered the knife incident. Lynne is poor. Although she has a wage, it is low, and her father takes control of most of it. She is not in a position to pay for extra help or buy her own home. Who would give Lynne a mortgage? In effect, she is dependent on her father to provide a roof over her head.

Lewis and Meredith found that economic necessity was often a factor in 'choosing' to become a carer; but that the demands of caring then ensured that the carer would not become financially independent, because they limited her ability to obtain well-paid employment.

Other social factors. Lynne is a woman with learning difficulties. She is not assertive, or well informed, or well connected to people who would give her advice and help her manage the system. She seems to know what she wants, or at least what she does not want, but feels powerless to do anything to change her situation for the better.

Although the Durrants are an unusual family in many respects, their situation highlights some important issues which apply to many carers. Families are not always the haven of loving feelings, respect and dignity that they are often assumed to be, and informal carers do need support.

3.4 The other side of the relationship: what is it like to be cared for?

So far, I have focused largely on the carer's perspective. But in any care relationship there are at least two people involved. How does it feel to be on the receiving end?

In fact, much less is known about the care recipients' point of view. We do not even have a convenient label to give them. Because informal carers have become part of the machinery of care provision, their situation has received far more attention.

Let's think about Arthur. We will need to use some imagination because he is not articulate about his feelings.

Lack of control

Kate Cooney, a 31-year-old woman, disabled with rheumatoid arthritis, wrote this description of being dependent on a relative for basic daily needs:

> *No, it's not easy being cared for. It's not just the messy bits. It's no longer being able to nick a chocolate biscuit out of the fridge, or experiment with*

make up, or grab just the right scarf to set off your jumper as you rush out of the door. Always, always, you have to ask.

Your carer has to run part of your body for you. If you insist it is run exactly the way you would have run it, you would be ridiculously demanding. But it still hurts to let go, and it's still hard getting used to the new circumscribed you – should I ask for that or shouldn't I?

(Quoted in Bornat et al., 1993, p. 89)

This is the other side of the coin. Is it what Lilian McSweeney's or Val Hollinghurst's mother would have said if anyone had taken the trouble to ask them?

It is hard to imagine Arthur spelling his feelings out as clearly. But we might interpret some of his *actions* as a protest against helplessness and frustration.

Feeling a burden

Arthur cannot pay Lynne, or anyone else, back for the help he gets. Many relationships depend upon a sort of social exchange – give and take. It is not easy for someone in Arthur's position to meet this unspoken expectation, although he might see himself as 'in credit' for all he has given Lynne in the past.

Fear of violence or abuse

Lynne threatened her father with a knife. He, in his wheelchair, out of reach of a telephone, out of earshot of neighbours, might have felt really frightened. Imagine it – enclosed within the four walls of your own home, dependent on another person for all your needs, and that person is, or becomes, violent. It is the stuff of nightmares. This happened to Vicky, a disabled woman interviewed by Jenny Morris for her book *Independent Lives*. Vicky fell in love with another woman, Lorraine, and they set up home together, with Lorraine responsible for all Vicky's personal assistance. Vicky describes an incident:

One night she was putting me to bed. When I lie on my back, my arms are up by my ears, they don't lie flat at my side and I have to have two pillows under my legs to be comfortable and while she was doing this she took up a pillow and held it over my face. And we weren't even having an argument. You know, when you're past that stage of holding your breath, you know, when you would take a gasp of breath, it was past that stage. And when she took it off I tried not to gasp, and there I was, she lifted it slightly and then she did it again hard. And then she took it off and carried on quite normally putting me to bed.

(Quoted in Morris, 1993, p. 84)

Later, when she plucked up the courage to ask Lorraine why she had tried to murder her, Lorraine said, 'I thought it was what you wanted'.

Leaving care to families *can* leave people quite vulnerable. Our nearest and dearest are not always well intentioned. But abuse is hard to find out about because it is so private, and many of those likely to be victims are exceptionally powerless – small children, older people with dementia, adults with severe learning disabilities. Abuse in care relationships is explored in more detail in Block 5.

Poverty

Like Lynne, Arthur is poor. He had been a factory worker but now he has only state benefits to rely on. The flat has been partially adapted for him: he has a hoist to enable him to get into bed unaided, but there is no shower and he cannot use a bath without help. The flat is on the fifth floor, and lifts are frequently out of order. The estate where they live is notorious for vandalism and worse. He does not dare to go out in his wheelchair. You will read in Block 2 about the difference the physical environment can make to the lives of people in apparently dependent positions. How different might things be if Arthur had money to pay for a care environment of his own choosing.

The estate where the Durrants live was notorious for vandalism and worse

Choice

How much choice does Arthur have in the situation? Who says he's better off in his own home? Has anyone ever asked him or taken the trouble to explore alternatives? Arthur has little idea of how care services work, who to go to if he is unhappy with his care or carers, what alternatives might be on offer.

In fact, although it is often assumed that families are the best people to care for older people, several research studies suggest that, when they have extensive care needs, older people themselves increasingly prefer the support of professional carers (Biggs, 1994, p. 126).

Stresses and strains affect those people who need care as well as those who give it. It is not only carers who may be adversely affected by the prevailing belief that families are the best providers of care: those on the receiving end may be equally disadvantaged.

3.5 Family duties and obligations

In this section, I have examined some of the strains care arrangements between family members can generate. I have also touched on some factors which can make those arrangements more or less successful and enjoyable for those involved. I have not yet questioned where the feeling of duty comes from. What is it that made this woman caring for her husband say:

I feel under pressure from him, from the family, from everyone. Who else will do it? If I fall ill, God knows what will happen.

(Quoted in Allen et al., 1992, p. 27)

We can examine this question by thinking about what Lil Durrant (Lynne's mother) said to the social worker who visited her when she first knew she had cancer. He was trying to get her to think about the future if, as seemed likely, her illness progressed. Here is how Lil described her life with Lynne:

I never go out and leave her, no, not ever. She would open the door to anyone who knocked. She never goes out anywhere on her own. I take her to her club on Monday evenings, and the transport picks her up to take her to the Centre every day, and brings her back to the door in the afternoons. I'm always here when she comes home. I fit my outings in around her. Ooh, no, she doesn't do any cooking. She makes a cup of tea for me sometimes, that's all she does. I wouldn't let her put a gas stove on anyway.

I wouldn't want her to go to one of those places when I can't look after her. She likes her own company. She wouldn't like to live with lots of people, all the noise. I went to one once. They have to do their own washing. She's never had to do her own washing, never. And I'd worry about, with men, you know. They might take advantage. Of course, she can't have children since that operation she had, but it wouldn't be right, would it? I want her to be cared for properly. I can still do that.

Lil didn't seem to resent her continuing lifelong commitment to what she saw as Lynne's welfare. Indeed, she said she wouldn't want it otherwise, commenting 'we're a very happy little family'. There is no mention of stresses and strains.

Activity 14   **Understanding Lil Durrant**

Allow about 10 minutes   Try to put yourself in Lil's shoes. Why do you think she saw the world like that? Make a few notes before you read on.

Comment   Perhaps the first thing you thought of was that she loved Lynne and wanted the best for her. As a mother, she was the person who ought to care for her. No one else would care for Lynne as well as she could. She felt that Lynne had particular care needs – to have her washing done, not to do her own cooking. She was worried about Lynne getting into a sexual relationship, and that Lynne's own preference to have time on her own in peace and quiet would not be met in 'one of those places'.

How much information did Lil have on alternatives? No one mentioned Lynne living independently in her own flat, which we now know is what Lynne herself wants. Lil based her dislike of residential care on one visit to what was, presumably, a large hostel. Maybe this was an inadequate basis for a decision, although understandable.

Lil wanted to take care of her nearest and dearest. This position is often reinforced by friends and neighbours. One woman interviewed in Lewis and Meredith's research study commented on the behaviour of the daughter of an elderly neighbour who showed no signs of taking her in: 'I'd be ashamed. It's a disgrace. We all think in the road it's a disgrace' (quoted in Lewis and Meredith, 1988, p. 23).

Finally, we should not discount personal preference and emotional needs. Although Lil did not say so in so many words, she probably gained something from Lynne's continued presence at home – a sense of identity, of being needed perhaps, affection for and from Lynne, companionship, a structure to her daily life. And perhaps Lynne's benefits helped financially. Would the family have lost income from, say, attendance allowance, if Lynne went to live elsewhere?

The Durrants are, as I said earlier, an unusual family. But what we can extract from this story is that some informal carers gain a strong identity from their role and are quite reluctant to relinquish it. Although there is a considerable amount of public support for carers' apparent unselfishness, the reality was that Lil's wish to protect and care for her daughter inhibited Lynne from taking responsibility for herself and developing her own lifestyle. This is not unique to Lynne. Even people who appear to be quite dependent on others may actually welcome the opportunity to make alternative choices.

The belief that families ought to care, that there is something morally superior about families who care for their own, is strongly held. It is reinforced in legislation such as the Children Act 1989, which emphasises the obligation of parents to care for their children. It does not always represent what people as individuals want, although it does coincide with the government's agenda of reducing expenditure on care. Sections 4 and 5 will explore where these ideas come from in more detail.

Key points

- Care relationships can be intensely demanding and stressful.

- Feelings about being in care relationships vary. Some carers stress the rewards of caring (love), others the stresses and sense of burden (work). It is usually a mixture of both.

- Support, choice, an adequate income and a well-adapted environment can make the experience more tolerable for both parties in the relationship.

- The sense of a duty to care for relatives is often a motivating factor for unpaid carers. In part, it comes from lack of knowledge or access to alternatives; it is also seen as morally right.

Study skills: Time management revisited

Did you reach your target time for Section 3? Did the activities hold you up longer than you had anticipated? Do you need to readjust your strategy for managing time? Perhaps it would be worth looking back at pages 33 to 40 of *The Good Study Guide* and re-examining your strategy.

At least in Section 3 you did not have any reading besides what is in the unit, whereas in Section 4 you will find that there *is* extra reading. Try to notice how much this adds to your study time. However, the point is not that you need to be able to estimate time precisely, or that you become obsessed with achieving targets. Rather it is to become aware of study time as something you need to manage – to get a feel for what kinds of work use up most time and where you can make up time if you need to.

Section 4
Motherhood and care

So far in Unit 1 we have looked at the 'care' side of family care. Now, in the last two sections we are going to explore the 'family' side. In this section we will explore why 'care in the family' tends to mean care by women, like Lil Durrant, Lynne herself, Lilian McSweeney and Val Hollinghurst. One way of explaining this is to see a close connection between mothering (by definition done by women) and care work.

I will tackle this in three stages. First, we will consider some commonsense ideas about the importance of mothers, through looking at a newspaper story. Then I will look at the work of a psychologist, John Bowlby, whose ideas have been highly influential in thinking about family life and the roles of mothers in particular. Finally, I will show how subsequent research and debate challenged Bowlby's early ideas and stimulated him and others to modify and develop them.

4.1   Introducing ideas about mothering

Caring for children is at the heart of the popular idea of family life. You only have to think of advertisements to see this. And alongside the lively, troublesome, demanding children is the patient, understanding, long-suffering, loving mother. We can pick up the strong feelings associated with the idea of a mother's care in a newspaper story, 'Lost and found' reprinted in the Offprints Book.

Activity 15

Allow about 15 minutes

Lost and found

Read Offprint 1 'Lost and found' and then jot down answers to these questions.

(a)   Is Sally Webster more concerned about having lost her mother's care than her father's? If so, why do you think that is?

(b)   From your reading of this story, what were the bad effects on Sally of being brought up (with her sister and brother) by the 'Aunt' in a small 'home', rather than in a family by her natural parents?

(c)   How well does Sally's story fit the popular picture of the family in decline?

Comment

The story does not offer a lot of detail, so you may not have found it easy to answer the questions. Here are some thoughts.

(a)   Sally talks more about the loss of her mother than of her father. Perhaps this is because her father had died anyway, whereas it was her mother who actually abandoned the children. On the other hand, Sally talks about the other children having known their mothers and doesn't mention their fathers. She was able to explain away her own father's absence as being to do with work. It seems it was her mother who 'ought' to have been there.

(b)   Sally apparently has a very close relationship with her substitute mother. She 'speaks to her daily'. With her brother and sister alongside her in a small home, she experienced at least some elements of family life. Yet Sally still talks about 'all the love I'd missed'. She also felt 'guilty' about not having parents. This takes us back to the discussion of stigma in Section 2 – the idea of being a 'problem child' from a 'problem home'. In spite of all the aunt's efforts, Sally feels that not being brought up by her own mother was very wrong.

(c) This story does not fit the popular image of 'the family in decline'. First it reminds us that families falling apart is not something new. And second, it shows that some people, such as Sally, still hold very strongly to the idea of a family where the father is breadwinner and the mother makes childcare her main priority. The story also goes against the common view that failures of parenting lead to children growing up to be poor parents themselves. It warns us not to assume that children simply learn by copying their parents. Sally went out of her way to behave differently from her own mother.

At no point in the story is it spelt out why being abandoned by your mother is a newsworthy item. A lot tends to be 'taken for granted' when people speak to journalists about motherhood and childcare – and equally when journalists write stories for us, the general public, to read. Much is not felt to be worth explaining. So what is it that we take for granted – and are we right? I begin by looking at the work of John Bowlby on the nature of the mother–child relationship.

4.2 John Bowlby: attachment and maternal deprivation

John Bowlby is a major figure in any account of motherhood and childcare. When he began to study childcare in the 1940s, Europe had been ravaged by war. Many families had been torn apart – children separated from their parents – for example, through the policy of 'evacuating' city children to unknown families in the country. Had these children suffered emotional damage – and how best could care be arranged for those who had lost their families during the war?

 In 1951 Bowlby wrote a report for the World Health Organization, reviewing expert opinion on these matters. Then in 1953 he published a very influential book, *Child Care and the Growth of Love*. In it he argued that the role of a mother in the first years of her child's life is critically important.

Activity 16

Allow about 10 minutes

Child care and the growth of love

Offprint 2 is an extract from *Child Care and the Growth of Love*. Turn to it now and read just the first paragraph.

Write down anything which strikes you about Bowlby's statement.

Comment

Were you struck by the assumption that the young child was 'him'? This was the convention in all writing about children at that time. To even the balance, I shall use 'she'. Did you notice the lack of any mention of the father?

Apart from that, at first sight the statement could seem almost 'common sense'. Don't we all know that babies need to spend a lot of time in a warm close relationship with their mothers?

But what do some of the words mean in detail. Does 'continuous relationship' mean all day, every day? And for how many years? Does the term 'permanent mother substitute' mean that a temporary mother substitute is no good? Can the father be a 'mother substitute' or does it have to be a woman?

Does every child whose mother does not provide a continuous close relationship inevitably suffer mental ill health? On closer inspection this statement begins to look rather alarming – both for mothers, who seemingly have to be 'chained' to their offspring at all times, and for children, who risk mental ill health if their mothers get it wrong.

Obviously, Bowlby's brief statement needs more explanation. In the next extract he puts some age limits on this 'continuous relationship'. First he explains how a small child depends on her mother, not just for food and other bodily services, but also for her general development.

Activity 17

Allow about 15 minutes

Bowlby's ideas of child development

Read the next section of Offprint 2, down to the points (a), (b), (c), ending '... for periods of a year or more'.

As you read, use a ballpoint pen, pencil or highlighting pen to mark anything that you find interesting or words that seem important.

Comment

How did you get on with marking the text? To give you something to compare with, here is an example for the first part of the section.

> *Just how we develop as <u>personalities</u> and how this development <u>depends on</u> our being in <u>constant touch</u> with some <u>one person</u> who cares for us during the <u>critical time</u> in our early years, whilst our <u>ability to adjust ourselves</u> to the outside world of things and of people is <u>growing</u>, is a very interesting question ...*

> *As our <u>personality develops</u> we become less and less at the mercy of our immediate surroundings ... and more and more <u>able to ... plan ahead</u> ... This means that we have to learn to <u>think in an abstract way</u>, to exercise our imagination and to consider things other than just our immediate sensations and desires. Only when he has reached this stage is the individual able to <u>control</u> his <u>wish of the moment</u> in the <u>interests of</u> his own more fundamental <u>long-term needs</u>.*

Study skills: Underlining and highlighting

You probably picked out different words – perhaps more, perhaps fewer. It's your choice – depending on the text and why you are reading it. People succeed with very different approaches. This is just to start you thinking about what helps *you* to get what you need from reading. I try to underline so that I can skim back over the text just reading the marked words and still make sense. I also put lines down the sides of bits I think are particularly important. To help you work out what is best for you, read the section 'Too much underlining and highlighting' on pages 118 to 119 of *The Good Study Guide* and the key points box on page 120.

A mother caring for her baby

Looking at your markings on this section, what were the points that stuck out for you? Here are my ideas.

• A key part of a child's development is learning to think abstractly, rather than always responding directly (knowing, for example, that the road is dangerous, and not running after a ball).

• Taking the difficult early steps in learning to think is achieved through close collaboration with her mother.

• This requires a very secure, close and continuing relationship.

Bowlby goes on to put some time boundaries around child development. A baby goes through the following stages in developing into a psychologically healthy adult:

1 By around *6 months* she must have formed a relationship with a particular person (normally her mother). Bowlby called this forming an 'attachment' to her mother.

2 From then to about *3 years old* the child feels happy and secure, and will make progress with her development, only if her mother is with her or nearby.

3 *After the first 3 years* there is a long period up to 'maturity' when the child's development continues to benefit from the close relationship, but she gradually becomes able to cope for longer spells on her own.

Bowlby went on to argue that if either:

• a child is prevented from forming an attachment

or

• after forming an attachment the relationship is disrupted

this has devastating effects on the child's development. He called such disruptions 'maternal deprivation'.

Activity 18

Allow about 15 minutes

Avoiding maternal deprivation

(a) Now read Offprint 2 as far as 'unable to make either himself or anyone else happy'. In this section Bowlby presents his explanation of why and how a child's development is affected by 'maternal deprivation' during each of the three phases. Read fairly quickly. The idea is to get the general gist of Bowlby's way of thinking. The details are not particularly important to the arguments in Unit 1. But you may find Bowlby's approach interesting, so make up your own mind about how long to take. You don't need to take notes on this section.

(b) Then finish the chapter, again reading quite quickly, but this time making a few notes of the main points as you go.

Comment

Here are some sample notes:

– Easy to provide continuous relationship in a family
  – v.v. hard outside family.

– 'Bad' parent at least gives continuity of care – and child trusts her to continue.

– Too often removal of children from family seen as solution to problem:
  – done without a proper plan

- without realising full consequences for child's future personality and mental health.

- First approach to preventing maternal deprivation should be to try to shore up families, not seek alternatives to family.

Study skills: Note taking

Do these notes look like yours? It would be surprising if they did, since everyone takes notes differently. In any case, my purpose in taking the notes was different. They were for *you* to read in this unit. Your own notes can be briefer and more messy. Quickly look at the bottom half of page 155 of *The Good Study Guide*, below the heading 'Making notes strategically', then read the Key points box on page 156.

Because Bowlby places a lot of emphasis on the psychological development of a child through her relationship with her mother, he comes across as a strong advocate of families. He also raises deep doubts about institutional care and fostering.

Key points

In 1953 Bowlby's argument ran as follows:

- A child's personality development is achieved through a close continuous relationship with her mother.

- The child must form an *attachment* by about 6 months, after which, until around 3 years, she has a strong need to be continuously with or close by her mother.

- Any obstacle to the forming of an attachment, or any subsequent disruption of the relationship, constitutes *maternal deprivation*.

- Maternal deprivation at phases 1 or 2 does deep damage to personality development. In phase 3 the damage is less fundamental.

- The secure attachment and continuous relationship a child needs is far more likely to be provided within her natural family than anywhere else.

4.3 Motherhood: the image and the reality

Bowlby's emphasis in his 1953 book was very clear – mothers take the central, and all but exclusive, role in early childcare. He makes little mention of any sharing of the burden and only occasionally mentions fathers. And there are dire warnings about disruptions to this intensive relationship. Does this mean that taking a job is out of the question for a mother? Are day care nurseries a dreadful mistake? A mother appears to have a 'biological' duty (unlike the father) to give up all else and devote herself to childcare in the early years. If not, her child will have personality problems later on.

Yet there have always been mothers who worked outside the home and now the government encourages them to do so. Has this inevitably led to disturbed children growing into unhappy and inadequate adults? Have women been irresponsible and selfish? In the rest of this section I explore arguments that have emerged to challenge this alarming interpretation of Bowlby's early ideas.

What do women think?

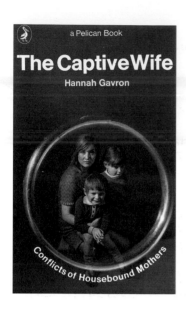

Bowlby's account of the mother–child relationship appears to fit with the 'traditional' idea that women achieve full maturity and a sense of identity through motherhood. It looks like natural harmony – children need mothers to be with them in the home and women need motherhood and domesticity. Women like Sally Webster's mother may not fit the picture, but perhaps they are 'unnatural'.

Yet when women themselves were asked about the experience of full time mothering a much less certain picture emerged. Many mothers of young children reported feeling isolated, frustrated and 'housebound' (Gavron, 1966). In one study 70 per cent of women interviewed were dissatisfied with housework and complained of loneliness and low self-esteem (Oakley, 1974). Another study uncovered high levels of depression in full-time housewives (Brown and Harris, 1978). So the role of 'mother' cannot be relied on to provide women with unalloyed happiness. What is more, some young children do not experience the family as the safe haven Bowlby depicts. Firm statistics are hard to come by, but there are plenty of cases, like that of Fred and Rosemary West and Victoria Climbié, which reveal appalling child abuse perpetrated by mothers and fathers, or by other relations or family friends (Malone *et al.*, 1996).

Victoria Climbié: appalling cases of child abuse at the hands of relatives have come to light (Community Care, 21-27 Feb 2002)

Study skills: Coping with the names and dates

You have come across quite a number of brackets like this: (Brown and Harris, 1978). What are you supposed to do? Learn the names and dates? The answer is an emphatic 'no!' I am simply 'citing' sources, so that you know where the idea comes from. In academic study you seldom make up new ideas off the top of your head. You generally build on other people's ideas. It is important to the reader to know where ideas come from, so that they can weigh up their value.

In this part of the unit I am reviewing a range of research that is relevant to Bowlby's ideas. Each time I quote from a research study I give the name of the person who wrote it up, the date it was published and the page number. Then, if you need to look up the research study, you can look at the list of references at the end of the unit to get the details. When there are lots of names, as here, you simply read past them. But they are there for you to come back to if you need them.

Maternal deprivation revisited

Bowlby's early work stimulated a lot of research, some of which raised doubts about his initial exclusively mother-centred account. For example, it was found that babies can, and generally do, form attachments to other people besides their mothers. Indeed, fathers can be equally effective in providing a safe continuous relationship. (In other words, care roles are not biologically predetermined.) What is more, brothers and sisters also play an important part. Michael Rutter, who undertook a review of the research in 1972, commented that when children are distressed in hospitals or nurseries it is not only the mother who can help:

> *The evidence that distress is much reduced by the presence of a brother or sister or a friend even when the mother remains absent strongly suggests that there is nothing specific about mother separation. Indeed it is curious that studies of children in hospital or a residential nursery are nearly always considered as examples of separation from mothers when in fact they consist of separation from mother and father and sibs and the home environment.*

> *(Rutter, 1986, p. 50)*

Rutter accepts that children need to form *attachments*, and that disruption of these attachments is distressing, but he argues that attending a day care centre, for example, is not inevitably traumatic, as Bowlby's 1953 account might lead us to believe:

> *... good quality day care does not disrupt a child's emotional bonds with his parents; moreover, children continue to prefer their parents over alternative caregivers.*

> *(p. 178)*

Rutter argues that it is important to distinguish between a child's need to form attachments, her need for basic care and her need for play. Meeting these needs can be shared among several people:

> *Bonding, caretaking and play are three separate functions, which may or may not be performed by the same person ... so long as all three are available, it is of no matter ... who provides them, and in particular it does not matter if the mother does so.*

> *(p. 108)*

It has also been found that new attachments can be formed at a much later age than Bowlby had originally indicated. For example, you saw how close Sally Webster became to her aunt. Finally, regarding the idea that damage caused by early separations from a mother is irreparable, a review of research concluded that with the right kind of care many of the effects can be reversed (Clarke and Clarke, 1976). Gillian Pascall concludes that:

> *Fortunately the evidence is altogether more cheerful ... No one argues that children thrive without love and care ... What is argued is the maternal deprivation thesis ... attaches too much importance to bonding with a*

single mother-figure, and is too pessimistic about the long-term
irreversibility of damage inflicted on young children ...

(Pascall, 1986, p. 76)

It is important to add that Bowlby himself played a leading part in the
debates stimulated by his book and in his later writings modified his
account to reflect newer research. However, like any author, he did not
have control over the way his ideas were interpreted and put to use.
Once published, his words had a life of their own.

Competing ideas of motherhood

It is perhaps no accident that Bowlby's original account of motherhood
was written at a time when there was great emphasis on rebuilding
family life. We always need to ask why a particular set of ideas took root
when they did. Men returning from war service wanted the jobs that
women had taken over during the war. Bowlby's ideas seemed to fit
well at a time when women were being asked to re-immerse themselves
in domestic life. Lynne Segal sees the 1950s as a period of:

> *... unprecedented attempts to reconstruct the family – and woman's place*
> *at its centre ... the idea of the happy healthy family was promoted by*
> *whatever means possible. Social scientists of all persuasions wrote of the*
> *institution of the family as universal and eternal, blaming any sort of*
> *social or individual discontent on the 'problem' family.*

 (Segal, 1993, p. 298)

The 'proper' care of children was not just a matter for individual
parents to decide. By the 1960s Bowlby's 1953 arguments provided the
basis for the accepted wisdom of (mostly male) civil servants. For
example, the Ministry of Health argued that nursery provision:

> *... must be looked at in relation to the view of medical and other authority*
> *that early and prolonged separation from the mother is detrimental to the*
> *child [and] that wherever possible the younger preschool child should be at*
> *home with his mother.*

(Ministry of Health, 1968, quoted in Hughes et al., 1980, p. 46)

In other words, although mothers might wish for nurseries, it would, in
the view of male experts leaning heavily on Bowlby's account, be bad
for children to provide them. The arguments had run the *other* way
during the war, when women had to be persuaded to leave their
children in nurseries to free them for work in munitions factories.

In fact the normal practice of many mothers has long been to share
childcare with other family members, older children and neighbours.
Yet for a time the dominant ideology was that women risked their
children's development if they did not stay at home. This view was
reflected in films, TV programmes and magazines. You saw it in Sally
Webster's account, and you will encounter it frequently in newspapers,
on TV, and in everyday conversations.

However, you will also encounter an alternative view, as in recent times
there has been something of a swing back. We see the image of the
modern woman who 'has it all', successfully combining a career with all
the demands of motherhood. It has even become government policy
that mothers should be supported in returning to work. Indeed, it is
now 'officially' seen as desirable that mothers should continue to
participate in society through paid work and that children also benefit
from spending time outside the family.

Ideology

Ideologies are sets of ideas, beliefs, and images which shape the way we look at the world and make sense of it. They make some things seem 'normal', 'natural' and 'right', and others seem 'abnormal', 'unnatural' and 'wrong'. For example, wartime ideology made it 'right' for children to be evacuated and for women to work in 'men's' jobs. But after the war there was a rapid change of ideology (into which Bowlby's writing fed). This ideology painted a picture in which family life was the heart of society, and it put motherhood at the centre of women's 'nature'. It remains powerful in some quarters today, as we see in Sally Webster's vision of a mother always at home, putting her children's welfare first. Women who did not conform to this ideology, such as Sally's own mother, may find themselves perceived as 'unnatural', whatever their reasons. On the other hand, as the competing ideology of the all-competent working mother has emerged in more recent times, someone like Sally may feel this makes her seem inadequate and lacking ambition.

Dominant ideologies are difficult for individuals to resist. In the 1950s, if women resisted, they risked being seen as irresponsible and uncaring and 'unnatural' – not proper women. However, by the 1960s and 70s the dominant ideology was being challenged by a new body of writing and research from a feminist perspective.

What is a feminist perspective?

Family care, health care and social care have all been important areas of feminist study because they affect women's lives very directly. Yet women's interests and women's own views were for a long time left out of accounts of child care and family life. For example, Bowlby's work involved studying children, not asking mothers for their views, and the Ministry of Health referred to the views of medical experts, not mothers, in debating policy on nurseries.

So what is a feminist perspective? There is no single description of feminism. Feminists differ considerably in how they explain the world and what strategies they advocate. Feminist theory has developed into a sophisticated subject that requires a course in its own right to untangle and assess. However, anyone who writes from a feminist perspective will be committed to a struggle to improve the condition of women. Academic writing and research from a feminist perspective can be expected to:

- *question* existing arrangements and ask about their implications for women

- *insist* that women's voices should be heard and should be given equal value

- *seek* to uncover patterns of exploitation and oppression in all areas of life.

Feminist writers began to unpick the seemingly 'natural' ideology of motherhood. They showed that the image of families as cosy havens, where contented mothers and children found protection from the hard world outside, could be far from the reality. Some families were more dangerous than the outside world – exposing women and children to aggression, violence and abuse (Mitchell, 1966). Equally, the idea of being provided for by a male 'breadwinner' could be turned upside down by men who spent most of the family income on themselves.

Having uncovered gaping holes in the cosy image of mother safe at home with her children, feminists went on to show that this version of motherhood also arranges society in such a way that women are burdened far beyond the demands of childcare:

> *Child-care is at the heart of the sexual division of labour. Responsibility for children keeps women isolated in the home and disadvantages them in the labour market. While raising children must often be more satisfying than the male side of the labour bargain, the ramifications ... spread into every area of women's lives ... Motherhood is central, both in the general social concept of woman, and in most women's experience. It casts women into marginal positions in public life. In this it is quite unlike fatherhood.*

> *(Pascall, 1986, pp. 96–7)*

How true is what Pascall wrote now, in the early twenty first century? Can we see a different ideology operating at the beginning of the twenty-first century, one that says mothers should go out to work however old their children, thus giving them a more central place in public life? Or is there still the expectation that good mothers stay at home for their kids?

Whatever your view on that, there is statistical evidence to prove another of Pascall's assertions that women are disadvantaged in the labour market which makes them more likely to resume caring roles in later life:

> *When women leave the labour market to have children, their return is usually to work with shorter hours, lower status, and lower pay ... When somewhat later in life, there are elderly or disabled relatives to care for, again the tasks fall to women. Not only is it in the 'appropriate' sphere, but they are by now even more badly placed in the labour market.*

> *(Pascall, 1986, p. 97)*

The Equal Opportunities Commission found that women in full-time work are paid 82% of men's wages, and women in part-time work only 60% of men's wages on average (EOC, 2001).

Reviewing the impact of Bowlby's ideas

Let us begin with a real-life scenario.

Anna

Anna is three and a half. Her mother, Jane, suffered from severe post-natal depression and as a consequence was placed in a psychiatric hospital when Anna was two weeks old. Anna was initially looked after by her grandmother, an arrangement which broke down after two months. She was then placed with foster carers who worked in partnership with the social worker to ensure that Anna had contact with her mother three times a week. After five months, Jane was discharged and Anna returned home to her. Jane began work full-time when Anna was 18 months old. Anna was placed with a childminder.

How does this case look from the perspective of Bowlby's original ideas of *attachment* and *maternal deprivation*? Is there any hope for Anna, given that she was living apart from her mother during much of those critical first six months, during which Bowlby originally suggested her attachment to her mother would need to form – and given that well before she was three she had begun to spend large parts of the day apart from her mother. From the perspective of the 1953 book, her prospects look poor. On the other hand, the efforts made to maintain contact between mother and child under difficult circumstances are consistent with Bowlby's insistence on the importance of *attachments*. And in the light of evidence from the later research stimulated by Bowlby's ideas Anna would, under the right circumstances, be able to make valuable attachments to carers other than Jane, such as her childminder. So, while Bowlby's ideas have been modified and reinterpreted, they continue to contribute to the way we think about how care should be provided for young children.

Yet Bowlby's early emphasis on mothers as the irreplaceable, ever-present carers of their children, was seized upon at the time as providing 'scientific' backing for established ideas about motherhood and the place of women in society. It is tempting to think of motherhood as a simple, straightforward, 'natural' idea, something people learn about from childhood through direct experience and through stories and play. But we have seen that motherhood is a concept over which battles rage. It has been used to define the fortunes of half of society. Not only has motherhood been used as a concept which allocates childcare to women, it has also made them more likely to pick up other unpaid caring work in the family.

Key points

- The extent to which childcare should be a mother's sole responsibility has been much debated and researched. Bowlby originally laid great emphasis on the mother taking the central care role, but subsequent research, including Bowlby's own, found that fathers and other carers can successfully share with, or substitute for, mothers. Familiarity, trust and continuity are what matters.

- Feminists have argued that allocating responsibility for childcare exclusively to mothers is at the heart of the sexual division of labour. It marginalises women in public life, and increases the likelihood that it is women who take on unpaid caring work in spheres other than childcare.

Section 5
Families: diversity and change

Families

I have argued that most care needs are met within families, and I have shown how the role women are expected to take on as mothers leads to expectations that they will take on caring roles in other contexts also. If most people rely on families for most of their care needs, this poses some difficult questions.

- Does everyone live in a family? In other words, can most people rely on a family to support them in times of need?

- Are we quite clear what we mean by the word 'family'?

- Is the family in decline, and can it continue to provide care?

5.1 Meanings of family

You can begin by thinking about your own family.

Activity 19   Exploring your idea of family

Allow about 10 minutes   Are you a member of a family? Do you belong to more than one, for example a birth family and a later one? Write down the names of the people in any families you belong to. Are there people you might add to the list whom you regard as 'family' but who are outside the immediate circles of those you have shared a home with?

Which of these family members do you think could possibly call on you to care for them in need? What would be the highest amount and degree of care they could expect?

Which of these family members do you think you could call on to care for you in need? What degree of care could you expect from each?

Is there a balance between the amount of care you might be expected to give and the amount you could receive?

Comment   Who did you count in your family – parents, brothers, sisters, children, partner? Did your family extend more widely than that? Or did you feel you are not significantly linked to any family? Your answers will depend on a range of things, including your cultural background, your circumstances and assumptions as to who has ties and duties to whom.

One of our course testers wrote:

> *I've recently started Spanish lessons and already we have been asked, 'How many people are there in your family?' 'How old are they?' and so on. I had to explain that I live as a one-person family, but I would talk about my brother, parents, etc. It seems OK to refer to your birth family until you are in your thirties, but after that it seems a bit odd. It struck me that this may be one of Lynne's problems too. To have to refer to your family of birth as your family becomes more embarrassing the older you get. It defines you as a daughter, not as an autonomous adult.*

Here are two other people with very different family ties.

Bipin and Devi

Bipin Shah is 40 years old. He has severe learning difficulties, and is also physically disabled. He lived with his parents until he was 36, with his mother taking the major responsibility for his care. When his younger brother married, Bipin moved in with him and his wife Devi, and she took on responsibility for his care.

(Walmsley, unpublished)

We have here one woman living independently, with ties to geographically distant family members, and another with a lifetime's commitment to sharing a home with, and providing daily care for, her severely disabled brother-in-law. Clearly, families are not one simple kind of thing. Yet we talk about 'the family' and whether it is changing for the better or the worse. So whose family are we talking about when we say 'the family'? Are some families 'proper' families, and others exceptions? Do the majority of people live in what we could call a 'typical' family?

To explore such questions we turn again to a feminist perspective.

Activity 20   'The' family and families

Allow about 15 minutes   Read Offprint 3 '"The" family and families' by Janet Finch.

Do some underlining as you go and when you have finished reading write answers to these questions:

(a) What is meant by 'the nuclear family' and have you ever lived in one?

(b) What are the two senses in which the nuclear family might be seen as the dominant form of family in Britain?

(c) Would you say it *is* the dominant form in *each* sense?

(d) What does Finch say is the difference between *families* and *'the family'*?

(e) Do most women marry and have children? What do the statistics in Finch's article tell us?

Comment   My response is as follows. How do your answers compare with mine?

(a) The 'nucleus' of a family is considered to be two parents and their children. Other relatives are spoken of as the 'extended' family. Part of the popular idea of a nuclear family is that the children are not yet adults and they all live together.

(b) The nuclear family might be seen as dominant in being the most common kind of family numerically. It might also be seen as dominant in being the 'idea' or image of a family which people take for granted when the word 'family' is used. You will recognise this as ideology as I defined it in Section 4.

(c) It seems quite clear that the nuclear family is dominant as an *idea*, but it is not so easy to say that it is dominant *statistically*. Most of us pass through a range of different family arrangements in our lives. At any given time a minority of people are actually living in a nuclear family. However, a majority of people *have lived* in one at some time.

So the nuclear family *is* numerically dominant compared with other kinds of family. But saying that should not mislead us into thinking that most people currently live in a nuclear family.

(d) According to Finch, 'families' refers to all kinds of households with children, whereas '"the" family' refers to the dominant form of family – the nuclear family, for short 'the family'.

(e) The answer seems certain to be 'yes'. But Finch gives figures only for women born in 1951 and 1955. Of those women more than 9 in every 10 had married and over three-quarters had had children.

So you see that when we are talking about families we need to be clear whether we are talking about 'the family', i.e. the nuclear family, as portrayed in advertisements and so on, and as generally assumed in ordinary conversation – or about families in a broad sense, including couples whose children have grown up and left home, a father and daughter living together as in Arthur and Lynne's case, lone-parent families, gay and lesbian couples, foster families (Sally's aunt), and families where the parents each have children from previous partnerships. 'The family' currently covers just under a quarter of households.

> **Key points**
>
> • Families come in many shapes and sizes.
>
> • However, when we are talking about families we tend to say 'the family', meaning the nuclear family.
>
> • This is one sense in which the nuclear family is the dominant form in Western societies – it is the form of family 'taken for granted'.
>
> • The nuclear family is also the dominant form in that there are more nuclear families than other types of family, and the majority of people have lived in a nuclear family at some time. However, the majority of people are actually not living in a nuclear family.

5.2 Historical and cultural diversity of families

As the nuclear family is the dominant form in Western society, it is easy to think it is a 'natural' form, which has always been dominant. However, if we look across different societies or at different periods of history we see a great variety of family forms. For example, Nelson Mandela in his autobiography recounts that:

> *All told, my father had four wives ... Each of these wives – the Great Wife, the Right Hand wife (my mother), the Left Hand wife and the wife of the Iqadi or support house – had her own kraal [homestead] ... The kraals of my father's wives were separated by many miles and he commuted among them. In these travels, my father sired thirteen children in all, four boys and nine girls.*
>
> *[...]*
>
> *My mother presided over three huts at Qunu which, as I remember, were always filled with the babies and children of my relatives ... In African culture, the sons and daughters of one's aunts or uncles are considered brothers and sisters, not cousins.*
>
> *[...]*
>
> *My father ... took turns visiting his wives and usually came to us for perhaps one week a month ...*
>
> (Mandela, 1994, pp. 5-6, 9, 14)

Nelson Mandela grew up with very different ideas from Sally Webster's as to what is natural in family relationships. Even her most basic assumption – that children belong with their two biological parents – was not a feature of his daily experience. Yet his story is of an idyllic childhood in the beautiful countryside of the South African Transkei. Other times and places illustrate many other family patterns. Reviewing writing on different cultures, Stevi Jackson concludes:

> *The precise configuration of kin and non kin who live together and co-operate economically varies greatly ... Husbands and wives do not always live together, nor are children necessarily reared by either of their biological parents.*
>
> (Jackson, 1993, p. 180)

She also points out that the model of the man of the house as breadwinner for a dependent wife back in the home is far from normal:

> *Women as wives and mothers are not generally wholly dependent on men. One of the most pervasive myths ... is that men are natural breadwinners and have provided for women since the dawn of history. In most non-industrial societies ... women make a substantial contribution to subsistence, and in many they are the main food providers.*
>
> (p. 181)

In fact the version of the nuclear family which Bowlby's account treated as normal and desirable – a stay-at-home mother with children and a breadwinning father – has a relatively recent history. Jackson argues that it emerged in the 1800s as an aspect of the Industrial Revolution:

> *Until the industrial phase of capitalism, most production, whether agricultural, craft or domestic industry, was centred on households. Everyone – men, women and children – contributed to the household economy. There was however a distinct sexual division of labour, and generally men controlled productive resources, including the labour of their wives ... With industrialisation the removal of commodity production from households reduced most of the population to wage labour, and separated family life from paid work. Among the bourgeoisie in the early nineteenth century these changes were associated with a new 'domestic ideology' which defined the home as women's 'natural' sphere ... This ideology was subsequently adopted by sections of the working class. Male-dominated labour organisations sought to exclude women from many forms of paid work and to establish the principle of the male breadwinner earning a 'family wage'.*
>
> (pp. 181–2)

The story that Jackson sketches starts with families in which all family members worked together in and around the home, both for their own needs and for sale. (Cloth, for example, was woven in people's homes.) But the shift to factory production took production of things for sale out of the home. If people wanted money, instead of making and selling things at home they had to go out and work regular (and long) hours for wages. Initially, women and children were popular as cheap and less troublesome employees. But gradually a combination of legislation and pressure from male-dominated trade unions led to the norm being seen as men going out to work as breadwinners and women going out to work irregularly or not at all:

> *By the twentieth century, normal family life had come to be defined in terms of breadwinning husband and domesticated wife, although this was not a pattern that many poorer members of the working class could afford to adopt. Even today, when the majority of married women are employed and women spend a far smaller proportion of their lives rearing children than they did a century ago, the idea persists that a woman's purpose in life is to care for home, husband and children.*
>
> (p. 182)

Thus the version of the nuclear family which many think of today as traditional is only a few generations old. Furthermore, the history outlined here is not shared by all groups within modern Britain. It has never been relevant to the upper classes, for example, many of whom assign their children when young to paid nannies, and when older to boarding schools. Nor is it necessarily relevant to the wide range of minority ethnic communities in Britain. There are other traditions and other ideas of what is a 'normal' family:

Black and white women's experience of family life are not the same, and there are differences between the various Black communities in Britain. For example, over 10 per cent of Asian households contain more than one family with children, compared with only 2 per cent of Afro-Caribbean households and 1 per cent of white households. Afro-Caribbean women, on the other hand, are more than five times more likely to head single parent households than white or Asian women ... This is not just a matter of ethnic diversity ... Slavery, colonization and, more recently, immigration and citizenship laws have had profound effects on Black families.

(pp. 178–9)

So different cultural histories give rise to different forms of families. However, because the nuclear family is dominant within the society as a whole, other types of family are often taken to be abnormal, unhealthy, inadequate, or in some way immoral:

The Afro-Caribbean family is seen as being too fragmented and weak and the Asian family seems to be unhealthily strong, cohesive and controlling of its members ... Afro-Caribbean women are stereotyped matriarchs, or seen as single mothers who expose their children to a stream of different men while Asian women are construed as faithful and passive victims ... identified as failures because of their ... refusal to integrate.

(Parmar, 1988, p. 199)

In other words, it does not matter in which direction alternative cultural patterns deviate from the nuclear norm, they are equally suspect just through being different. Yet, as you have seen, what is taken to be 'normal' has quite shallow foundations. Throughout the course you will see how ethnic diversity challenges the norms on which care services have been unthinkingly constructed.

So the type of nuclear family which tends to be taken for granted is not a universal 'natural' form. It is the product of a particular historical time and place. Families across different periods of history and different cultures show great diversity. To understand caring in families it is important to recognise that diversity.

Key points

- The modern nuclear family is neither the 'natural' family form nor the most common through history or across the world.

- In any modern society there is considerable diversity of family forms.

- Minority ethnic families are sometimes condemned as abnormal because they do not conform to the Western ideology of 'the family'.

5.3 Changing families

Not only is there a diversity of forms of family, but these forms are constantly changing. As the economy has changed, offering men fewer jobs and women more, and in general offering more short-term, part-time work, the male breadwinner model has been steadily undermined; many households depend on two or more breadwinners. The legal dependence of women on men has been eroded. At the same time attitudes, ideas and beliefs have changed. The mass media project images of ways of living which would have shocked earlier generations. These and many other changes have affected family life greatly. You can see some of these changes in the charts in the next activity.

Study skills: Working with numbers

What do you do when you come across numbers, percentages and charts as you are reading? Do you stop to take in what they mean, or do you skip ahead and carry on reading? You will miss a great deal if you do skip. Numbers can tell you a lot very quickly. You may be quite comfortable with numbers, in which case this box is not addressed to you. But if you aren't, we shall aim to help you in K100 by:

•   bringing numbers and charts into the course a little at a time, starting with easy ones

•   giving you advice about charts and practice in reading them

•   asking you to read some easy figures from charts as part of your assignment work.

You can make a start by doing Activity 21.

Activity 21

Allow about 15 minutes

Working with pie charts

You will see some diagrams known as 'pie charts' on the opposite page which we have drawn from General Household Survey information (Office of Population Censuses and Surveys, 1996).

(a)   Figure 1 shows two pie charts. Look at Figure 1(a) and work out what it is telling you. Then write a sentence summarising it. Figure 1(b) is very similar, but it is for a different year and the sizes of the slices of pie are different. Write a sentence summing up the change the two pies are showing.

(b)   Figures 2 to 4 are of exactly the same kind as Figure 1, but they are about different aspects of families. Look at each and make a note of the change it shows.

(c)   Then write a few sentences describing recent changes to families, as shown by Figures 1 to 4.

If you get stuck with one of these questions look at the explanation in the Comment before coming back here to do the next question.

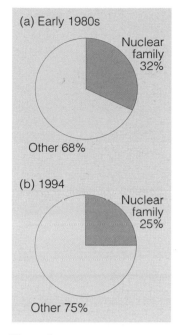

Figure 1
Households containing a
'nuclear family' (married or
cohabiting couple with
dependent children)

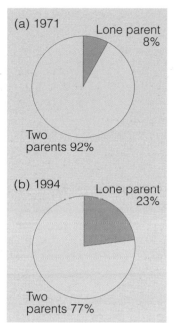

Figure 2
Families headed by a lone
parent

Figure 3
Women aged 18–49 married
at date of interview

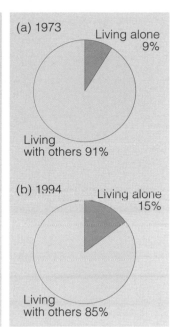

Figure 4
People living alone

26
26
52

Comment

Datum means an item of information. The plural is *data*, meaning lots of items of information. Notice the sentence says that data *were* collected (not data *was* collected).

Here are my answers.

(a) In Figure 1(a) it says 'Early 1980s'. This tells us when the data in this chart were collected. In the circle we see a small dark slice of pie marked 'Nuclear family 32%'. Here 32 per cent means 32 households out of every 100 households. So, in the early 1980s, 32 households in every 100 were composed of nuclear families.

The other slice is twice as big. The dark slice is nearly one-third of the pie and the light slice is just over two-thirds. So we can say 'in the early 1980s nearly a third of households contained a nuclear family'.

Figure 1(b) is for 1994. Here the dark slice has shrunk to 25%. It is now just a quarter of the whole pie. So we can say that 'between the early 1980s and the early 1990s the number of households containing nuclear families dropped from a third of all households to a quarter'.

(b) You can read Figure 2 in exactly the same way. It shows that in 1971, 8 per cent of families were headed by a lone parent, whereas by 1994 the figure had risen to 23 per cent. Twenty-three per cent is nearly three times as large as 8 per cent. So we can say that 'the proportion of families headed by a lone parent trebled between 1971 and 1994'.

Figure 3 shows that, in 1979, 74 per cent of women were married, in other words about three-quarters. By 1994 the figure had dropped to 57 per cent. This is not much above half.

Figure 4 shows that, in 1973, 9 in every 100 people lived alone and, by 1994, 15 in every 100 did (about 1 in every 7).

(c) Over the 25 years from 1970 to 1994 there were a number of changes in people's domestic arrangements. Nuclear families dropped from a third to a quarter of households. Meanwhile, the number of households with only one person rose to over 1 in 7. The proportion of families headed by a lone parent rose even more sharply to nearly a quarter of all families. And the proportion of women who were married fell sharply.

These figures could be taken to show that the family *is* after all in decline as popular opinion suggests. However, it depends what is meant by family and what is meant by decline. Certainly, if the nuclear family is what we are talking about, there are signs of a decline in numbers, but some of the other changes are more ambiguous. For example, the growth in single-person families has a lot to do with people living longer and bereaved spouses having enough financial independence not to need to move in with children. Living alone is not necessarily a sign of having left a family.

Even the rising rates of divorce are not necessarily a sign of rejection of marriage.

> *If current rates continue, then 37 per cent of marriages are likely to end in divorce. Divorce, however, ends only a particular marital relationship. It does not necessarily undermine the institution of marriage itself. Most of those who divorce subsequently remarry, many only to divorce again. Women's discontent with marriage does not seem to be experienced as disillusionment with the institution, but rather with the particular relationship.*

> (Jackson, 1993, p. 183)

There have certainly been changes in family patterns, and you will be learning more about them in Unit 6, but the meaning of the changes is not easy to untangle. In thinking about care in the family, we need to know about change, but we should be careful not to rush to conclusions. On the other hand, it is likely that changes *will* produce new stresses and strains in some quarters and leave gaps in others.

How are these changes in family patterns relevant to practice in health and social care? They are a warning not to assume norms and expectations where they are not appropriate, the sorts of norm that Rita tried to impose on Lynne when she told Lynne she was under an obligation to care for her father because he had cared for her. If sensitive support is to be offered, then it is important to appreciate diversity and difference.

Key points

- The word 'family' has many meanings and covers a wide diversity of domestic groupings.

- When people think about families, what seems 'right' tends to be very much influenced by the history of their own particular cultural group.

- As society changes, families also change. It is difficult to untangle whether these are changes for better or worse. But they are likely to affect the type and amount of care which families can provide, and the sort of support they need.

Conclusion: is caring a family affair?

In Unit 1 we have explored families and caring. We have seen that caring and families often do go together:

- most caring takes place in families behind the scenes, usually unnoticed and unpaid

and

- close caring relationships which matter profoundly to people often exist within families.

You have also seen that it is most often women who take on the caring. Ideas of women as biologically destined for caring roles have long had a hold on the popular imagination. At one time, psychologists such as Bowlby seemed to support this thinking – arguing that small children required continuous contact with their mothers. The 'nuclear family', with a mother and a 'bread-winning' father, is widely seen as the 'natural' way of organising close relationships and of managing the work of care. So, not only do 'caring' and 'families' tend to go together in practice, but the ideology of motherhood and the family acts to persuade us that they *should* go together. The persuasion is all the more effective because it harmonises with some very basic human needs for connection, warmth, closeness and protection – needs which are often well met within families.

You have seen, however, that in actuality families are very diverse and that they are changing. When you think about care, you cannot take the membership of families for granted, nor the roles that members play. Present day psychologists – and Bowlby himself in his later writing – have acknowledged that people other than mothers can provide the support that small children and other family members need.

We should also recognise that families serve many functions other than early childcare, including, as with Lynne, care for people who are unable to manage tasks of daily living. And we should not take for granted that change or diversity means 'families in crisis' or 'families in decline', a favourite rallying cry of politicians and the popular media, although we should try to understand what they mean for care provision.

What we want you to take from this unit is a recognition that there are questions to be asked about caring in families. The family cannot be seen as the dumping ground for all society's care needs. It will absorb some, but will simply not meet others, regardless of what policy makers or moralists might wish.

Study skills: Rounding off your first week's study

Congratulations on reaching the end of your reading for Unit 1. As you will see below you have one more significant task. But just before you turn to that, now is a good time to reflect on your experiences of working on Unit 1. Do you feel you have made a good start? To help you think about this, read through the first four sections of Chapter 1 of *The Good Study Guide* (pp. 9–18) and Section 2.4 of Chapter 2 (pp. 40–44). It won't take long because you have already read quite a lot of it. Section 1 will clarify the kind of help you can expect to find as you use *The Good Study Guide* during the year. Sections 2 and 3 will remind you of some of the strategic choices you made as you studied (whether or not you were aware of them at the time). They will also start you thinking about how to approach Unit 2.

Practice essay

Your last piece of work for Unit 1 is to write a very short essay (TMA 07) just to make contact with your tutor and get yourself started on the writing part of your studies. This only counts for a quarter of the marks of a normal assignment, so think of it as a practice run. You will get advice back from your tutor, which will be very helpful when you reach the first proper assignment in four weeks' time at the end of Block 1. For full details of what to do, look in the Assignment Book.

Difficult personal issues

Perhaps some of what you have read in Unit 1 has touched very close to your own experiences, past or present, in ways that were difficult or upsetting to think about. Caring situations often have stressful or painful aspects. It is particularly important that a course like K100 recognises these issues and discusses them, using real cases to help draw out just why particular situations can be difficult and what might be done to help. The course writers have tried very hard to discuss all issues sensitively and responsibly, but it is possible that at some point you will come to a case, or a discussion, which arouses emotions you have difficulty coping with. If this happens, and you feel you need to stop reading the topic under discussion and move on to the next section of the course, you should feel free to do so – though you might want to consult your tutor first. Alternatively you might feel the need to talk to a friend, a counsellor, or a helpline. Perhaps it would be a good idea to think now about who that would be.

References

Allen, I., Hogg, D. and Peace, S. (1992) *Elderly People: Choice, Participation and Satisfaction*, Policy Studies Institute, London.

Arber, S. and Ginn, J. (1990) 'The meaning of informal care: gender and the contribution of elderly people', *Sociological Review*, Vol. 39, No. 2, pp. 260–91.

Biggs, S. (1994) *Understanding Ageing: Images, Attitudes and Professional Practice*, Open University Press, Buckingham.

Bond, H. (1995) 'Working together', *Community Care*, 14–20 September, p. 22.

Bornat, J., Pereira, C., Pilgrim, D. and Williams, F. (eds) (1993) *Community Care: A Reader*, Macmillan, London.

Bowlby, J. (1953) *Child Care and the Growth of Love* (2nd edn, 1965) Penguin, Harmondsworth.

Briggs, A. and Oliver, J. (eds) (1995) *Caring*, Routledge and Kegan Paul, London.

Brown, G. and Harris, T. (1978) *Social Origins of Depression*, Tavistock, London.

Burke, P. and Signo, K. (1996) *Support for Families*, Avebury, Aldershot.

Bytheway, B. and Johnson, J. (1997) 'The social construction of carers', in Symonds, A. and Kelly, A. (eds) *The Social Construction of Care in the Community*, Macmillan, London.

Clarke, A.M. and Clarke, A.D.B. (1976) *Early Experience: Myth and Evidence*, Open Books, London.

Department of Health (2000) Caring about Carers: a National Strategy for Carers, 2nd edn, The Stationery Office, London, http://www.doh.gov.uk/carers.htm [accessed 15.5.02]

Equal Opportunities Commission (1980) *The Experience of Caring for Elderly and Handicapped Dependants*, EOC, Manchester.

Equal Opportunities Commission (1982) *Who Cares for the Carers? Opportunities for those Caring for the Elderly or Handicapped*, EOC, Manchester.

Fisher, M. (1994) 'Man made care: community care and older male carers', *British Journal of Social Work*, Vol. 24, pp. 659–80.

Gavron, H. (1966) *The Captive Wife*, Penguin, Harmondsworth.

Graham, H. (1984) *Women, Health and the Family*, Harvester Wheatsheaf, London.

Green, H. (1988) *General Household Survey 1985: Informal Carers*, Series GHS No 15, Supplement A, HMSO, London.

Henderson, V. (1960) *Basic Principles of Nursing Care*, International Council of Nurses, Geneva.

Hughes, M., Mayall, B., Moss, P., Perry, S., Petrie, P. and Pinkerton, G. (1980) *Nurseries Now: A Fair Deal for Parents and Children*, Penguin, Harmondsworth.

Jackson, S. (1993) 'Women and the family', in Richardson, D. and Robinson, V. (eds) *Introducing Women's Studies*, Macmillan, Basingstoke.

Keith, L. and Morris, J. (1994) 'Easy targets: a disability rights perspective in the "children as carers" debate', *Critical Social Policy*, Issue 44/45, pp. 36–57.

Kestenbaum, A. (1996) *Independent Living: A Review*, Joseph Rowntree Foundation, York.

Lee-Harmony, A. (1996) 'Dream parents', unpublished.

Lewis, J. and Meredith, B. (1988) *Daughters Who Care*, Routledge, London.

MacRae, H.M. (1995) 'Women and caring: constructing self through others', *Journal of Woman and Aging*, Vol. 7, No. 1/2, pp. 145–67.

Malone, C., Farthing, L. and Marce, L. (eds) (1996) *The Memory Bird: Survivors of Sexual Abuse*, Virago, London.

Mandela, N. (1994) *Long Walk to Freedom*, Little, Brown and Co., London.

Mitchell, J. (1966) 'Women: the longest revolution', in Mitchell, J. (ed.) *The Longest Revolution: On Feminism, Literature and Psychoanalysis*, Virago, London.

Morris, J. (1993) *Independent Lives*, Macmillan, London.

Oakley, A. (1974) *The Sociology of Housework*, Martin Robertson, London.

Office of Population Censuses and Surveys (1992) *General Household Survey: Carers in 1990*, OPCS monitor SS92/93, HMSO, London.

Office of Population Censuses and Surveys (1996) *Living in Britain: Results of the General Household Survey*, HMSO, London.

Parker, G. and Lawton, D. (1994) *Different Types of Care: Different Types of Carer*, HMSO, London.

Parmar, P. (1988) 'Gender, race and power: the challenge to youth work practice', in Cohen, P. and Maines, H.S. (eds) *Multi-Racist Britain*, Macmillan, London.

Pascall, G. (1986) *Social Policy: A Feminist Analysis*, Tavistock, London.

Rutter, M. (1986) *Maternal Deprivation Reassessed* (2nd edn), Penguin, Harmondsworth.

Segal, L. (1993) 'A feminist looks at the family', in Muncie, J., Wetherell, M., Dallos, R. and Cochrane, A. (eds) *Understanding the Family*, Sage, London.

Tredgold, A.F. (1947) *Mental Deficiency*, Bailliere, Tindall and Cox, London.

Tucker, S. and Liddiard, P. (1997) 'Young carers', in Brechin, A., Katz, J., Peace, S. and Walmsley, J. (eds) *Care Matters*, Sage, London.

Acknowledgements

Grateful acknowledgement is made to the following sources for permission to reproduce material in this unit:

Text

'Dream parents': courtesy of Anastasia Lee-Harmony.

Illustrations

p. 13 (top right): Ed Clark; *p. 13 (top left and bottom)*: John Birdsall Photography; *p. 30*: reproduced from A. F. Tredgold (1947) *Mental Deficiency*; *p. 31 (right)*: Philip Hatfield Photography; *p. 39*: Sunil Gupta; *p. 40*: courtesy of the Carers National Association; *p. 41*: Dan Chung/ News Team; *p. 44*: Paul Stewart/Digital News Associates; *pp. 50, 58*: Sally and Richard Greenhill; *p. 52*: copyright Graham Bishop/Penguin Books Ltd.; p. 52 (*right*) courtesy of PA photos.

Unit 2
Caring for Health

Prepared for the course team by Celia Davies and Geraldine Lee-Treweek
Updated by Geraldine Lee-Treweek

While you are working on Unit 2, you will need:

- Course Reader
- Offprints Book
- *The Good Study Guide*
- Audio Cassette 1, sides 1 and 2

Contents

Introduction

Focusing on the family, as you have seen in Unit 1, offers one way of thinking about the work of caring. It draws attention to ordinary people caring for others as part of their understanding of themselves – as parents of young children, as partners or, as in the case of Lynne Durrant, as adults with obligations to their own, now-ageing parents who need help with the activities of daily living. Some forms of care, however, require more knowledge and skill than family members can provide. This is particularly true when we start to think about caring for health. You can't attempt to remove your brother's appendix yourself and, when your child is feverish and vomiting, you will want to turn to health professionals for advice and action.

In this unit I will examine some of the perspectives of those on the providing end and the receiving end of health care. Doctors and nurses are probably the first people we think of as providers of health care, although there are many others who work with them in health care settings. As you will see at the beginning of the unit, it is also important to recognise that we all do things to care for our own health and for that of others, although this kind of health care is often overlooked. Just as in Unit 1, I will be encouraging you to take a critical look at different concepts of care, pointing to limitations as well as strengths, and exploring stresses and strains associated with caring in different ways.

Core questions

- What is health care and who does it?

- How important are medicine and medical ways of thinking to caring for health?

- How is health care work – especially the most complex health care work – organised?

- What does it mean to be on the receiving end of health care?

You will find that this unit involves more additional reading than Unit 1. Be sure to leave yourself enough time for this. The readings are designed to help you make sense of the themes in the unit and to introduce you to different styles of writing and to arguments based on different kinds of evidence. As you work through the activities connected with the readings, you will also get valuable practice in summarising ideas and assessing them.

Section 1
Health care at home

It is easy to think that health care is what happens in hospitals – it is what other people do to us. As the old saying goes, 'doctor knows best'. In practice, however, we all do a great deal of health care in our daily lives. No one takes everything they see as a health problem to a doctor's surgery.

Activity 1 **Keeping yourself healthy**

Allow about 10 minutes   Jot down if you can at least four things that you have done over the last week to care for someone's health, your own or that of others – your children perhaps, or your partner, relatives or friends. (You don't necessarily need to think of crises – include some things that you do on a routine basis too.)

Comment   When the course testers tried this activity they gave very varied answers. Here are some of them:

- cleaning my teeth
- taking the dog for a walk
- buying vitamin tablets
- taking my son to the doctor's
- going to the gym
- taking an old friend out for a meal and just listening to her troubles
- buying a pot of anti-wrinkle cream
- finishing the course of antibiotics that the doctor had given me

- making sure my little girl has her inhaler with her
- dosing myself up for a cold
- booking an aromatherapy session
- making sure the family eats plenty of fruit
- getting Gran a mobile phone for her birthday
- awarding myself the occasional bar of chocolate

The people who produced this list thought in different ways. They often interpreted caring for health as including things they do to maintain good health and to prevent illness. We can think of this as taking a positive health maintenance and health-promoting approach rather than one oriented to disease – waiting for ill health and then seeking to get it fixed when it arrives. Also, many of the items in the list are not 'treatments' in the ordinary sense of the word. A balanced diet, exercise, lending an ear to a friend going through a crisis, are all actions that we might well say contribute to a sense of health and well-being, although no-one is going to write out a prescription for them – certainly not for the chocolate!

So we do lots of things on a daily basis to keep ourselves and others healthy. Your list, particularly if you started to think about day-to-day family life in a home with children, may have been quite different. Hilary Graham (1984), a sociologist whom you met in Unit 1, made a detailed study of the role of women in the health of their families, and pointed out that often we do not even notice a lot of what we do for health. She organised the various activities, such as those the course testers – and probably you – have listed, into five main kinds of health task that families accomplish every day.

Providing for health. This is crucially important but easily forgotten. It includes ensuring that there is: clean and warm accommodation which protects against danger and disease; a diet meeting nutritional needs; and a secure set of relationships in the home, allowing for growth and development of children.

Nursing the sick. This is the most obvious kind of health work and probably the kind you first thought of – but it covers a range of activities. It entails additional domestic work, contact with health professionals, and following their advice, and it can mean finding ways of meeting additional costs for heating, special diets, laundry, and transport to and from care settings such as health centres or hospital outpatient departments.

Teaching about health. Most of us first learn about health inside families and carry our mother's warnings in our heads ('don't go out with wet hair'; 'don't take a bath right after a meal'). Some people make a great effort to find out about health issues and to learn about illnesses and their signs and symptoms. Intentionally or not, however, parents work as health educators, setting standards and, as Graham puts it, 'transmitting a culture in which health can be understood'.

Mediating with outsiders. Here Graham means meeting the health professionals, for example 'the doctor and health visitor, the social worker, and the district nurse, the school nurse and the health education officer' (p. 151). (One member of the course team remarked that it was only when his daughter was born that he really began to notice that all these people existed – he and his partner had become 'a family', having to meet, understand and relate to the health care system.)

Coping with conflict/crisis. The need to make ends meet can lead to hard decisions about how important health care is compared with other family needs and about whose health has priority. Having studied families in poverty, Graham points out: 'in meeting the children's need for food, the diet of the parents can suffer: in providing a car for the male breadwinner, the children's access to medical services is restricted' (p. 152).

You saw in Unit 1 that caring is very often women's work and it is taken for granted that women will do it unpaid and unseen in the home. By setting out health-related aspects of care in this way, Graham is drawing attention to another dimension of women's roles and is also underlining the extent of knowledge, skill and responsibility that is involved.

Let us think about health knowledge for a moment. If you work in the field of health you will probably have had training in health issues relevant to your job. But if you are a lay person – the man on the bus or the woman in the street – where have your health ideas come from? Did you get them from your mother? Have these ideas changed since you were a child at home? If they have, what brought about these changes?

Activity 2   ## Sources of health information

Allow about 20 minutes   There are probably a number of newspapers or magazines lying around at home or perhaps in your workplace. Glance through one or two of these now and note how items about health appear and what form they take.

Comment   I thought that there would be plenty of material to list here but I was surprised at just how much I came across. There is news about health services – as much news about cuts in services or restricted budgets as about breakthroughs in treatment. There are advertisements for books on particular forms of illness – irritable bowel syndrome seems to be a frequent one. There are also advertisements for treatments and products, promising cures for anything from baldness to incontinence, from impotence to dandruff.

In women's magazines there is much direct health advice about the care of children and about women's own health. In this type of magazine there is often a regular column written by a doctor. In other magazines, such as *Here's Health*, the whole focus is health and wellbeing. The reader of this type of magazine is exposed to health issues on every page – from recipes for healthy eating to a discussion of managing stress or the latest exercise fad used by celebrities. Other specialist magazines can provide advice on specific issues such as slimming and diet, on food and nutrition or natural beauty products. There are newspaper features, with advertisements for exercise machines, and for lotions and potions aplenty that promise healthy hair, youthful skin, cold cures, and so on.

Health information and advice is not directed only at women. Teenage magazines feature health, and newspapers often have a central feature about a health topic. *Men's Health* is a well-established publication and other general men's magazines, such as *Loaded* and *GQ* have health features. One course tester expressed her surprise at how many

Health advice is a consumer industry

advertisements she found in women's magazines relating to frail elderly people – for stair lifts, for special baths to soothe muscular pain, for vitamin supplements, and so on.

We are bombarded with stories about health and illness, with information, advice and advertisements for products connected with health, and we are encouraged to spend money on it. Health advice is a thriving consumer industry as well as a publicly provided service and medical advice books sell well. In addition, what used to be called 'alternative therapies' such as acupuncture, osteopathy, herbalism and reflexology are increasingly popular forms of treatment. These therapies are now frequently termed 'complementary therapies', a change in terminology which reflects the way people often use them alongside medicines and treatments they may get from their doctor. Health and fitness clubs too are flourishing. Our ideas about what it is to be healthy and the actions that we take are influenced by all these factors as well as by face-to-face encounters with those working for the NHS. Therefore, people are presented with an array of information and choice of treatments to help them seek health and treat disease.

Key points

- Everyone cares for their own health in a variety of ways, and many people also care for the health of others.

- Women as mothers are key health workers, particularly in caring for children in the family and making contact with the health services.

- People build up a knowledge of health from their families, from the media, from information given by health professionals and from health books written for a lay audience.

Section 2
Concepts of health

What is known about how people think about their health? Since the mid-1980s there has been a growing attention to finding out both how people think about health and what they do to keep healthy. We will concentrate in this section on a classic large-scale health and lifestyle survey, the results of which started to emerge in 1987 (Cox, 1987) and which continued to be the focus of attention in the 1990s. Over 9,000 people in England, Scotland and Wales were interviewed in the first survey, a follow-up was conducted seven years later (Blaxter, 1990; Cox et al., 1993) and a similar study was also carried out in Northern Ireland (Barker et al., 1988). The survey provided a great deal of information on matters such as diet, exercise and alcohol consumption as well as measuring weight, heart rates and other health indices. It also asked people to state what they meant by health, how they would describe a healthy person, and how they would describe being healthy themselves.

Study skills: Making sense of survey findings

In Unit 1 you looked at some numbers in the form of pie charts. Now we continue your introduction to reading numbers by looking at a table of figures. Care policy and care provision always depend on having detailed information about the public at large – the needs of various groups, people's habits and attitudes, the circumstances in which they live. Consequently, surveys are vital, and anyone who wants to understand care provision needs to know how to make sense of survey findings.

Before you can understand the meaning of the numbers that come out of surveys, you need to have a general awareness of how surveys are carried out – what kinds of questions are asked, what kinds of answers people are allowed to give, and what the researchers then do to turn the answers into numbers and charts. So, in Activity 3, before looking at the numbers themselves, we begin by exploring how the answers to a particular question were grouped into categories.

Activity 3

Allow about 10 minutes

Survey on meanings of health – making categories

The people taking part in the health and lifestyle survey were asked a series of questions designed to get them thinking about what it meant to them to be healthy. One question put to them was:

'At times people are healthier than other times. Describe what it is like when *you* are healthy.'

To begin this activity, jot down your own answer to this question now. If there is someone else you can easily ask, break off from reading for a moment and see what response they give to the question. Or you might like to try this part of the activity later, with work colleagues for example, or with older and younger family members or friends.

People in the survey gave very varied answers to this question. In order to make some overall sense of the answers, the researchers sorted them into broad groups. If you look at the left-hand side of Table 1 you will see the main categories the researchers arrived at.

(a)   Do these categories make sense to you as ways people might describe feeling healthy? Try fitting your own answer and any others you have collected into these categories.

(b)   What does 'All' mean at the top of the right-hand column?

(c)   What does the figure 43% underneath 'All' tell us? Try writing down a sentence starting 'Table 1 shows us that for 43% of people ...'

Table 1   What does it mean to be healthy yourself?

	Age			All
	18–39 (1)	40–59 (2)	60 and over (3)	(4)
A Feel psychologically fit, happy, relaxed, able to cope	41%	47%	41%	43%
B Fit, strong, energetic, physically active	40%	30%	14%	30%
C Able to do a lot, work, get out and about	22%	32%	38%	29%
D Not ill, no disease, never see a doctor	13%	13%	13%	13%
E Can't explain, or don't know what it is to be healthy	13%	9%	9%	11%
Total	*100%*	*100%*	*100%*	*100%*
(Number)	*(3,818)*	*(2,836)*	*(2,349)*	*(9,003)*

(Source: supplied by Blaxter, M., based on Blaxter, 1990)

Note: Percentages add to more than 100 since some people gave more than one answer.

Comment (a)   Did your answers fit easily into these categories? Perhaps you felt, for example, that categories B and C overlapped? Why were they not put together as one category? Researchers have to use their judgement in choosing categories which do justice to the answers they have gathered. Here they judged that a large number of answers emphasised feeling *physically active*, whereas another large group put the emphasis on being able to *function* in daily life at home and work. So they set up two separate categories. As you will see in a moment, each was indeed a large category. Separating the two revealed some interesting differences between age groups.

Perhaps your answer spread over more than one category. This is what happened in the survey, so people whose answers had several parts were counted in every category they mentioned. This means that the numbers in each column can add up to more than 100% (i.e. for each 100 people there would generally be more than 100 answers in the category boxes).

(b)   Most tables have headings at the tops of the columns to say what the columns refer to. So does Table 1. Below 'Age' we first see 18–39. So the first column of figures is for people aged between 18 and 39 years old. Then there are two other age groups – the 40–59-year-olds and the 60 and overs. These three columns between them cover all adults. Obviously, the final 'All' column must show figures for all three age groups lumped together.

(c) If you look across to the left of the row containing the figure 43%, you can see that it relates to category A. It also comes under the 'All' heading. So this figure is telling us that 43% of *all* people gave an answer which fell into category A. To complete the sentence you need to look back to the question in the table title, as well as at the wording of category A. Here is my version.

Table 1 shows us that for 43% of people being healthy means feeling psychologically fit, happy, relaxed and able to cope.

Activity 4   **Survey on meanings of health – interpreting the numbers**

Allow about 20 minutes   Now we'll look at some of the other numbers.

(a) Staying with the right-hand column – do most people think of being healthy as not being ill or having to visit a doctor?   No

(b) In which age group are people most likely to think of being healthy as feeling fit, strong, energetic and physically active?   13-39

(c) In which age group are people most likely to think of being healthy as being able to work and get out and about?   13-39 60 + over

(d) Comparing the under-40 age group with the 60-and-over age group, how do ideas of health differ? A same view, D same view
Differences in B & E

Comment   (a) In their accounts of what being healthy means, only 13% of people mentioned not being ill or having to visit the doctor.

(b) It is adults under 40 who are most likely to think of health in terms of being fit, strong, energetic and physically active (40% of them compared with 14% of 60 and overs).

(c) It is people aged 60 and over who are most likely to think of health in terms of being able to do a lot, work and get out and about (38% of them).

(d) For all age groups feeling psychologically fit, happy and relaxed was the most commonly mentioned ingredient of being healthy. However, young people also tended to emphasise physical fitness, strength and energy, whereas older people tended to emphasise ability to function in daily life.

Thinking about it, you may feel that these findings are largely what you would have expected.

The survey went on to explore these results further. It showed, for example, quite marked differences between women and men in their concepts of being healthy. More women than men defined health in psychological terms. More men than women could not give a definition. It also showed that people in white-collar and professional jobs are more likely to have a 'fitness' concept of health, whereas those doing manual work are more likely to stress function. Why should this be? It may well be because manual workers' jobs require more strenuous activity and are more insecure, or that manual workers have fewer resources to devote to a healthy lifestyle – the survey is open to different interpretations here.

The survey has recently been re-analysed, matching the 129 Asian people and 94 African-Caribbean people with white people of similar class, sex and region, to see if differences emerge. The findings show many similarities, with high proportions in all communities stressing psychological well-being as an important part of their idea of health. Asian people are more likely to stress functional health, whereas African-Caribbean people stress strength and fitness. Again there are different ways of interpreting the findings, but it is interesting to note that in answer to an earlier question – asking them to think about someone who was very healthy – more Asian and African-Caribbean people than white people did not actually know such a person (Howlett *et al.*, 1992).

As well as being asked about what health meant to them, people were also asked to assess their own levels of health. I won't go into all the details, but it is worth looking at the results for just one group. Table 2 concentrates on people aged 50 and over. If you look at the left-hand side of the table you will see they were asked to assess their health as excellent, good, or only fair or poor. The table divides people into different income groups.

Activity 5

Allow about 10 minutes

Wealth and feelings of health

Look at Table 2.

(a)   What general conclusions would you draw about the health of people aged 50 and over?

(b)   Write a sentence about the health of people aged 50 and over with high incomes.

(c)   Write a sentence about the health of people aged 50 and over with low incomes.

(d)   In one sentence, summarise the relationship between income and health for people aged 50 and over.

(e)   Note I mentions 'rounding'. Do you know what this means?

(f)   Can you think why the category '£996 and above' may not be as useful as some of the other income categories used in the table?

Table 2   How do people aged 50 and over, with different income levels, assess their own health?

	Household income per month				
	£996 and above	*£581–995*	*£231–580*	*£230 and below*	*All*
Own health is:					
Excellent	45%	24%	24%	31%	28%
Good	43%	50%	42%	34%	42%
Fair/poor	11%	26%	34%	36%	30%
Total	*100%*	*100%*	*100%*	*100%*	*100%*
(Number)	*(337)*	*(472)*	*(1,669)*	*(797)*	*(3,275)*

(Source: supplied by Blaxter, M., based on Blaxter, 1990)

Notes:
Some of the percentages do not add up exactly to 100, owing to rounding. About 20% of the sample, for whom no information about income is available, are excluded.

Comment

I deliberately tried to put my answers in a way that would be different from yours. See whether our answers amount to the same thing.

(a)   Roughly speaking, out of every 10 people aged 50 and over, 3 say they are in excellent health, 4 say they are in good health and 3 say they are in fair or poor health.

(In other words, looking at the 'excellent' category, 28% is close to 30% – and 30% means 30 out of every 100, which is the same as 3 out of 10. Similarly, for the 'good' row 42% is close to 40%, which is 4 out of every 10, and so on.)

(b)   Of people with incomes of above £1,000 per month (I have rounded up from £996), nearly half describe their health as excellent, and only about 1 in 10 say their health is fair or poor.

(c)   Of people with incomes of less than £230 per month, just under a third describe their health as excellent, about a third describe it as good, and just over a third describe it as fair or poor (a third is about 33%).

(d)   Among people aged 50 and over, those with the highest incomes are most likely to say they enjoy excellent health and those with the lowest incomes are most likely to say they experience fair to poor health.

(In fact, the sharpest changes are between the top income group and the next to top – a drop from 45% to 24% for excellent health, and a rise from 11% to 26% for fair to poor health. Is this because the wealthiest people can afford to live a lot more healthily? Perhaps they can also get quicker access to some kinds of health care through private medicine.)

(e)   Rounding is what you do when, instead of thinking 'that CD costs £9.99', you think 'that costs £10'. In other words, when there is a figure after the decimal point, you simplify by going to the nearest whole number instead. If, instead of 2.85, you say 3, then you have rounded *up*. If, instead of 4.2, you say 4, you have rounded *down*.

(f)   The category of people whose monthly income is '£996 and above' is very broad. For instance, under this category there may be people who earn £996 per month and others who earn £5,000 – we just do not know from the information provided. The other bands of income on the table are narrower. This is something to look out for when you are using tables of information.

The conclusion we can draw from Table 2 therefore is that, among people aged 50 and over, the best-off say that they enjoy considerably better health. In other words health is not just a matter of biology and the body you inherited – it is related to wealth. Not surprisingly, differences in social and economic circumstances affect people's abilities to care for their own health and for the health of their families. But health itself, as we have seen, is more than just absence of illness and disease; it is also a state of mind. The World Health Organization, for example, has defined health as 'a state of complete physical, mental and social well-being' (World Health Organization, 1996). If health is such a broad concept and is linked to so many different factors – age, income, gender, ethnicity – then caring for health is clearly linked to every aspect of our lives and how we live them with the resources available to us.

You have been studying a one-off, large-scale survey. Are there other sources of information on health? Health and well-being in Britain is monitored by a variety of national agencies, including the Department of Health, the Scottish Executive, Northern Ireland Department of Health and the National Assembly for Wales. The most recent survey of self-reported health in England (Health Survey for England Trend Data for Adults 1993–2000) showed that reports of good or very good health have remained stable since 1993 (at 75% and 73% for men and women respectively) as have reports of very bad health (at 7% and 6%). Studies like the one we use above, which try to understand what people mean when they report they have 'good' or 'bad' health, are not so common. Other health data is regularly collected about areas such as smoking behaviour, eating patterns (in particular about the consumption rates of fruit, vegetables, fat and lower fat foods) and how much exercise the population is taking. This aids in the planning and delivery of services and can identify regions or groups of people who are particularly at risk of ill health. For instance, the most recent Scottish Health Survey (2000) has found that, in general, fewer people are smoking and more people are eating at least one portion of vegetables or fruit a day than in the past. However, on the downside, exercise rates remain poor with 38% of men and 35% of women deemed to be inactive and there was a 3% increase in the number of people who were clinically obese. As you can see, this data allows health professionals to have both a snapshot of people's health-related behaviour (as in the percentage of people currently taking exercise) and also allows them to compare change over time (as in the rise in obesity since the last study).

The government compiles a range of statistics that are available to the general public on the internet. Having looked at the statistics here you might wish to have a look at some other health statistics. The Department of Health (DoH) website (http://www.doh.gov.uk) allows you to go in and search through a range of topics, including statistics relating to health and social care. You can even look at statistics on health in your own local area by going to the address, http://www.statistics.gov.uk/statbase/geog.asp and then following the links for the 'all fields postcode directory'. You can choose to put in your postcode area to look at statistics on, for instance, chronic illness rates and you can also search by town, city or county. From December 2002 statistics from the Census 2001 will start becoming available. These will include some health and social care related data and will be accessible from the web address: http://www.statistics.gov.uk/census2001/default.asp. Published sets of statistical data are also available in many libraries and one of the sources you might like to look out for is called Social Trends (published by the Office for National Statistics). This includes key statistics about a whole range of areas and the findings are represented in an accessible way.

At work with the World Health Organisation

Campaigning for positive health worldwide

The World Health Organization (WHO) was set up in Geneva in 1948, as the United Nations specialised agency for health. It is well known for its work in combating infectious diseases and helping to bring basic health care to developing countries. It has also challenged governments of the West, arguing that they spend too much on disease and not enough on health promotion, too much on specialist hospital services and not enough on primary health care and health education. Its 'Health for All by the Year 2000' initiative, started in 1978, finally began to bear fruit in the UK from the mid-1980s onwards. This developed into the new WHO programme 'Health for all in the 21st century'. This continues to focus on health promotion and urges western governments to place prevention at the heart of their health care systems. Present (2002) policy for England is set out in a White Paper 'Saving Lives: Our Healthier Nation' (Department of Health, 1999). It involves strategies and targets for public health – improving diet and nutrition, reducing drinking and smoking, and reducing death rates for certain preventable diseases.

Key points

- People's concepts of health are varied; feeling psychologically fit and energetic is valued strongly.

- Older people tend to stress being able to function while younger ones emphasise fitness, energy and strength.

- Economic circumstances affect our health and our assessments of health.

- The WHO has questioned the extent to which government health policies should rest on a disease concept rather than a health one.

Section 3
Health care and medical care

3.1 The biomedical model

As you saw in the previous section, there is a lot more to being well than not seeing a doctor. Where do doctors' concepts of health and illness fit in this? Do they see health differently? Here is one account of what guides doctors:

> ... the model of health and disease which came to dominate Western thinking after about 1800 ... was grounded in biology and other sciences. Overriding importance was given to learning about anatomy and physiology, in particular to understanding mechanisms such as the heart, arteries, nerves, brain and so on. The body was conceptualised as a machine in which all the parts functioned together to ensure health; if some parts broke down, clinicians intervened to limit and treat damage.
>
> (Jones, 1994, p. 377)

Dissection of a cadaver by an anatomist making an abdominal incision, 1345

Historians of medicine explain that it was only when medicine came to dissect corpses that anatomical changes and inflamed internal tissues could be observed and then related to the outward signs and symptoms that the patient could report and the doctor could examine (Armstrong, 1993). The challenge for the doctor is to examine and – sometimes by opening up the body, sometimes by offering a chemical substance – to attack and destroy or suppress the source of malfunction. The doctor's starting point, in other words, is that the site of the problem lies within the individual and that the biological sciences will reveal an appropriate course of action. More attention is given to the body than the mind in this way of thinking, and extensive training in the biological sciences is crucial. How you feel about being ill is less relevant than identifying the diagnosis (i.e. which disease in the established classification you are suffering from) and then ensuring that you comply with the treatment.

It is cure that doctors concentrate on, and those with the highest status are the specialists whose knowledge and skill in the relevant area of medical sciences can produce results. Underlying this approach, too, is a notion of what is normal and what is abnormal or pathological. The doctor is looking for defects and working with what is considered an acceptable range of the normal. All these ideas are features of what has been called the 'biomedical model'.

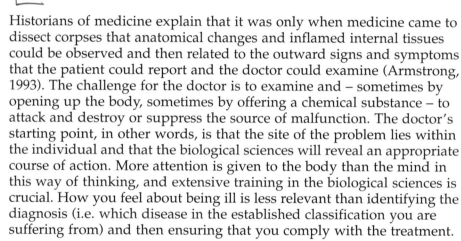

The biomedical model

Health care is medical care, and medical care is seen as:

*   a quest to conquer and cure disease

*   focused on the disease not on the whole person

*   concerned with what is normal and what is pathological and making judgements about the boundary between them

*   a rational activity based on scientific knowledge that is secured through a lengthy formal training.

Results achieved through use of the biomedical model can be dramatically successful.

Activity 6   **The accomplishments of biomedicine**

Allow about 10 minutes   This brief activity is designed to help you use your own experience to think about the accomplishments of medicine. As we have noted above, biomedicine is the dominant way of thinking about and treating illness and disease and as such we often take for granted its successes and positive contribution to our lives.

- In *your own life* you will have experienced times when biomedical care or treatments helped you through perhaps a course of drug treatment or an operation. Note down two of these occasions and try also to note down how you felt about the treatment you received at the time.

- There will also be examples that you can think of where biomedicine can be seen to have *helped a lot of people*. Note down two main examples of this.

Comment   You may have identified a number of different ways in which biomedicine has positively helped your own life. In terms of feelings you may have noted feeling 'relief' or being 'grateful'. However, when doing the exercise, I noted that after receiving treatment for illness I have very rarely thought about how biomedicine has helped me and have just been glad to be feeling better! This illustrates the way that we often take for granted the contribution of medicine in our lives. For the ways in which biomedicine has helped a good deal of people you may have noted a range of breakthroughs, such as the development of successful treatments for some kinds of cancer or the development of particular drugs.

To see the accomplishments of biomedicine from a different perspective, two health professionals were asked what they felt were the three principal achievements of biomedicine.

Midwife

Maureen Harris, a Senior Midwife at Derriford Hospital (Plymouth Hospitals NHS Trust, Devon), selected these three areas:

- *vaccination programmes*
- *the development of antibiotics*
- *advances in anaesthetics, in particular increased safety.*

General practitioner

Dr Tom Heller, a member of the course team and a general practitioner, identified these three areas:

- *antibiotics*
- *analgesia and anaesthetic developments*
- *surgical developments, such as new hips, heart valves and transplants.*

However, he offered some words of caution about the way we often think of medical progress in these areas as involving 'breakthroughs':

'The media wants to tell a story, with dramatic discoveries in the "fight against cancer" etc., but in truth there are many examples of incremental improvements which together add up to greater benefit than any one medical researcher suddenly finding the answer to a single question.'

From considering our own experience and the views of the health professionals we can see that biomedicine has been successful in tackling many areas of disease and illness and examples of this are all around us.

Many of us would not be here without the services of modern medicine and the biomedical model. But is it always an appropriate way of caring for health?

Activity 7   **Thinking about the doctor's diagnosis**

Allow about 15 minutes   Think back to the case study of Lynne and her father, Arthur, in Unit 1.

Remember how that was followed by accounts of research showing the stresses and strains and the toll of exhaustion that doing the work of a carer can sometimes entail. Imagine now that it is some years later, that Arthur's health has deteriorated, and that Lynne is finding it more and more difficult to provide for his needs and hold down her job. She feels exhausted and at the end of her tether – she goes to see her general practitioner (GP). What actions would a doctor, thinking within the biomedical model, be likely to take? Try to think of more than one.

Comment   One response that fits within the biomedical model would be to check for anaemia. 'You are a bit run down', the doctor might say, having examined her, 'I'm going to give you some iron tablets.' Another possibility would be to question Lynne about how much sleep she is getting and to offer her sleeping pills. A third possibility, faced by her agitation and distress, might be to prescribe tranquillisers. These actions all fit with the view of the body as a machine in need of repair – the equivalent of drying the spark plugs or changing the oil!

Let us take this a little further. You might feel that a response in terms of the biomedical model is *too narrow*. It might make Lynne feel better for a while but in the long term her overall situation needs to be addressed. A different response might be to ask a little more about Lynne's life and what has brought her to this state of exhaustion, to see if there is a remedy that can be applied, not at the level of Lynne's body, but at the level of her daily life and the obligations in which she is enmeshed. Suppose the doctor then suggests that Lynne give up her job and concentrate on caring for her father? Knowing what you know about Lynne's history and her needs, you might feel that a doctor who did this had gone too far. What right has a doctor to prescribe what Lynne's obligations as a daughter are, and to decide that her father's needs for care must be given priority? Lynne has needs for the things that her work gives her (not only money, if you remember, but company, self-esteem and a sense of being like other people).

In yet another approach, the doctor might decide that Lynne needs support from other kinds of health and social care staff. That might involve asking a community nurse to call, or referring Lynne to the social worker to see what additional support and respite can be arranged, or setting in motion a new needs assessment for her father or for Lynne herself.

As the first port of call, a GP faces a wide array of medical and social problems and is also sometimes able to get to know individuals and their circumstances in some depth. This is a different position from a doctor in an acute hospital who is a specialist in particular forms of disease and receives patients referred from a GP. Medical training has increasingly come to emphasise the importance of getting to know the patient and the family and of effective communication that can help draw out any more important problems that lie beneath what is called the presenting problem. But the main strength, even of GPs, who are often referred to as family doctors and thought to be known to all members of the family, lies in their ability to offer individual solutions within the biomedical model – treatments for disease. A GP, after all, can hardly prescribe more resources for social services to support a carer, or central heating in the homes of those with recurrent respiratory disease, or a change in transport and retail sector policies so that young mothers living on low incomes on out-of-town housing estates have access to fruit and vegetables that are both fresh and affordable. Some say it is outside their remit to be concerned about this; others join campaigns for change.

Doctors do not always act only within the biomedical model, but it is an important part of their frame of reference and often both they and we assume that caring for health means there is 'a pill for every ill'.

Key points

- The biomedical model has many successes and is firmly established.

- But it is not the only way of understanding health and disease, and other solutions – e.g. changing the environment or providing social support – may also be important to health.

- Although the biomedical model is firmly entrenched, doctors can and do sometimes take a broader approach.

3.2 Medical care and chronic illness

A key distinction in health care is between acute illness and chronic illness. An *acute illness* is fairly sudden. It flares up and it goes away again. It may run a natural course (like a bad cold or flu), but it may need specialised treatment. The medical profession has been particularly successful in treating what are often called 'acute illness episodes' with drugs or surgery. It may be a matter of a few minutes' consultation with a GP in the surgery or health centre where you are registered. It may take a considerable time if the GP refers you on to see a specialist at a hospital outpatient clinic and if you are then booked for a hospital stay. In all these cases, however, there is an end point of full recovery or of very considerable improvement.

In *chronic illness* there is no cure that medical science can offer. Tactics for preventing a flare-up, relief of symptoms, and ways of managing and controlling pain have to be the goals. You might know a number of people who suffer from chronic illness. Perhaps you have a child who is asthmatic or a friend who is diabetic, or perhaps you are feeling the onset of rheumatism. In these cases, there is something that medicine can do, but it cannot work the miracle of taking the condition away. There may be other kinds of help – things that other health professionals can do or that you can do for yourself, that are as important, or even more important than the actions of a doctor trained in the biomedical model.

Update: Is the patient an expert?

As we have seen throughout this unit, we all use skills to keep ourselves healthy or cope with illness in the home. But there are cases in which people may become very knowledgeable indeed about a particular disease and develop skills that may be considered to be expert. For instance, people with chronic disease often become highly proficient at dealing with their symptoms. They may also become very knowledgeable by learning about their own disease from health professionals, the media and the internet. Patients' groups and chronic illness self-help groups, such as the Multiple Sclerosis Society and the Coeliac Society UK, have campaigned for many years for people with chronic disease to be given a greater say in their own health care. The government now recognises that the chronically ill person can be said to be an 'expert patient'. That is, they are well informed and can make decisions about their own care (Department of Health, 1999).

Recent government recommendations state that patients' groups should now be supported to run self-management classes. These can use the experience of people with chronic illnesses to help other patients (Department of Health, 2001). The kinds of help offered at such classes may build upon the support already provided by patients groups and self-help organisations. They may focus upon a particular problem faced by patients, such as pain control. Such groups may also provide a place for patients to meet one another, talk and share information. The 'expert patient' approach appears to demonstrate a shift towards health professionals and people with chronic diseases working together in a more equal partnership.

In principle, it sounds a good idea that people with chronic diseases should have their knowledge and experiences recognised by heath professionals. Many patients will have had years of practice managing their disease at home and may know as much as their doctor about the condition. However, it is worth considering how these recommendations might work in reality. I question whether the patient will become an equal partner with health professionals in making key decisions. Wilson (2001) argues that although chronically ill people may be listened to more in future, it is likely that health professionals will remain in charge of directing their care. Furthermore, will enough resources be made available to help patients and support groups? As the concept of the 'expert patient' is new, it remains to be seen whether people with chronic diseases will now be treated as experts.

In the next activity you will read Chapter 13 in the Reader by Ruth Pinder, entitled 'Striking balances: living with Parkinson's disease'. Ruth Pinder is a sociologist who worked for the Parkinson's Disease Society. In the longer article from which the extract is drawn (Pinder, 1988), she explains that she wanted to understand in depth how people experienced living with this chronic illness; she found that telling people that her husband had multiple sclerosis (MS) helped to establish a relationship and also helped her to establish a framework for understanding her findings. She carried out 39 interviews over a 10-month period with 10 people suffering from Parkinson's disease (PD). On average, they were seen four times, the interviews lasted about an hour and a half, and they were tape recorded. Pinder checked the transcripts with her interviewees and asked for their comments on what she had written.

Activity 8

Allow about 45 minutes

People with Parkinson's disease

Read Chapter 13 in the Reader now. Read it all the way through and then make some notes to remind you of the key points that you feel Pinder is making. When you have done this, ask yourself what this piece of research has to say about the limitations of the biomedical model. What are they and how important are they? Is there an alternative?

Comment

Here is my set of working notes based on a reading of Pinder. Yours are unlikely to be exactly the same, but they will probably overlap.

As a summary of the argument, I wrote:

- Pinder's main theme concerns the way in which PD sufferers seek *actively to control their lives*. When she refers to 'striking balances', she is drawing attention to the way the people in her study have to accommodate to the disease but try hard not to let it take over their lives. She demonstrates that preserving a semblance of normality is crucially important for them.

- This is particularly *difficult to achieve*, (i) because the course of the disease is unpredictable, (ii) because the effects of the drugs are also unpredictable, and (iii) because these two interact.

- She is able to show that people have *different priorities* (you could fill in some examples) and that priorities also change over time.

- Patients seek but do not always gain information about their disease and about the rationale for the drug regime that they have been given. Some clearly are very *hungry for knowledge* – they get it not necessarily from the doctor, but from books and magazines and from the PD Society. Some become *experts* on PD.

On limitations of the biomedical model, I wrote:

use to support essay

- PD is an example where the goal of cure is not attainable. This illness is not an acute episode 'solved' by the doctor, but an ongoing reality for the patient and something that needs to be managed. Pinder suggests that the patients' need for control is not being acknowledged by doctors and that the medical model may need to change for chronic conditions like this. Specifically, she suggests that the emphasis in medical training on intervention may need to shift towards support and to greater understanding of patient preferences.

- Pinder also acknowledges the importance of the patients' friends and families. Their needs should not be neglected if the aim is to create as healthy a life as possible for those facing chronic illness or disability. She also introduces the role of the PD Society as a source of information and support apart from the doctor.

- The chapter affirms the argument at the beginning of this unit that we are, or can become, knowledgeable about our own health. It raises the idea that patients should have a voice and in some cases want a more equal partnership with the doctor.

An important question to ask when reading small-scale studies such as this is 'how far can we generalise?' A sample of 10 can hardly be treated as representative of the whole population of PD sufferers, let alone of all those who suffer from chronic illnesses. On the other hand, sensitively conducted studies, where the researcher builds a relationship with those being researched and allows them to speak in their own words and to reflect, can give us considerable insight into the significance of illness and the way in which people are likely to behave.

Another example which underlines the way in which the biomedical model is based on cure, and may not be at all appropriate as a model of care, relates to the care of those who are dying. The box shows how a critique of the biomedical model can help set out what form an alternative care model could take – a model which has been developed and put into practice in the hospice movement in the UK. The medical emphasis on cure can crowd out alternative ways of thinking about and acting on care. The summary in the box below, devised by a nurse working with dying people, gives you a glimpse of how a different model of care could be put into words.

Replacing cure with care?

Care of people who are dying involves:

- a recognition that dying is not a symptom but a process, and *that people need more than just physical care*

- a recognition of *the role of the family and friends*, and the impact on them of the patient's process of dying and subsequent death

- a recognition of *the contributions needed from a range of disciplines* in order that all needs are met – emotional, spiritual and social in addition to the physical needs of the dying person

- a recognition that death does not have to be seen as a negative experience, but that it can be a positive and enriching experience.

(Adapted from Biswas, 1993, pp. 133–4)

Study skills: Making notes

How did you get on with the note-making exercise? Were your points anything like those in the text? As you will remember from Section 6.6 on page 155 of *The Good Study Guide*, your notes are for *you*, so there is no reason why they should be the same as someone else's. On the other hand, you do want to try to catch the main points. How did you set about doing it? I underlined some points on my first read through and occasionally wrote a few words in the margin. Then I looked back over what I had underlined and marked the margin where a point seemed particularly important. Finally, I jotted down the main points to make the list in the comment on Activity 8. In other words, I was looking for points that were *interesting to me*. I was reading 'actively' with my pen at work – which made me think about what I was reading.

3.3 What kind of care for women in childbirth?

This topic concerns challenges to the biomedical model that stem in particular from the rise of the women's movement and its campaigns for change in medical practice. I will concentrate on childbirth as a particularly striking example of the way that lay and medical perspectives can come into collision.

Activity 9   **Critics of medicalised childbirth**

Allow about 30 minutes   Read Chapter 14 in the Reader by Lesley Doyal entitled 'The new

obstetrics: science or social control?' As you did for the previous reading, summarise the key points that are being made and then consider what this says about the relevance of the biomedical model. Consider too what Doyal's answer to the question in her title is – are the practices she describes positive or do they represent control over women?

Comment   As a summary of the argument, I wrote:

- Doyal points out that childbirth occurs in an unfamiliar place and among strangers. There can be a lack of information and support.

- She refers to a longstanding approach of 'active management of childbirth' by obstetricians (e.g. inductions and caesarean operations), and to a 'new interventionism' (monitoring of the foetus). She shows that there is not always good evidence that these procedures are beneficial.

- Developments in obstetrics can be life-saving but, while some women are reassured by and grateful for being surrounded by high-tech medicine, others feel they have had procedures foisted on them that are unnecessary and sometimes harmful to them and their babies. (You might want to note down some of the research evidence questioning routine use of procedures.)

On relevance, I wrote:

- This is another case where care for health seems to call for an adjustment in the doctor's model of practice. Unlike the case of chronic illness, where doctors do not have a cure, here doctors can do something if things go wrong, and most of us would want them to intervene. The complaint is that, instead of standing back and only coming in if needed, doctors are treating all births as potentially abnormal and denying women the opportunity to deliver their babies in the place and the way they choose.

On the question of science or control, I wrote:

- Both! The new obstetrics represents an important set of developments in high-tech medicine that have advanced understanding and enabled doctors to intervene more effectively. But if doctors, with their emphasis on what can go wrong, take the lead, women are denied control over a key event in their lives that has the potential to be positive and rewarding.

In some ways, the challenge to doctors here is a stronger one than you saw in the chronic illness case. Women are arguing, in effect, that they are doing something entirely normal, that for the most part they are healthy and well, and that they want to be able to make choices and feel in control of a significant life event. You can see from some of the language of the commentators what strong feelings are evoked. Doyal cites, for example,

Use some of these comments to support essay finding

p
P. 129
(reader)

an American writer, Rapp, who has described women as being made into 'unwitting "pioneers" on the road to medicalised childbirth'. Note, however, that this is not just rhetoric from feminists who want to see more control in women's hands. Two kinds of evidence are apparent.

First, there are the studies of women's experience during pregnancy and childbirth. Ann Oakley has been a leader here, in her classic research study interviewing women at regular intervals during their pregnancy, and finding ways to encourage women to speak about their experiences (Oakley, 1979; 1980). The newspaper article below shows how this work continues. There is also a clinical literature questioning the outcomes of some of the procedures. Study and campaigning have borne fruit. Early 1990s government policy, expressed in the document *Changing Childbirth* (Department of Health, 1992b), marked a significant change towards hearing the voices of service users in this area of care. Some people, however, are saying that the impact on the organisation of care has been disappointing.

Women 'forced into taking' antenatal tests

Chris Mihill Medical Correspondent

Pregnant women should have the right to decline tests that might detect deformities in their babies, the National Childbirth Trust said yesterday.

Antenatal tests were being virtually forced on some pregnant women, with health professionals making assumptions that screening was needed and that a handicapped foetus would automatically be aborted, the charity said.

The trust has carried out a survey of some 2,700 women, with 38 per cent being pregnant at the time and 68 per cent having had a baby less than 18 months earlier.

It found that in some cases the right of parents to choose not to have antenatal screening was being undermined by health professionals, who made assumptions that screening – and termination of pregnancy if the baby had a disability – was in parents' best interests.

One woman said that during her antenatal visit the consultant commented: 'If there's something wrong with the baby, we just get rid of it.'

The charity looked in detail at the response of 352 of the women, who were told they had a greater chance of carrying a baby with a disability, asking who they felt had made the decisions about the next step.

Sixty-three per cent of the women said they had made all the decisions, and 32 per cent that they had been fully involved in decisions. But 17 per cent said the hospital had made assumptions and 10 per cent had felt pressurised. Seven per cent did not feel they had a real choice and 2 per cent said the hospital made all the decisions.

Some women said that their decision to decline tests was not accepted, with health professionals asking them at successive antenatal appointments to have scans. Two women said their blood was tested against their will.

Other women said they were only offered tests if they agreed in advance to a termination of pregnancy if their baby had a disability.

The report concluded: 'Women should have a right to choose or refuse each test or scan. Health professionals should not make assumptions about what is in the best interests of parents. They should never put any pressure on parents.'

The antenatal tests most commonly undergone by the women included ultrasound, amniocentesis and chorion villus sampling, to look for conditions such as Down's syndrome or neural tube defects such as spina bifida.

(*Guardian*, 8 February 1997)

Key points

The biomedical model has many strengths and is strongly valued, but:

- the priorities of the medical profession and of users of its services may not always coincide

- the patient, relatives and friends have a role in instances where cure is not an appropriate or feasible goal

- the views of user groups should be heard not only about delivery of care but also about priorities for research and further development of medicine.

In the next section, I will consider the 'disease palaces' where the biomedical model is most dramatically successful in terms of its results. How does 'care' fit into this setting where the doctor has a number of co-workers and where the patient is more sick and perhaps less able to take an active part in care than the instances I have considered so far?

Study skills: Managing time

Apart from this Unit 2 text, you are being asked to read several other pieces. Being 'ambushed' by these additional tasks can throw your time plans out. That is why we put a book symbol in the margin – so that as you flick through the pages ahead, you can see any extra reading. We suggested that you allowed half an hour for the last reading. How long did it actually take you? You need to notice how long different kinds of reading take, so that you can adjust your reading speed according to circumstances. To help you think about strategies for getting through the reading ahead of you, take a quick look at Sections 5.4.2 and 5.4.3 of *The Good Study Guide* (pp. 114–16).

Section 4
A day in the life of a hospital ward

To explore care in the setting of an acute hospital, I visited Leeds General Infirmary (LGI) in the winter of 1996. The hospital provides a service of medical and surgical care for local people and, because it is a specialist teaching hospital with a medical school attached, patients are referred from all over the region for specialist advice, treatment and care. The hospital occupies a bewilderingly large, sprawling site in the centre of Leeds. It is a mix of the old and the new, and at the time I first visited it staff were particularly looking forward to the opening of a new building, providing a brand-new accident and emergency service and another 14 operating theatres. Its improved facilities for heart and brain surgery, people were saying, would make this hospital one of the best in Europe. LGI was part of what was then called the United Leeds Teaching Hospitals Trust. In 1996, the trust employed over 7,000 staff and managed another six sites in Leeds and the surrounding area. It dealt with well over 1,000 inpatients, another 500 day patients and more than 7,500 outpatients every week. Like other trusts it acknowledged severe financial difficulties, its waiting lists for admission remained high and certain areas of much-needed investment were on hold.

Update: Change at Leeds

In 2002 I contacted David Lee, Head of Continuing Professional Development at Leeds, to find out about changes there since this section was written. He noted that the General Infirmary at Leeds has become part of a group now called the Leeds Teaching Hospitals NHS Trust, one of the largest in Europe. It was created in 1998 following a merger. There are eight hospital sites and over 15,000 staff serving a local population of over 250,000. As a centre for regional specialities it needs to cater for a population in excess of 4 million. David has contributed to sections 4 and 5 and provided us with a view of the change going on in Hospital Trusts.

Some of the buildings of the Leeds Teaching Hospitals NHS Trust

See Care Systems and
Structures, Figure 1

The formation of NHS trusts

Under the NHS and Community Care Act 1990, health care
providers in the hospital and community sectors could for the
first time bid to become self-governing trusts. Trusts are in
principle free to develop their own management arrangements, to
use their assets as they see fit, and to set terms and conditions for
their staff. A first wave of 57 units was granted trust status in
April 1991, and successive waves of successful applications in
subsequent years meant that over 95 per cent of providers were
trusts by 1996. Trusts bid for contracts with GP fund-holders and
with health authorities to provide services for an area. They
compete with directly managed units, with private and voluntary
providers and with each other. They are still part of the NHS,
accountable to the Secretary of State through outposts of the NHS
Management Executive.

Primary Care Organisations (Trusts) have been established and
are in the process of maturing their services and the ways in
which they will work with the Acute Trusts to provide seamless
care for patients.

In 1996, we visited Ward 29, one of two gastroenterology wards in the medical unit, and recorded the views of patients and staff. The ward has 24 beds. Its patients were women and men, across a wide age range, suffering from digestive disorders – for example, stomach ulcers, Crohn's disease, ulcerative colitis, cancers of the digestive system or problems with liver function brought on by alcohol abuse. Because it was winter the ward had more elderly people than it would have at other times of year, and staff underlined the pressure they were under to find enough beds.

Probably everyone would agree that Jackie, the ward sister, is the linchpin of Ward 29. She qualified as a general nurse six years ago and has been working in this post for about 18 months. Hers will be the first main voice that you hear on the audio cassette as she describes her morning shift. Dave, the senior registrar, speaks next. One rung below the consultant, he is the doctor who oversees day-to-day medical work on the ward. Ann, the health care assistant, is voice number three. Although she started hospital work as a domestic, she explained that she 'always wanted to do more'. Once her children were older, she moved on to the direct care role that she describes. (Later in this part of Audio Cassette 1 you will hear James, a nurse, and Susan and Jack, a patient and her husband.)

These are all real people, talking about a real day in the life of a real ward. With their permission, we have used their first names (as they indeed use them in speaking to each other). However, we have edited the tape at points where they use the full names of patients to protect patients' confidentiality.

Activity 10   **The ward sister's day**

Allow about 10 minute

Listen to part 2 of Audio Cassette 1 (side 1), stopping at the point where Jackie goes home at 3.30 pm. At this point, just jot down as you are listening the different types of people that she deals with in the course of her day. If you have worked on a hospital ward yourself, or been in a hospital ward as a patient or as a visitor, see if you can add other people who might well be on the ward on any one day.

Comment   We tend to think of a hospital ward as a place where doctors and nurses work. In fact, as you have just heard, many more people than this both work on the ward and visit it. Jackie referred to the nursing staff from the night shift who hand over to her at 7.30 am. The need to consult the pharmacist was mentioned when she was interacting with a patient and a doctor, and she talked about 'jigging in and out' of the more formal doctors' round to deal with the physiotherapists, dieticians, social workers, occupational therapists. In the afternoons, she said, she spends a lot of time talking to relatives as well as sometimes going off the ward for a while for a sisters' meeting or a meeting with her manager. There are plenty of other people she might have mentioned. She did not talk about the regular visits of the phlebotomist to take blood (you will hear her at work later on the cassette) or her interactions with the ward clerk or the housekeeping staff. These, and the person bringing newspapers, are a very visible part of the busy ward scene. Nor did Jackie mention any kind of maintenance work. (I came up in the lift with the plumber, who was trying to find which ward had blocked drains.) Jackie did, however, mention the many phone calls that she makes, dealing with social problems, carrying out procedures that care assistants cannot do and, as you will hear later, trying to ensure that things are right for a patient returning home.

An example of one ward and one morning like this is not necessarily representative of others. But it is certainly the case that large numbers of people routinely visit acute wards in hospital. In a study of the management arrangements of 14 wards in Wales, a team of observers recorded comings and goings over a period of three days. They calculated that each day an acute ward is visited on about 125 occasions by staff who are not based on the ward (e.g. doctors, physiotherapists, porters, chaplains, phlebotomists and nurses from neighbouring wards). The demands they make upon the time of staff varies from zero for a porter collecting pathology samples to over four nurse-hours for a medical ward round:

> *The authors further calculated that a member of the ward staff had to stop what he or she was doing on average more than 36 times in each day. And the figure of 125 people did not even include family and friends of patients – a large number if open visiting was the norm. The pattern did vary, however, between different types of wards. A more specialised ward or a longstay ward for older people for example might have many fewer people in evidence.*
>
> *(Hawley et al., 1995, p. 261)*

Certainly, as Jackie's description on the audio cassette makes clear, there is a lot of co-ordinating to do if care arrangements are to go smoothly.

Activity 11   **Contrasting routines of staff on the ward**

Allow about 20 minutes   Listen now to the next bit of Audio Cassette 1 where two more of the staff
    describe their day – Dave, the senior registrar, and Ann, the health care assistant. Finish listening at the point where Ann says that her job is very much like a nurse's job. As you listen, consider the following questions.

(a)   What are the main differences in the daily routines of the three speakers you have now heard?

(b)   Who is most available to care for a patient, and what concerns other than patient care does each of these three have?

You may find that you need to listen to all three of them once again in order to prepare your answers.

Comment (a) There are different ways of approaching this, but I was struck by how very different Dave's day is from that of the other two. For Jackie and Ann, the ward is their workplace. They are there for the whole of their working time although, as Jackie says, she might leave for an hour for a meeting. A doctor, by contrast, might be in any number of places in the hospital. For a start, Dave's patients are on five wards, not one. Not only does he visit the wards, but the patients from this ward, other wards, and indeed from outside, visit him in the endoscopy department. There are of course differences between Jackie and Ann. Ann spends much of her time doing hands-on care. Jackie, you might remember from earlier, does get to do some hands-on care, and there are some procedures which Ann as a health care assistant cannot do – administering medicines for example.

(b) Of the three, Ann is the one who is most available to care for patients. Did you notice how she emphasised the importance of talking to patients? She does other things too, for example attending to stores. Jackie, you heard earlier, does a great deal to ensure that things run smoothly on the ward. She is co-ordinating, sometimes minute by minute, she is filling the gaps, dealing with crises, offering support and advice to the nurses on her ward, as well as some of the time engaging in direct patient care tasks herself. Dave carries out technical procedures and discusses their care with patients face to face. He sees an important part of his role, however, as supervising more junior medical staff and he also teaches medical students. Although he did not mention it, he is also studying when he can in order to pass the exams which will mean he can apply for a post as consultant (see the box below).

Jackie, Dave and Ann all have responsibilities that go beyond direct patient care.

Who's who among the doctors?

Would-be doctors spend five years as *students* in medical school. They must then complete one year as *House Officer* (six months in medicine and six months in surgery) before they are registered. Then come two to three years in *Senior House Officer* posts and, unless they train as general practitioners at this point, three to four years as *Registrar* followed by perhaps four to five years as *Senior Registrar* before they can apply for *Consultant* posts. Few can hope to move out of the training grades into consultant posts before their late thirties or early forties. Moves are afoot to shorten this time by creating new specialist registrar posts and abolishing the two grades of registrar.

If two consultants have patients on a ward, counting all the junior grades, there are likely to be at least ten doctors who might visit the ward.

Activity 12 **Different approaches to care?**

Allow about 30 minutes

Now play section 2 of this part of Audio Cassette 1. First, James, a qualified and experienced nurse, describes the way work is organised into what nurses call 'primary nursing' teams to provide greater continuity of care, and Jackie comments on this from her own point of view. You will then hear Jackie and Ann planning the details of a patient's discharge. Ann had been on a home visit with the patient. Concentrate in particular, however, on the later part of this section, where first Ann, then the others, discuss nurses and doctors and their contributions to care.

(a) Do the speakers feel there are real differences in how they relate to patients?

(b) Do they all value each other's work equally?

Comment   (a) Different people pick out different things as rewarding. James, the primary nurse, singles out an emotional problem he was able to address. Ann, the health care assistant, says that she likes patients who need a lot of physical help. Jackie talks at length about caring for the person as a whole, taking into account all their needs. Although she does not use it at this point, 'holistic care' is a term she and other nurses use a lot.

(b) Ann says that she doesn't believe doctors understand what nurses actually do, although James believes that much has happened to change doctors' narrow focus on disease. As a doctor, Dave is clear that nurses are vital. He singles out the emotional support that nurses give and reflects on the strains this brings. On the other hand, his examples seem to be about the nurse as 'assistant' to the doctor. On that basis, one might be inclined to agree with Ann. Notice though that the organisation of the work means that neither doctors nor nurses are well placed to observe fully the work of the other.

In the next activity you will listen to the final section of this part of the cassette, and hear something about how the ward feels from the receiving end. Susan is the patient. Seven years before, then in her early forties, she had a stroke and was nursed by Jackie, who at the time was a staff nurse. Susan, her husband Jack, and her grown-up children all knew that with a diagnosis of liver cancer Susan had only a short time to live. The week before our visit she had collapsed at home. She had been rushed into hospital where staff had been able to stabilise her condition. When I met her, she was cheerful and alert. She and Jack listened carefully to what I was trying to do and agreed that they would like to take part. Susan sounds lively and energetic on the cassette. She and Jack were hoping that she would be back home in another week and said that they planned to 'just take it from there'. Sadly, that was not to be. Susan did not leave Ward 29; about 10 days after my visit she lapsed into a coma and died.

Activity 13   **Patient perspectives**

Allow about 20 minutes

Now listen to section 3 of this part of Audio Cassette 1 (side 2). Jack speaks first, describing Susan's emergency admission. Then Susan talks to a friend who came to visit. Listen to the whole of the remaining cassette first, and jot down your first impressions. Next, read through the questions, and then play the scene again, noting down your answers.

(a) Jack and Susan have a great deal of praise for the care that they have received. What kinds of things do they value most?

(b) Alongside the praise, there are also hints of ways in which things can go wrong from a patient's point of view. What criticisms, for example, do they have of doctors? Are there any criticisms of nurses or of the nursing care they receive?

Comment   (a) Jack couldn't praise the staff enough for the support that they gave him as he stayed by Susan's bedside. There was always someone ready to talk and he was particularly grateful for the way they would talk to his children too. Information is another need that he and Susan had. They wanted straight talking and they got it. Friendliness and informality were something Susan valued. She says that nurses have time; she feels she is a name not a number.

(b)   Neither had any direct criticisms of the present doctors, but they were aware of what can go wrong. Some doctors, Susan says, talk over your head. She feels she is well able to challenge them and deal with it, but she observes that 'you've got to ask'. Jack points out that doctors are so busy that perhaps they don't know they are doing this.

It is hard to find any real criticism of the nurses. Susan does describe how confusing it can be with all the different people who come to your bedside – but she says she is a person who adjusts easily and is not afraid to ask. She and her visitor do complain about slowness in providing the diet supplements that she needs. Comparisons with home offer more clues to how hard it can be to adjust to the hospital. 'You're more one to one at home', says Susan (thinking perhaps of the fragmentation and specialisation when so many people come to attend to different things). 'You can do things in your own time', says Jack (thinking perhaps of the routines of the hospital day).

There are a number of published accounts of patient experiences in hospital which are more negative than the one you have been considering. You met some earlier in the unit in reading about childbirth. Deborah Lupton, an Australian social scientist, who has gathered together and reviewed a number of published accounts, sees in them recurrent themes of helplessness and loss of control. She regards hospitals as settings where, from a patient point of view, confidence in your own knowledge and power is challenged and your sense of your self is diminished. She cites a number of accounts by people who have become ill, particularly by social scientists used to studying other settings and by doctors who become patients and are moved to observe what is happening to them. Here is just one example from Dr Oliver Sacks, a doctor who spent a long time in hospital as the result of a leg injury. Things he already knows take on a new significance from the other side of the fence:

> One's own clothes are replaced by an anonymous white nightgown, one's wrist is clasped by an identification bracelet with a number. One becomes subject to institutional rules and regulations. One is no longer a free agent; one no longer has rights; one is no longer in the world at large. It is strictly analogous to becoming a prisoner, and humiliatingly reminiscent of one's first day at school. One is no longer a person – one is an inmate.

(Sacks, 1984, quoted in Lupton, 1994, p. 97)

The idea of 'total institutions', the depersonalisation, control and even abuse of patients that can occur are themes we take up at several points later in the course. For the moment, I shall return to the perspectives of staff as they try to provide treatment and cure alongside good continuity of care for the patient in hospital. The next section will examine in more depth the ways of working of the doctor, the nurse and the care assistant – how they define themselves in relation to others and what effect this has on the caring that is offered.

Key points

- The work of many different people must be co-ordinated to care for health in a hospital setting.

- Each occupational group tends to have a different work routine and a somewhat different outlook on care.

- Patients, at a time of often great anxiety, face the challenge of adjusting to hospital routines and of understanding and participating in their care.

Section 5
Working together for health in hospital

5.1 Doctors: the 'Great-I-Am'

We pin a lot of hopes on doctors. We expect them to know all that is relevant about the classification and treatment of diseases. We expect them to be able to make us better, and to give us an indication of what will happen to us next. There are strong pressures on doctors to respond to this expectation – to be knowledgeable and confident, to set themselves apart from ordinary mortals. Lesley Mackay is a researcher who, in 1989–90, carried out an extensive study involving over a hundred interviews each with doctors and nurses in five hospital settings in England and Scotland, exploring in depth how they saw themselves and their work. She coined the phrase the 'Great-I-Am' to try to capture the perspective of the doctors and the ways in which they related to nurses, patients and others in the hospital setting. I will quote a series of excerpts from her book (Mackay, 1993) to build up a picture of her argument about how doctors think. For many of them, she believes, life in medical school and subsequently in a hospital sets them apart from other health care workers. I will then look at Mackay's argument in the light of the material on the audio cassette and the experience of course testers.

Mackay calls attention to the image of junior doctors striding purposefully to the next patient, 'the tails of their unbuttoned white coat flapping, stethoscope prominently dangling from one pocket' (p. 63), a reflection, she says, of an attitude that 'only I can deal with this'. She then develops this idea:

> *It is easy to see how junior doctors can see themselves as being the centre of everything. The doctor arrives, decisions are taken, the action begins. Nurses, perhaps cross and impatient about any delay in the doctor's arrival, will be critical of any failure to take a speedy decision. The doctor learns to act (and it is an act, in the beginning at least) quickly and decisively. The adopted persona of decisiveness becomes convincing, and the doctor rushes onto the wards, makes the necessary decision, and rushes off again, with smaller tasks perhaps left uncommunicated or undone.*
>
> *(Mackay, 1993, p. 68)*

Mackay argues that accepting decision-making responsibility, as doctors do, can be a stressful responsibility that they admit is 'scary'. It should not, but often does, mean that the doctor ignores the contribution of others, failing to listen to those who have more contact with and knowledge of the patient.

Here is another aspect:

> *... a continual effort is made to present a united front through which the patient is kept calm and protected. The way the performance is played is that the doctor has the leading role, the nurse acts as the assistant ... The doctor can question a nurse's actions ... [but] ... if a nurse were to question a doctor in front of a patient, the doctor's presentation of confidence and competence would be undermined.*
>
> *(pp. 112–3)*

Activity 14   **Thinking about doctors and caring**

Allow 20 – 30 minutes   (a)   First, summarise Mackay's argument by reference to the following
                            questions:

(i)   What does Mackay mean by the 'Great-I-Am'?

(ii)   How does she say that the 'Great-I-Am' attitude is produced?

(iii) What results does she argue that it has?

(b)   Next, jot down your own reaction to this argument. Do you think it is
accurate? Do you think it is fair to doctors?

Comment   (a)   (i)   The 'Great-I-Am' is an expression Mackay coined to draw
attention to doctors' belief in their centrality to health care. It can
mean arrogance on the part of the doctor who might refuse to
listen to co-workers or to the patient. (But Mackay's account
shows another side – where doctors feel that they are required
to behave as if they are omniscient and always certain about a
course of action, and have instilled in them a very strong sense
of their own personal responsibility for outcomes and of the
enormity of the consequences of error.)

(ii)   The 'Great-I-Am' attitude, she argues, is also sustained in the
daily organisation of work by nurses, and by the 'golden rule' of
no disagreement in front of the patient.

(iii) She points out that the 'Great-I-Am' can give the patient
confidence that the doctors know what they are doing. But it
can also feed doctors' sense of their own importance and result
in devaluing the contributions of others – particularly nurses.
Where nurses do not speak up and challenge there is the
potential for harm to the patient.

(b)   Reading about the 'Great-I-Am' provoked some strong reactions in
our group of course testers. Some were dismissive:

*This is obsolete and of no value to the course; it's one-sided, good
doctors do not have this stance, doctors are not the 'Great-I-Am' –
they are humans!*

For others, it struck a chord:

*Some doctors I have come across in hospital, also GPs, when
asking for information they look right through you and ignore you –
you do not need to think the 'Great-I-Am' to help people; I have
experienced doctors' wrong opinions three times – I think the
doctors should listen to what people are saying.*

It would be wrong to interpret what you have read as saying that all
doctors behave in a 'Great-I-Am' way, or that they are always
'uncaring'. Mackay's point is that the preparation that doctors receive
encourages them to be active, to decide quickly on a course of action,
and to use their knowledge to get results. The model of medical activity
that they learn is primarily about *cure* rather than care in the sense that
we have been discussing it in this course. A cure perspective –
stemming from the biomedical model – can mean keeping quite *distant*
from the person who is the site of the disease. Indeed, doctors can see
this distancing as important in helping them think calmly about courses
of action without getting entangled with individuals. Both James and
Dave on the audio cassette indicated that they thought that doctors
today are more alert to these issues than they have been in the past.

A very different approach from the 'Great-I-Am' can be seen in the
words of Tom Heller (Chapter 5 in the Reader), recounting how he feels

as a GP faced by uncertainty at the end of a long day. We will be asking you to read this in detail for Unit 10 but you might like to look at it briefly now. It is certainly an antidote to the attitudes and behaviour I have been discussing. Tom Heller comments too on how he shifts between the biomedical model and a more holistic model of care.

Key points

- Both the biomedical model and ways of working in the hospital tend to set doctors apart from others in the hospital health care team.

- This can produce tensions among co-workers and can distance doctors from patients.

- There is awareness of this among doctors, however, and not all behave in this way.

Update: A move towards patient-centred care?

David Lee of Leeds Teaching Hospitals NHS Trust, commenting on recent changes towards patient-centred care, said 'The modernisation agenda stemming from the National Health Service Plan (Department of Health, 2000) is requiring major shifts in organisational and cultural thinking. The patient is increasingly being placed first and at the centre of every aspect of health care. In essence, health care and indeed ward routines are now expected to be driven by the needs of patients and users of the services, rather than by caregivers. This is closely related to the need for the Health Service, and the staff who work within it, to be responsible and accountable for the patient's experience.' Clinical governance is the term used to encompass, among other things, ensuring quality of care, learning from mistakes and reducing risk to patients. All staff are now expected to share responsibility for clinical governance. David Lee also drew our attention to the existence of independent bodies such as the Commission for Health Improvement which are also indications of the move towards making health services responsive to the wishes of patients.

5.2 Qualified nurses: working in the shadow of medicine?

Dave, the senior registrar at Leeds General, made a strong statement about nurses on the audio cassette:

> *Nursing staff are vital. I can't be there all the time. They are my eyes and ears. So they basically watch over the patients for me and will let me know of any changes either good or bad that may be important. If you are performing a procedure ... it's very helpful to have an assistant there, someone who can help you with the practicalities of it and also talk to the patient ... about bits and bobs to relax them.*

Jackie, you might remember, said something rather different in describing what good care was to her as a nurse:

> *I think giving good care is listening to what the patient and the family want first and foremost ... keeping [them] well informed is another thing, making sure that they feel physically as well as they can do ... making sure that they know their way around ... treating everybody with respect and with kindness – I think that's giving good care.*

Activity 15 **The role of the nurse**

Allow about 15 minutes What are the main differences between Dave's perceptions of the role of the nurse and Jackie's? How would you account for these differences?

Comment These two accounts are some way apart. Dave stresses ways in which the nurse can help him. He describes the nurse as an assistant to the doctor. He does not actually say that the patients are 'his' patients, although he seems to come close to it. What the nurse does, in this excerpt at least, is very much to play second fiddle. Even the reassurances that Dave knows he or she gives is downplayed as 'bits and bobs'. Jackie, on the other hand, has a much wider view of what it is that nurses do. Her account is oriented to the patient and the patient's family, not to the doctor – indeed the doctor does not figure at all!

3. PURSUING OUR PHILOSOPHY

Our aims in pursuing this philosophy are:

3.1 To work towards the continual improvement of Quality in all areas of nursing, midwifery and health visiting.

3.2 To deliver nursing, midwifery and health visiting care in partnership with those who need it wherever this is possible, working in response to their needs and expectations and acting as an advocate where appropriate.

3.3 To pursue a research-based approach to care and evaluation of personal practice.

3.4 To be committed to professional development and maintenance of personal competence in order to respond to current knowledge, thinking and attitudes in health services and society.

3.5 To assess, plan, implement and evaluate nursing, midwifery and health visiting care, in hospital and the community, in order to meet agreed standards.

3.6 To promote unity of purpose between the Trust's Governing body and nurses, midwives and health visitors, whilst recognising and valuing these professional roles. Also, to work in partnership with other health care workers and value them individually and professionally for their contribution to the service.

3.7 To promote similar unity of purpose between and within nursing, midwifery and health visiting; and, whether working in clinical practice in hospital or community, in education, management or research, this cohesion should be fostered and maintained.

UNITED LEEDS TEACHING HOSPITALS

PHILOSOPHY OF NURSING, MIDWIFERY AND HEALTH VISITING

MARCH 1993

Caring for Patients within the National Health Service

United Leeds Teaching Hospitals Trust: nursing philosophy

David Lee comments that, since this was written, the nursing philosophy has been subsumed within the new merged organisation (Leeds Teaching Hospitals NHS Trust). However, its principles remain relevant and continue to evolve with increased emphasis upon continuing professional development (CPD), responsibility and professional accountability.

The differences stand out particularly sharply because these are short extracts. No doubt, if challenged, Jackie would acknowledge that part of the job of the nurse was to do some of the things Dave describes, and Dave too would want to add that the nurse's role was rather broader than his remarks here imply. Dave certainly makes clear that he is aware that doctors can be accused of just looking at the disease, and adds his own belief that 'you care whichever branch of caring you are in'. But the audio cassette (like the excerpts from the trust's philosophy statement) does indicate that nursing works with a different model, which emphasises care rather than cure.

The single mostly frequently used definition of nursing in textbooks and classrooms is the following:

> *The unique function of the nurse is to assist the individual, sick or well, in the performance of those activities contributing to health or its recovery (or to a peaceful death) that he would perform unaided if he had the necessary strength, will or knowledge. And to do this in such a way as to help him gain independence as rapidly as possible.*
>
> *(Henderson, 1966, p. 3)*

Jackie's description of good care very much accords with this rather more formal statement. In some ways nursing seems to be the mirror image of the biomedical model.

- In place of the focus on disease, it brings the person to the fore and stresses the different goals that people might have.

- In place of striving for cure, it accepts that there are other outcomes – developing or regaining independence in the context of a chronic disease or disability, for example, or aiming for a peaceful death.

- In place of emphasising expertise and special techniques, it aspires to work with, rather than working on.

But:

- Instead of the very clearly decisive and interventionist stance of the curer, it seems deliberately to hold back and reflect. It seems altogether a more nebulous activity.

In practice, it is probably fair to say that nursing looks both ways. Nurse education undoubtedly draws on the biomedical model with its emphasis on bodily systems and disease, but it also stresses that health and healing involve more than arresting the course of a disease by surgical or chemical means. Nursing emphasises care for the whole person, and pre-registration education brings a wide range of social sciences – including aspects of sociology, psychology, economics and social policy – into the curriculum more strongly than does medicine.

Holding a biomedical model and a broader, more holistic notion of care at the same time is not an easy matter. Nurse researcher Pam Smith, through observation on hospital wards and interviews with student nurses and qualified staff, has taken a direct look at student nurses. Her work shows that, although people come into nursing because they want to 'care' and initially value care very highly, caring slips down the agenda – even though no one deliberately is devaluing it (Smith, 1992). How could this happen?

First, there are the clinical placements that students do in the course of their training. As they pass through surgical, medical, gynaecological, paediatric, geriatric wards and so on, they are, in effect, moving through medical specialties. And the way in which students talked about their experience showed them shifting from an initial orientation towards people to a biomedical approach – in other words towards a medical *cure* model, not a nursing *care* one.

Second, students found the learning offered by the high-tech specialties altogether more tangible and more exciting. They were learning new and more technical procedures:

> ... *one student, less than six months into training, compared the 'heavy' routine work of her first allocation to the neurological ward where she was now assigned. 'It's unlike most other medical wards' she said in a thrilled voice 'because there are loads of different illnesses and multiple sclerosis and all that and people coming in for tests and lumbar punctures and things.' In her excitement she saw neurology as exotic diseases and tests, rather than uncertainty, unpleasant symptoms and long-term suffering for patients and their families.*
>
> (Smith, 1992, pp. 54–5)

A comment from one of the nurses' tutors conveyed, albeit for different reasons, that she too liked the medical model – because it was 'nice and logical and it's scientific and you can do it in school beautifully' (p. 38).

The third point in some ways is the reverse of this. When the course *did* deal with emotions and with interpersonal skills, it did so in a third-year module where students were encouraged to identify and explore critical incidents that they themselves had experienced and to comment on them in discussion. The informal nature of the sessions reinforced in them a sense that this was something that could not be taught. You 'just picked it up', they said, and they concluded that this was 'stuff you learned as you went along'. Being caring, it seemed, resulted from experience and from coping with difficult situations.

These three points suggest that the learning experience of student nurses at the time of Smith's study was unwittingly *devaluing care*. Developments in nurse education have combated this in a number of ways. Student nurses spend more time in a structured educational setting and less as apprentices in hospital wards. They also now begin with a common foundation programme which emphasises health rather than disease and deliberately gives placements in community settings as well as in hospital wards.

If care tends to be devalued, cast into the shadows compared with the glamour of medicine in this way, it is important to develop concepts that can describe its contribution more clearly. *Emotional labour* is one such concept, designed to draw attention to the importance of offering support to patients, listening, getting involved with families, managing your own emotions and responding in helpful ways to others. While emotional labour is something people do for each other in day-to-day life, there are particular skills linked to emotional labour in the hospital and other health settings. For one thing, the nurse needs to make assessments of need and to respond appropriately to patients from different cultures and classes and at different points in the life cycle. There is skill too in organising emotional care, making the necessary time among the routines of physical care for work that can easily look and feel like doing nothing. Nicky James, a nurse researcher who has made a study of hospice nursing, argues that

care = organisation + physical labour + emotional labour

and she emphasises the centrality of emotional labour, the importance of the time to build emotional closeness and the logistical difficulties this can present in settings requiring 24-hour cover (James, 1992, p. 503).

The nursing staff on the ward in Leeds would no doubt identify with this – and Susan and Jack gave testimony to what they achieved. But often what will contribute most to the emotional well-being of a patient is something that seems on the face of it a very trivial and minor task – on a geriatric ward, for example, making sure hearing aids work and glasses are clean (Smith, 1992, p. 1). Nicky James and Pam Smith are among a number of researchers who suggest that emotional labour is a key concept in caring, which should be studied more carefully and incorporated into nurse education and into our understanding of the nature of nursing.

Activity 16   **Constraints on nursing care**

Allow about 15 minutes

Read the two quotations that follow. You have seen how emotional labour can be overshadowed by the glamour of cure and not be fully acknowledged in nurse education, or well understood as part of nursing. What else, do these excerpts suggest, interferes with the possibility of doing emotional labour?

> *A nurse has been closely watching a post-operative patient whose psychological depression had been impeding his recovery. For days he has been silently brooding, unresponsive to all efforts to make contact with him. Finally, one evening, he begins to respond to the nurse, talking about his worries and concerns for the first time. As she sits with him, listening sympathetically, using all of her interpersonal skills to support his emotional catharsis, she feels that this is one of the rare and precious moments when she is really 'doing nursing' in the way she was trained.*

> *Unfortunately, just after the patient began talking, the dinner trays came up from the kitchens. It is dinner time, the food is getting cold, the other patients are hungry and restless. Organisational efficiency requires that patients be fed at a certain time. But if the nurse leaves her patient to serve dinner to the others, the patient may withdraw into his shell again. The optimal time for talking to a patient cannot be regimented, controlled, or even predicted.*

> (Cherniss, 1980, p. 87)

> *One of the characteristics of nursing work is that it is difficult to specify with any precision. This is particularly true of general hospital nursing where, at different periods, nurses have done (and do) work which could be considered the province of cleaners, dieticians, porters, clerks, secretaries, ward housekeepers, receptionists and doctors ...*

Traditionally, one of the most valued attributes of a nurse has been her ability to 'cope and get the work done'. Since nurses in hospital settings are the group in continuous direct contact with patients, they tend to be the ones to cope with the absence of other staff. This is particularly true outside of office hours and at weekends, where nurses may take on secretarial or clerical tasks, run errands, or act as extension therapists.

(Beardshaw and Robinson, 1990, p. 8)

Comment

The first quotation deals with the importance of *organisational routines* in the hospital, the need for a predictable pattern of events, and scheduling and co-ordination of activity. Care, on the other hand, as you saw in Unit 1 in the context of the home and unpaid carers, is not easy to schedule and predict. It can play havoc with planned activity in a large organisation. You heard on the audio cassette about one way of trying to reconcile the two – the shift to primary nursing. Organisational demands, therefore, mean that emotional labour can be devalued and sometimes actually driven out.

The second quotation continues the theme of devaluation. Caring, it seems, often amounts to coping with whatever needs to be done at the time and seems to be something that we can 'naturally' expect of nurses – something that is unremarkable, that goes unnoticed and unsupported. Doing other jobs can mean nurses have no time to care, and report that they are not doing 'real nursing'. In short, then, if the doctor seems to be the 'Great-I-Am', the nurse seems to be the (not so) great 'Can-Do'!

It is frequently said that nursing is 'women's work' and that this too contributes to its devaluation. Caring in the home, as you saw in Unit 1, is often done by women on an unpaid and unnoticed basis. An important question, therefore, is where gender fits in.

Activity 17   **Images of nurses**

Allow about 20 minutes

This activity is designed to start you thinking about public images of nurses and the message about nursing work that they give. Consider the two advertisements for nurses overleaf. Both these advertisements ran in the national press as part of a campaign to attract more people to nursing. They are taken, as you can see, from some time ago. What message were they giving about the nature of nursing work and nursing care?

Comment

It is just as true today as it was in the 1960s, as the small print says, that most women who go into nursing marry, and that most take a break from nursing for childbearing and then return. It is also true that nurse training will help with the health care that women do in families. But it would not be surprising if nurses were annoyed at this portrayal of them. One message we might receive is that nurses are warm, attractive, caring people. Another message, conveyed by the headline and the picture is that marriage is more important for women than work, and that nursing is not really a job in its own right at all. The words say that nursing is a 'real job', but the context devalues it. The 1980s advertisement could also be said to devalue the work of nursing, although in a different way. By associating it with 'women's work' – something that comes naturally to girls – it is portrayed as a job that hardly seems to warrant formal training at all.

In the 1980s nurses campaigned against the kinds of image, in recruitment posters and in the media more generally, that portrayed them as angels or sex symbols or battle-axes (Salvage, 1985). Such

A 1960s recruitment advertisement

Nurses make the best wives

You can say that again!

Most nurses marry – and because of their training make better wives and mothers than most. When their children have started school, a great many of them return to part-time nursing, providing a good extra income for the family.

A fine training. It's the training that turns a girl into an exceptional woman. Your develop both as a nurse and as a person. Your talents and capabilities are brought out to the full. You become confident, resourceful, poised. And you're paid while training.

Good pay and long holidays. Because of this training, you qualify for a well-paid, secure job. A Staff Nurse works a 42-hour week, starts at around £700 a year. By the time she's 26, she can be earning £1,000 a year as a Ward

Sister – a lot more than most women. In addition a nurse gets up to 6 weeks paid holiday a year (even in the first year of training it's 4 weeks). She can afford to make the most of this time . . . be enterprising . . . go abroad . . . really relax and enjoy herself.

A real job. On top of this, a nurse knows she is doing a job that counts . . . that is respected by the community. She has the satisfaction of knowing her work is vital to the people who need her. She is a really important person in this modern world, and is treated as such. Thousands of girls like you are qualifying as nurses every year. Join them, and share their full, satisfying life. *Send in the coupon today for full details of how to become a nurse.*

NURSING SURELY THE MOST REWARDING JOB IN THE WORLD!

HOW TO BECOME A NURSE

	Minimum age of entry	Educational Requirements
Three-year Nursing Courses General, Sick Children or Psychiatric	18	In most cases, five years Secondary Education, up to G.C.E. standard, with the "O" level passes or the passing of the G.N.C's educational test.
Two-year Nursing Courses General, Sick Children or Psychiatric	18	A good general education; no special examination qualifications

For the older woman, there are opportunities too, especially in the two-year course.

To: The Chief Nurse Officer, Ministry of Health, P.O. Box 244, London, S.W.1. (In Scotland: The Chief Nursing Officer, St Andrew's House, Edinburgh.)
I'd like to know more about these careers.
I am particularly interested in . . . (tick whichever interests you most)
a 2 year course ☐
a 3 year course ☐

Name
Address
Age

A 1980s recruitment advertisement

The best nurses have the essential qualifications before they go to school.

Providing you have what it takes to start with, you could qualify as a State Enrolled Nurse in two years or, if you have 'O' levels as well as a State Registered Nurse in three.

Send us the coupon and we'll send you more information. Post to the Chief Nursing Officer, Dept of Health and Social Security (G/QT2, PO Box 702, London SW20 8SZ.

Name & Address

Age   Sex

Nursing. Make a career out of caring.

images are not so prominent today, but they have not disappeared completely. And today's fictional nurses do not necessarily give what nurses themselves would see as an accurate representation of the skills and the demands of their work. Sometimes in TV soap operas it is the careful attention the nurse gives that teases out information vital to treatment. But nurses' love lives figure in such stories more often than their skills as nurses. The recruitment posters, however, have changed. They now pay attention to the range of work and the diverse career opportunities in different fields of nursing. And at least one early 1990s campaign specifically addressed men. 'Nursing is an Equal Opportunity Employer' was its headline but, it went on, 'we're very much aware that men and women aren't attracted to it in equal numbers'. It then challenged ideas that a man who nursed was 'soppy' or that he was there just to do the heavy work.

In some of the textbooks for nurses of a hundred years ago, describing and prescribing their place in health care, the hospital was compared to a family – the doctor as father, nurse as mother, and patient as child. The doctor made decisions, the nurse helped and respected him, and the patient followed orders, since daddy knew best (Gamarnikow, 1978)! The gender stereotypes of the time were clear – that women/nurses are naturally more nurturant, caring and motherly, and that doctors/men are calm, decisive, and scientific and rational in their approach.

Have such ideas been overturned completely? Of course, a great deal has changed in the course of a century. Although the proportion of men in nursing remains low, at about 10 per cent overall, numbers of women doctors have risen sharply in the 1990s, so that women are now about half of all entrants to medical school. Nursing is organised in the same way as medicine, as a profession that registers its members and sets conditions for entry, which has its own specialist journals and research. Yet pay differentials are considerable; nursing only became a university subject on any scale in the early 1990s; and the lack of investment in a strong programme of funded nursing research comparable with that in medicine has been a focus of enquiry and concern (Department of Health, 1992c). Has nursing ever been granted the resources and the autonomy to show what it can do? Certainly there have been nurse-led initiatives in areas where medicine has less to give – well-person clinics, care of the dying, and pain clinics, for example. We could say that in these cost-conscious days it is surprising that all this is not more developed. I am on record as arguing that medicine and nursing remain a prime example of legacies of gender-stereotyped thought and of the devaluation of the skills of caring (Davies, 1995). Others, however, point to the power that stems from being on the ward and having more knowledge of the patient under the primary nursing structure that James described on the audio cassette (Hughes, 1988; Svensson, 1996). There is more about this and about what has been called the 'doctor–nurse game' in Unit 4.

Study skills: Using references

The usual academic convention is to refer to people by their surnames, like Hughes or Svensson. But what if you wanted to follow up what either Hughes or Svensson has to say on this subject? Where would you go? The first thing is to turn to the list of references at the end of this unit. Look at it now and see if you can make sense of it.

References are presented according to a strict format. They usually begin with the writer's *surname and initials*, then the *date* of publication. (The date can sometimes be misleading. I have a book by Sigmund Freud with a publication date of 1964, yet I know Freud died in 1939. How can this be? In fact the original was published in German in 1933 and this English translation was published in 1964.) Then we get the *title*. With the Hughes piece the title is shown in ordinary type with quotation marks round it, but if you look at some of the others in the list you'll see the title is in italics, without quotation marks. Why? In fact, the part in italics is always the title of the publication. So in the case of Hilary Graham's *Women, Health and the Family* that is the title of her book. But in the case of Hughes, D. the publication is the academic journal *Sociology of Health and Illness*. (If you look down the list you'll see that a few of the references are from this journal.) The Hughes piece is just one of the many articles in Volume 10 of the journal. The Svensson piece was published eight years later and sure enough the volume number is 18. The final information is the page numbers, so that you can find the article easily. To look up a journal article you will generally need to go to an academic library at a university, although you could enquire at your local library about any alternative sources.

If you look up the author Gamarnikow, you'll see that the reference is to a chapter in a book edited by Kuhn and Wolpe. So the title of the book is in italics, not the title of the chapter. For books, the publisher and the place of publication are also given.

With a bit of practice you will get used to these conventions. You need to understand them so that you know what you are looking for when you go to a library or a bookshop. You also need to be able to list your own references correctly at the end of your essays. You can see examples of referencing in Erin's essay on page 252 of *The Good Study Guide*.

Key points

- The cure work of doctors and the care work of nurses are both important for patient care, yet nursing often seems less important.

- The caring that nurses do is devalued in several ways, for example by its association with women's work.

- Challenges for nurses are to re-examine the care they provide, work with others on ward towards multi-disciplinary working and to devise organisational arrangements that enable high-quality care to be given.

5.3 More carers: still deeper in the shadows?

What can be said of the others who work on hospital wards? There are, as you heard on the audio cassette, care assistants, there are domestic staff, and sometimes too there are nursing auxiliaries and clerical assistants whose role is to take some of the paperwork away from the nurses, to enable them to get on with the business of giving direct patient care. You have already seen that the division of labour between doctors and nurses is not always clear-cut. You will now see that there are important overlaps between nurses and those who assist them in the work of patient care. What a care assistant does, and also what a domestic or a clerical assistant does, rather like what a nurse does, can depend on who else is available, varying from ward to ward or even varying on the same ward depending on what time of day it is. This can lead to frustration all round, with the qualified nurse feeling that she is not doing the work she is trained for and wants to do, and others feeling that no one is acknowledging the skills of the work they do.

'On the wards', the offprint you will read for Activity 18, is an excerpt from an account by anthropologist Liz Hart of the time she spent working as one of over 200 domestic staff on the wards of a large teaching hospital in the West Midlands. Her method was open participant observation – that is to say she had permission to carry out the research, and staff and management knew that she was a researcher. But she worked shifts alongside the others, doing the same work and sharing breaks with the domestic staff.

Activity 18   **Hidden contributors to care**

Allow about 20 minutes   Patient care in a hospital is not restricted to care by doctors and nurses – it includes care provided by staff who are not professionally qualified.

   Read Offprint 4 now and try to set out the different ways in which Hart's findings support this statement.

Comment   Hart shows that in the case of a teaching hospital domestic staff do many activities that can be classified as care.

- Domestics carry out a range of tasks for patients (fetching things, finding things in the locker, helping them to drink, even sometimes lifting) in response to patient requests and in the absence of nursing staff.

- Domestics converse with patients in an ordinary and everyday way which they, and some nursing commentators, claim is helpful to the patient and can be therapeutic. Relatives also sometimes turn to domestic staff for information and advice. Domestic staff can sometimes even be an 'anchor' in a setting where staff changes are rife.

- Often domestics have long years of experience in a particular ward, and wish to and successfully do build up knowledge and relationships that mean an extension of their role.

- Patient contact can be a source of job satisfaction for domestic staff, some of whom intend moving into care assistant work.

There are plenty of other examples that could be given to show that caring work is not the exclusive province of those who are qualified and registered as nurses. You will see in Block 2 that a great deal of care for elderly people in residential homes, for example, is carried out by care assistants. This can be true in hospital settings too. Qualified nurses plan, assess and supervise the work, delegating to others. This was clear when James described his role as a primary nurse on the audio cassette and when Ann, the care assistant, gave an account of her day. Care assistants and auxiliaries, however, are likely to have had some training for their face-to-face responsibilities for patients. Domestics are not. One of our course testers argued that Liz Hart's account was too positive – without careful training and supervision, the interventions of the staff that she describes could risk sometimes doing harm.

One of the members of the course team, Jan Walmsley, interviewed Val, a care assistant in a psychiatric setting, and then shadowed her as she worked for a day – recording what she did and what she had to say about her work. Val said that she was 'unqualified but not untrained'; she had had a lot of experience as a care assistant, and in practice she found that she was 'training' the junior doctors, the student nurses and the nurses with much less experience than herself. Earlier in this unit, you met the work of Nicky James (1992), studying hospice care. In this setting the sister admitted that care assistants were the 'backbone of the unit' and that she was sometimes 'a tinge jealous' of how close some were to the patients. A staff nurse from the same hospice went further and recognised that some of the care assistants possessed skills that she herself did not. Remembering one particular incident she said:

> At the time I just didn't know how to cope. And luckily the older auxiliaries were there. If Maggie hadn't been on that day I don't know what would have happened. I just didn't know what to do with this poor woman. She just completely broke down and collapsed in front of me. And I went to get Maggie, and said 'come and help me, please'. And Maggie was very firm with her, but very sympathetic at the same time.

> (Quoted in James, 1989, p. 36)

Can we ever generalise about what different grades of staff do? Can we get neat job descriptions? The answer, from workers at least, seems to be no – there is too much variation across the settings and in day-to-day resourcing. One care assistant summed it up neatly:

> I think of myself as polyfilla. Filling in the gaps, doing things the nurses haven't got time for, or making it easier for the nurses, or talking to patients when no one else has got the time to talk to them. Really just anything and everything.

> (Quoted in Ahmed and Kitson, 1993, p. 27)

There is considerable debate over what training should be provided for workers such as care assistants, by whom, and for how long. But over the last decade there has been growing recognition of the contribution made by non-qualified and non-clinical support workers. Substantial Department of Health funding has been made available to enable trusts and other health care organisations to develop education and training for these groups. National Vocational Qualifications (NVQs) and Scottish Vocational Qualifications (SVQs) are available to help staff in training for their important role in patient care. This issue will be considered in more depth towards the end of the course.

Key points

- Care assistants, and others who are sometimes not formally qualified or registered, carry out much hands-on care on hospital wards.

- Their work can overlap with that of registered nurses, and boundaries can be hard to draw.

- Although care assistants can play a key role for the patient, their training and responsibilities are not always well defined.

- New opportunities are emerging, however, which enable support workers to be formally and vocationally prepared for their roles.

Section 6
Changing contexts of health care

Spending time with Sue, the Manager of Nursing Services on the
Medical Unit at Leeds Trust back in 1996, cast a different light on direct
care relationships. As manager of 755 staff across a number of wards
and units, she could see pressures for change from a number of
directions that were altering the relationship between occupational
groups and the quality of the care experienced by the patient. Health
service managers often get a bad press. We think of them as pen-
pushing bureaucrats, far removed from an understanding of the
pressures on staff, spending money on the wrong things, not able to find
the resources that care staff need. Sue was certainly preoccupied with
resources at the time I interviewed her. It was mid-winter. As we spoke,
there were more than 50 'outliers' – overflow patients housed in surgical
wards since all medical beds were full. 'In the last two weeks', she said,
'I've done nothing but beds.' It was a matter of negotiating, but also of
getting some agreement about delaying the booked admissions when
faced with the high numbers of emergencies especially among old
people as a result of the cold weather. But there was much more on her
agenda than this.

The gastroenterology wards had been set up only two years earlier.
Before that patients went to a general medical ward. The new
arrangement was part of the consultant's vision of integrating medical
and surgical work in a new digestive diseases unit. A closer-knit,
specialised team was the result. Sue was now thinking about the
boundary between gastroenterology work and care for older people.
'We will be delivering a more complex service to an ageing client base',
she said. 'How can we organise our services to manage that more
effectively?' She was alert too to the recent reduction in hours of work
for junior hospital doctors and the consequent effects for nurses. 'You
can't wait 24 hours for a doctor to re-site a cannula, but is it the right
direction to go for the most skilled nurses to be the ones who can take
technical procedures away from doctors?' This is being explored at
national level, as the nursing profession debates the kinds of advanced
roles it needs. Changing the ways doctors work can make a difference.
The trust had introduced ward-based house officers, working a shift
system. Just by being there, they now worked more closely with the
nurses, they got involved in the care plan and the handover. Sue's
conversation was peppered with talk of new models of care and of the
need for nurses to get involved in designing them.

But Sue was looking outside the hospital too. NHS policy documents
stress the need to move as far as possible from costly specialist services
in hospitals and to make the service more primary-care led. This means
more preventive and health promotion work, a bigger role for GP
services, and care in the community as far as possible rather than
inpatient care. Also, pressure on beds and calls for more efficient use of
the most costly health care resources mean that patients are moving
through the hospital much faster and needing more nursing care once
they get home. The roles of doctor and nurse, dietician, physiotherapist,
occupational therapist and social worker are blurring in the joint care
teams being set up in the community. 'None of us can work within our
professional boundaries any more', Sue observed.

Sue identified four themes in all these changes.

1   The health needs of clients and the nature of client groups are both changing.

2   New medical and technical developments need to be accommodated.

3   New ideas about organising care delivery in the hospital and in the community are being tried.

4   A forward-looking response is needed to the changing priorities of the NHS and its relationship with other providers.

One more thing that Sue mentioned, although she said little about it, was change in 'public expectations'.

Update: Changing roles and responsibilities

Sue was making these comments before the Labour government came to power in 1997 and started to create what it called the 'New NHS'. After 1997 there were changes to nursing and medical education to create more shared learning and break down the boundaries between professions. There were initiatives designed to create more flexible ways of working and encourage nurses to expand their responsibilities and move into leadership roles. The National Health Service Plan (Department of Health, 2000) laid out the government's plans for investment and reform of the NHS, and placed the breaking down of rigid working roles at the centre of improvement. Although increasing the number of trained staff was to be part of the drive for improvement, this document also placed importance upon reviewing roles and responsibilities and broadening the role of nurses in hospitals. 'The new approach will shatter the old demarcations which have held back staff and slowed down care. NHS employers will be required to empower appropriately qualified nurses, midwives and therapists to undertake a wider range of clinical tasks including the right to make and receive referrals, admit and discharge patients, order investigations and diagnostic tests, run clinics and prescribe drugs' (Department of Health, 2000). However, the agenda for change encompassed within the NHS Plan is not solely about the use and deployment of professionally trained nursing staff: all staff are increasingly being seen as part of an integrated team approach to health care provision on the ward.

Sue's concern with care for older people was reflected in the publication of a National Service Framework – one of many such documents setting out the standards of care that NHS providers should meet. One thing Sue did not mention was the join between hospital care and care in the community. An emphasis on primary care and better connections between health and social care has been very much a focus of government policy since 1997. There is more discussion of this area in Unit 27.

Activity 19   **Changing expectations of the health care professional?**

Allow about 15 minutes   For the final activity of this unit, reflect for a moment on how far patient expectations of health professionals are changing. Do you think the passive patient, deferential to the doctor, is a thing of the past? Think about attitudes in your own generation and those of your parents or your children. Think too about whether the unit has supplied any clues.

Comment by Celia Davies

This activity took me back to my childhood in the 1950s. The visit of the GP was a major event. Kitchen, bathroom and living room had to be spotless lest he wish to enter. I was posted to listen for the sound of the car (a rare event in our street). My mother would hover anxiously. No one else was ever addressed in this 'yes doctor', 'no doctor' fashion. He (and it always was a he), with his education and accent, his car and his clothes, seemed in my eyes to be from a different planet!

Jack, on the audio cassette, contrasted how Susan was cared for and how more formal things had been in the past. I was struck by the bulletin board full of explanatory leaflets on the corridor in the ward. I thought of the many self-help groups and disease societies that there is today, like the Parkinson's Disease Society that you came across earlier. The childbirth example is the most dramatic one in the unit – where women have organised to challenge doctors and to provide alternative sources of information and interpretations of medical knowledge. Today there are even support groups and health information resources on the internet.

The changing face of the general practitioner

One text proposes that the biomedical model is under attack from at least four main social trends (Cooper *et al.*, 1996).

1   *A questioning of the objectivity of science and scientific enquiry.* There is a recognition, for example, that its explanations are not complete and that it is not entirely value-free; also that the social sciences have something to offer to the understanding of illness.

2   *Growth in confidence of the professions surrounding medicine* and a readiness among them to develop their own more socially oriented models of illness and of healing. The authors cite nursing and social work in particular.

3   *The rise of health promotion* drawing on multidisciplinary input and challenging practitioners to cross traditional boundaries in sharing knowledge with each other and with lay people.

4   Various forms of what the authors call *alternative caring*. They refer to palliative care (citing the hospice movement and the work of Biswas (1993) which I described in Section 3.2). They also mention contemporary use of complementary medicine, and an interest in Eastern cultures and alternative lifestyles.

For Cooper and his colleagues, the future lies in developing a bio-psychosocial model of caring for health, where care is more integrated, where different professionals take the lead at different times, and where patients themselves are more involved. Whatever the future holds, it seems clear that the biomedical model no longer enjoys an uncontested dominance in contemporary society (Williams and Calnan, 1996).

Conclusion

This unit has covered a great deal of ground, selecting from the many people who contribute to caring for health. Let us look again at the core questions with which the unit started.

- *What is health care and who does it?* A very wide variety of activities contribute to our health. Many of them we can do for ourselves; others require the help of health professionals, not always doctors and nurses.

- *How important are medicine and medical ways of thinking?* The biomedical model has had, and will continue to have, a profound impact on caring for health, but sometimes it needs to be used in alliance with other approaches, and sometimes other approaches even need to take priority.

- *How is health care work organised?* We have examined this in the hospital setting in particular and considered some of the occupational groups whose work needs to be co-ordinated. As you progress through the course you will meet many other settings, from the GP surgery to the residential home, from the contribution of nurses and home care assistants in private homes to health projects set up by activists in the community.

- *What does it mean to be on the receiving end of health care?* You have met many different answers to that question in this unit. Examples have ranged from those for whom health care is an entirely negative experience, involving loss of control and depersonalisation, to those – like Susan and Jack – who are deeply thankful for the information and support they have received. The one thing that is certain is that patterns of caring for health will change in the future, influenced by a wide array of factors inside and outside the health care system.

Study skills: Keeping a study diary

Having completed two weeks of K100, how do you feel it has gone? Are you getting what you should out of the course? Do you feel you have learned a lot – or are you just confused? Do you feel you have the skills to cope with the course? Now is a good time to reflect on your first experiences.

How to become an effective student is something you have to work out for yourself. You have to think about what *you* want from the course – what time and energy *you* have available – what strengths you have already and what weaknesses you might need to work at. Then you devise strategies for tackling the work ahead of you. Later you reflect on how things have gone and reconsider your strategies. You can't afford just to trudge on hoping for the best. Your time is too precious.

One excellent way of encouraging yourself to reflect is to keep a study diary. Just write a page each week or so, under headings such as 'Main achievements', 'What didn't go well?', 'Good feelings/bad feelings', 'Points for future study', 'Worries ahead', 'Strategies for tackling them'. Just thinking about these things will make you more analytical about your approach to study. But when you come to look back over these notes after a month or two, you will be able to see patterns in your studies, and to think strategically about them. Even if you only manage to keep a diary for short spells, every now and then, it can bring a big change to the way you think about your studies. Why not try starting a diary now? To help you think your way into it, complete your reading of Chapter 1 of *The Good Study Guide*, by looking at Sections 1.5 to 1.7 (pp. 18–26).

References

Ahmed, L. and Kitson, A. (1993) *The Role of the Health Care Assistant within a Professional Nursing Culture*, Report No. 3, National Institute for Nursing, Centre for Practice Development and Research, Oxford.

Armstrong, D. (1993) 'From clinical gaze to regime of total health', in Beattie, A., Gott, M., Jones, L.J. and Sidell, M. (eds) *Health and Wellbeing: A Reader*, Macmillan, London.

Barker, M., McClean, S., McKenna, P., Reid, N., Strain, J., Thompson, K., Williamson, A. and Wright, M. (1988) *Diet, Lifestyle and Health in Northern Ireland*, University of Ulster, Coleraine.

Beardshaw, V. and Robinson, K. (1990) *New for Old? Prospects for Nursing in the 1990s*, Research Report No. 8, Kings Fund Institute, London.

Biswas, B. (1993) 'The medicalization of dying: a nurse's view', in Clark, D. (ed.) *The Future for Palliative Care*, Open University Press, Buckingham.

Blaxter, M. (1990) *Health and Lifestyles*, Tavistock/Routledge, London.

Cherniss, C. (1980) *Staff Burnout: Job Stress in the Human Services*, Sage, Beverley Hills.

Cooper, N., Stevenson, C. and Hale, G. (eds) (1996) *Integrating Perspectives on Health*, Open University Press, Buckingham.

Cox, B. (1987) *Preliminary Report of a Nationwide Survey of the Physical and Mental Health Attitudes and Lifestyles of a Random Sample of 9003 British Adults*, Health Promotion Research Trust, London.

Cox, B., Huppert, F. and Whichelow, M. (eds) (1993) *The Health and Lifestyle Survey: Seven Years On: A Longitudinal Study of a Nationwide Sample, Measuring Changes in Physical and Mental Health, Attitudes and Lifestyle*, Dartmouth, Aldershot.

Davies, C. (1995) *Gender and the Professional Predicament in Nursing*, Open University Press, Buckingham.

Department of Health (1992a) *The Health of the Nation: A Strategy for Health in England* (Cm 1986), HMSO, London.

Department of Health (1992b) *Changing Childbirth: Report of the Expert Maternity Group chaired by Baroness Cumberlege*, HMSO, London.

Department of Health (1992c) *Report of the Taskforce on the Strategy for Research in Nursing, Midwifery and Health Visiting*, HMSO, London.

Department of Health (1999) *Saving Lives: Our Healthier Nation*, Department of Health, London.

Department of Health (2000) *The National Health Service Plan, A plan for investment*, Department of Health, London.

Department of Health (2001) *The Expert Patient: A new approach to chronic disease management for the 21st century*, Department of Health, London.

Department of Health, http://www.doh.gov.uk [accessed 30.4.02]

Department of Health, http://www.statistics.gov.uk/statbase/geog.asp [accessed 30.4.02]

Department of Health, http://www.statistics.gov.uk/census2001/default.asp [accessed 30.4.02]

Gamarnikow, E. (1978) 'Sexual division of labour: the case of nursing', in Kuhn, A. and Wolpe, A.M. (eds) *Feminism and Materialism*, Routledge and Kegan Paul, London.

Graham, H. (1984) *Women, Health and the Family*, Wheatsheaf Books, Brighton.

Hawley, C. *et al.* (1995) *Nurses Manage: Issues of Nurses and Management in the General Hospital*, Avebury, Aldershot.

Henderson, V. (1966) *The Nature of Nursing: A Definition and its Implications for Practice, Research and Education*, Macmillan, New York.

Howlett, B., Ahmad, W. and Murray, R. (1992) 'An exploration of white, Asian and Afro-Caribbean peoples' concepts of health and illness causation', *New Community*, Vol. 18, No. 2, pp. 281–92.

Hughes, D. (1988) 'When nurse knows best: some aspects of nurse/doctor interaction in a casualty department', *Sociology of Health and Illness*, Vol. 10, No. 1, pp. 1–22.

James, N. (1989) 'Emotional labour: skill and work in the social regulation of feelings', *Sociological Review*, Vol. 37, No. 1, pp. 15–42.

James, N. (1992) 'Care = organisation + physical labour + emotional labour', *Sociology of Health and Illness*, Vol. 14, No. 4, pp. 488–509.

Jones, L. (1994) *The Social Control of Health and Health Work*, Macmillan, Basingstoke.

Lupton, D. (1994) *Medicine as Culture: Illness, Disease and the Body in Western Societies*, Sage, London.

Mackay, L. (1993) *Conflicts in Care: Medicine and Nursing*, Chapman & Hall, London.

Oakley, A. (1979) *Becoming a Mother*, Martin Robertson, Oxford.

Oakley, A. (1980) *Women Confined*, Martin Robertson, Oxford.

Pinder, R. (1988) 'Striking balances: living with Parkinson's disease', in Anderson, R. and Bury, M. (eds) *Living with Chronic Illness: the Experience of Patients and their Families*, Unwin Hyman, London.

Salvage, J. (1985) *The Politics of Nursing*, Heinemann, London.

Scottish Executive (2000), The Scottish Health Survey, http://www.show.scot.nhs.uk/scottishhealthsurvey/ [accessed May 2002]

Smith, P. (1992) *The Emotional Labour of Nursing: How Nurses Care*, Macmillan, London.

Svensson, R. (1996) 'The interplay between doctors and nurses – a negotiated order perspective', *Sociology of Health and Illness*, Vol. 18, No. 3, pp. 379–98.

Williams, S. and Calnan, M. (1996) 'The "limits" of medicalization?: modern medicine and the lay populace in "late" modernity', *Social Sciences Medicine*, Vol. 42, No. 12, pp. 1609–1620.

Wilson, P.M. (2001) 'A policy analysis of the expert patient in the United Kingdom: Self-care as an expression of pastoral power', in *Health and Social Care in the Community*, Vol.9, No.3, pp.134-142.

World Health Organization (1996) *Basic Documents* (41st edn), WHO, Geneva.

Acknowledgements

Grateful acknowledgement is made to the following sources for permission to reproduce material in this unit:

Text

Mihill, C. (1997) 'Women "forced into taking" antenatal tests', *Guardian*, 8 February 1997, © The Guardian 1997.

Illustrations

p. 78: cover of *Health & Fitness*, May 1997, courtesy of Nexus Media Ltd; cover of *Men's Health*, May 1997, courtesy of Rodale Press; cover of *Here's Health*, May 1997, courtesy of EMAP Elan; *p. 86 (top left and bottom right)*: L. Taylor/World Health Organization; *p. 86 (top right)*: J. Moquillaza/World Health Organization; *p. 86 (bottom left)*: H. Anenden/World Health Organization; *p. 88*: Wellcome Trust Medical Photographic Library; *pp. 99, 109*: courtesy of Leeds Teaching Hospital NHS Trust; *p. 101*: from Carol Hawley *et al.*, *Nurses Manage*, Aldershot, Avebury, 1995, © Crown Copyright is reproduced with the permission of the Controller of Her Majesty's Stationery Office; *p. 114*: Advertising Archives.

Tables

Tables 1 and 2: courtesy of Professor Mildred Blaxter.

Extra information on Leeds Teaching Hospitals NHS Trust

David Lee

Unit 3
Social Care in the Community

Prepared for the course team by Jan Walmsley
Updated by the author with advice from Jo Warner

While you are working on Unit 3, you will need:

- Course Reader
- Offprints Book
- *The Good Study Guide*
- Audio Cassette 1, side 2
- Care Systems and Structures
- Wallchart

Contents

Introduction

So far in Block 1 we have visited two major areas of care activity: the family and informal care in Unit 1; and health and health care in Unit 2. Unit 3 is about what happens in the grey area between the private sphere of the family and the highly public sphere of medical care, a huge range of activity we have called, for want of a better term, social care.

To mention just a few of those who work in what could be broadly called social care, we could be talking about social workers, childminders, day care staff, community workers, counsellors, sheltered housing wardens, home carers, befrienders, meals-on-wheels volunteers, residential childcare workers, foster parents, and so on. If we wanted instead to think about those on the receiving end, we might mention under-fives, frail older people, people with learning disabilities, adult survivors of child sexual abuse, children on child protection registers, homeless people ... Or we might use another framework altogether, and refer to clients or customers, users or residents.

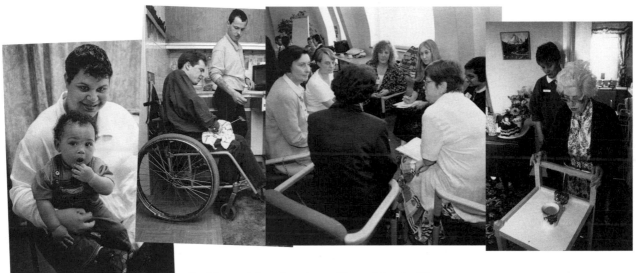

Social care takes place in a wide variety of settings

Unit 3 explores *changes* in social care, in particular the impact of reforms known as 'community care'. It also examines ideas about how care should be organised and developed by service users themselves.

The focus is home care services for adults, because the thrust of community care is towards more care being delivered at home. You will have the opportunity to consider other dimensions of social care in other parts of the course.

Core questions

- What is community care?
- What is the effect of changes in community care policy on who does the caring and who pays for care?
- What is meant by a 'market' in health and social care, and what impact does it have on relationships between care providers, informal carers and people who use services?
- What do people who use care services want?

Section 1
What is community care?

Community care is crucial to understanding social care in the 1990s and beyond. But community care is a chameleon term whose meaning has changed over time, and according to who is using it. In this section I untangle some ideas about community care.

1.1 Care: from the community to institutions and back again

When people talk of community care they might mean many things, but I shall begin by looking at some changes in the way care has been provided over time, specifically the shift from community to institutional care and back again over the past two centuries.

Arrangements to support people who need care in their own communities have a long history. In England and Wales before the 1834 Poor Law Amendment Act, which sought to make entering and living in a workhouse the only way for the poor to get help, a system of cash payments to paupers called 'outdoor relief' operated in some country areas. It was common practice for locally elected overseers responsible for collecting and spending the parish poor rate to make provision for 'community care'. Institutions like hospitals were few and far between, and very expensive. The eighteenth-century Overseers of the Poor records for Marston Mortaine in Bedfordshire contain many entries like the following:

- *10th March 1759 – pd. Mary Bushby for nursing Widow Doulton ... 1s (5p).*

- *26th May 1760 – pd. Wm. Battersham's wife for Jane Buckingham being sick ... 1s 6d (7.5p).*

(Quoted in Walmsley, 1990, p. 13)

The records of Aspley Guise, also in Bedfordshire, contain references to payments to family members for care, showing that some families needed financial help if they were to fulfil their obligations:

- *October 2nd 1826 – Kitty Marriot to have 7d for nursing her sister.*

- *November 17th 1827 – It was resolved that Susan Marriot, a pauper, should have 1s 6d a week for attending her mother and father.*

(p. 13)

It is not surprising that the overseers should make such arrangements. In 1770 transporting Eleanor Burton, a resident of Aspley Guise, to St Luke's hospital in London cost £3 18s (£3.90), and her fees were an additional £1 12s 6d (£1.62). Then, as perhaps is also the case nowadays, home-based care was less expensive.

If care by community members is not new, but something that has gone on and been supported by the institutions of government for a very long time, why is community care so often seen as something recent? To appreciate this, it is important to recognise that placing people in institutions like workhouses became a preferred solution to the 'problem' of care for people who were unable to fend for themselves between the early nineteenth century and the mid-twentieth century.

You can see some of the stages in this preference for institutional solutions on the wallchart. The first group for whom state asylum provision was made were people with mental illness, with the first publicly funded lunatic asylum opening in Bedford in 1811; while provision for older people who were chronically sick and whose families were unable to provide for them was initially in workhouses (from 1834) and subsequently in public assistance institutions (from 1929), in effect workhouses by another name. In practice, institutional care never provided more than a minority of care for any group but it did command a lion's share of resources, which meant that there was little in the way of support for people living outside the large institutions.

You'll be learning a lot more about institutional care in the course, especially in Blocks 2 and 4. But for the moment I list three features of institutional care which distinguish it from community care.

1 Institutional care involved people leaving their homes and their families behind to live in hospitals or homes which were often at a considerable distance.

Institutions were often remote from people's homes

2 Institutional care was largely a public responsibility where costs were paid out of taxation and care was provided by paid workers.

3 Services which provided institutional care were often under-funded, and conditions for residents were poor.

Modern ideas about community care can be seen as a reaction to the idea that the best place for care was in institutions where people were housed in large groups. This happened in two stages.

 1 In the 1960s and 1970s 'community care' was a term which referred to the relocation of older people and people with learning difficulties and mental health problems from institutions (often hospitals) to large-scale hostels or old people's homes, i.e. 'the community' was defined as 'not hospital'. This is often referred to as 'care in the community'. People were physically in the community, but usually not included in its daily life.

2 Since the 1980s 'community care' has come to refer to the dismantling of large-scale provision in any kind of institution and bringing care back home. As one recent author put it:

Broadly, it [community care] means helping people who need care and support to live with dignity and as much independence as possible 'in the community'. The 'community' is hard to define. It most often means ordinary homes, but for some people it includes special forms of housing, or residential or nursing homes.

(Meredith, 1995, p. 16)

This version of community care has been dubbed 'care by the community' to distinguish it from 'care in the community'. The ideal is that people are actually part of communities, not merely placed in specialist homes within its spatial boundaries, and that members of the community contribute to doing the caring.

1.2 Community care: forces for change

You can see that community care has been around for a very long time. But I have suggested that the modern concept of community care can be seen as a reaction to institutional care. There were three major forces for change: changing ideas about care, an economic agenda, and a political agenda.

Changing ideas about care

Institutions came to be seen as unsuitable places for care. The influences leading to this view can be summarised under three headings: research, scandals and new ideas.

Research. In 1962, Peter Townsend published *The Last Refuge*, a report on conditions in homes for older people. There is an extract from this in the Reader (Chapter 1 'Anthology: voices from the institutions'). He reported on the depersonalising regime and the hopelessness of both residents and staff. He was followed by others, for example Maureen Oswin in *The Empty Hours* (1971) showed the emotional deprivation of disabled children living in hospitals.

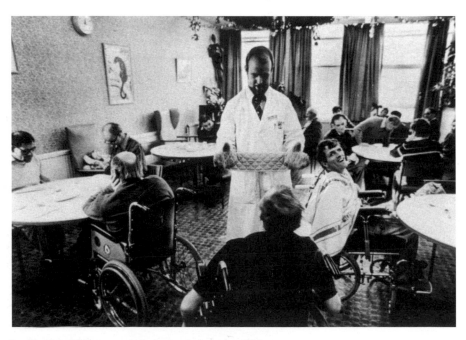

Institutional life came to be seen as depersonalising

Hospital scandals. During the 1960s and 1970s, a series of hospital scandals hit the headlines. Investigations into conditions in long-stay hospitals for people with learning disabilities and mental illness revealed large-scale neglect and ill-treatment of patients.

New ideas such as 'normalisation' began to take root. Pressure groups like Campaign for Mentally Handicapped People (CMH) argued that people who needed long-term care should have the opportunity to live an 'ordinary life' in the community (Kings Fund, 1980), not be shut away in hospitals.

An economic agenda

At the same time as changes in ideas about where care should best be delivered came concerns about the *costs* of long-term care, especially for older people. This concern was fuelled by two financial calculations.

1   Statistical projections of increasing numbers of older people in the population were used to stir up fears that their care would burden an ever-shrinking number of able-bodied adult tax payers. The bar chart in Figure 1 shows the projections.

2   Because of the way public funding worked to encourage private residential care rather than support for local authority provision, public expenditure on private residential care increased from £10 million in 1979 to £1,872 million in 1991 (Means and Smith, 1994).

Care by the community, because it was expected to draw on the energies and resources of existing 'informal support networks' – families, friends and neighbours – promised to be a cheaper option.

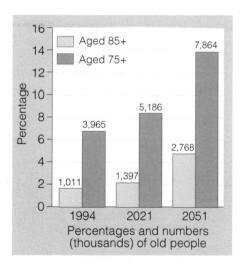

Figure 1
Projected changes in the age structure in the UK population 1994 –2051 (Joseph Rowntree Foundation, 1997, p. 3)

Study skills: Reading bar charts

In Unit 1 you read pie charts to find out some statistics about families. Figure 1 is another kind of chart, this time telling you about the numbers of older people in our society, both now and as projected into the future.

Reading a bar chart is usually a matter of diving in, selecting one of the bars and trying to work out what it is telling you by:

• looking to the key to see what a bar with that shading stands for

• looking below to see what the bar is labelled

- looking to the left of the chart to see what the height of the bar means

- looking at the title of the chart to see what the whole thing is about.

Don't worry if you find the bar chart difficult at this stage – we'll be coming back to it in Unit 5.

A political agenda

Alongside changing ideas and economic forces was a political agenda, most strongly associated with the Conservative governments of the 1980s. Advocates of change argued that:

- the welfare state set up in the 1940s had created a culture which encouraged people to rely too much on state welfare – if possible, individuals should manage without help from the state, and instead rely on their families

- the welfare state had become a vested interest largely run for the benefit of those who worked for it – health and care professionals, civil servants – and not for those who used it: the power of such groups should be broken

- introducing competition and a market in health and social care would improve quality and drive down costs.

Taken together, these three forces – changing ideas about care, and the economic and political agendas – brought a wide-ranging consensus on the desirability of moving care out of publicly funded institutions into 'the community'. Community care, it was argued, would not only be better care, offering a better quality of life, it would also be cheaper because it could harness the resources held in 'the community'; and it would promote a culture which encouraged initiative and self-help rather than reliance on the state.

1.3 The community care reforms: supporting care by the family

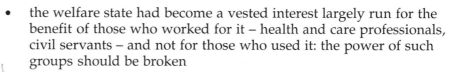
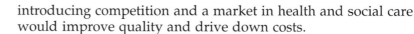

Community care meant more than just closing down large-scale institutions. If that was to work, then support services in the community were needed. The reforms ushered in by the NHS and Community Care Act 1990 (and equivalent legislation in Northern Ireland) established the present framework of community care. The Act's effects will be examined at various points in the course, and its key features are described in Care Systems and Structures. Here I will examine how it set out to change the emphasis of services.

An important dimension of the community care reforms is a changed vision of where the major responsibility for care should rest. Putting people who needed care into institutions placed the costs of care on to public expenditure and the work of care on to paid workers.

One way of looking at more recent changes is to see them as shifting the balance of responsibility for providing care. The emphasis moved away from services, such as hostels or old people's homes, which *replace* family care towards services which *supplement* family care and other types of unpaid care. The aim is to enable the family to continue to care and thus make it possible for people who need care to stay in their own homes. It is an approach which harnesses the willingness of relatives to care for loved ones and makes use of the resources that families can provide.

The role of families in caring for dependent members was clearly spelt out in the White Paper *Caring for People* (Department of Health, 1989a) which preceded and largely informed the 1990 Act (see Care Systems and Structures).

This describes community care as meaning:

> *providing the right level of intervention and support to enable people to achieve maximum independence and control over their own lives.*
>
> *(Department of Health, 1989a, para. 2.2)*

The White Paper refers to:

> *[a] spectrum of care, ranging from domiciliary support provided to people in their own homes, strengthened by the availability of respite care and day care for those with more intensive care needs, through sheltered housing, group homes and hostels where increasing levels of care are available, to residential care and nursing homes and long stay hospital care for those for whom other forms of care are no longer enough.*
>
> *(para. 2.2)*

but adds that:

> *the reality is that most care is provided by family, friends and neighbours.*
>
> *(para. 2.3)*

The idea that services should supplement, rather than replace, family care is clearly stated in this extract:

> *The Government recognises that many need help to be able to manage what can become a heavy burden. Their lives can be made easier if the right support is there at the right time, and a key responsibility of service providers should be to do all they can to support and assist carers. Help may take the form of providing advice and support as well as practical services such as day, domiciliary and respite care.*
>
> *(para. 2.3)*

The White Paper also states that:

> *Helping carers to maintain their valuable contribution to the spectrum of care is both right and a sound investment.*
>
> *(para. 2.3)*

The ideas expressed in this White Paper about the importance of carers were re-emphasised ten years later in the National Strategy for Carers which you read about in Unit 1.

You might recognise the situation the Durrants are in as being in part a result of community care policies. Lynne cares for Arthur with help from home carers, a social worker, and the community nurse

Parallels to this new emphasis on families caring for their own are to be found in attitudes to caring for children. The cardinal principle of the Children Act 1989 (see Care Systems and Structures) is that it:

> *... rests on the belief that children are generally best looked after within the family with both parents playing a full part.*
>
> *(Department of Health, 1989b, p. 1)*

As far as local authorities are concerned, their duties are to:

- support children and their families

- return a child looked after by them to his or her family unless this is against the child's interests

- ensure contact with parents whenever possible when a child is looked after by them away from home.

So, as well as meaning care provided outside institutions, community care came to mean *in addition* that the family is the best place for care, for adults and children, and services should be geared to support family care.

1.4 Community care: exploitation or ideal?

So far, I have built up two different but connected meanings of the term 'community care'. You have seen that in the 1960s and 1970s it was a term used to refer to the closing of large-scale institutions, and that in the community care reforms of the 1990s and the Children Act 1989 the term refers to changing the emphasis of services from *replacing* to *supporting* family care.

We turn now to a major set of criticisms of community care policies, made from a feminist perspective, which argue that in effect community care means care by the family. You may recall from Unit 1 that feminist perspectives:

- question existing structures and assumptions and ask about their implications for women

- insist that women's voices should be heard and given equal value

- seek to answer and understand patterns of exploitation and oppression of women in all areas of life.

Community care has been the subject of considerable research by feminists. You encountered some of it in Unit 1 where I quoted from research by Jane Lewis and Barbara Meredith on 'daughters who care'.

Gillian Pascall, a feminist sociologist, argued that, like the concept of 'the family' you encountered in Unit 1, community care is a term which legitimates minimal state activity in the private sphere of home and family. It also disguises minimal men's activity (1986, p. 85).

She went on to argue that the language of community care hides its real intentions:

> *Its use has been in justifying low government spending on the elderly and the handicapped, and in disguising policies whose real effects are to burden and isolate individuals. Irony is plentiful. For community one can read its virtual opposite. The heavier the demands of caring, the less likely the 'community' will care to be involved. An expression which appears usually to cover everyone disguises the fact that whether as paid workers or as relatives, it is generally women who do the 'caring'. And for 'care' when it comes to state activity, one may often read 'neglect'.*

(Pascall, 1986, pp. 85–6)

By putting its impact on women at centre stage, Pascall and other feminists launched a devastating attack on the whole idea of community care.

Activity 1   **Who benefits from community care policies?**

Allow about 5 minutes   Using Pascall's analysis, make two lists:

(a)   who benefits from community care policies

(b)   who does not benefit.

Comment   (a)   Those who benefit appear to be:
- governments, because community care justifies minimal state activity
- men, because it disguises their minimal activity in care
- tax payers, whose bill is lower.

(b)   Those who do not benefit appear to be:
- women relatives (informal carers)
- 'individuals', who are often burdened and isolated.

Research undertaken from a feminist perspective in the 1980s tended to demonstrate that in effect 'the community' did very little to support the work of care. An Equal Opportunities Commission survey into informal care for older people stated:

> *Only in one case were relatives cited as giving 'frequent' help; more commonly it is 'hardly ever' or 'none at all'. Help from voluntary organisations or neighbours was even more rare, and where given, it was on a fairly casual basis. Ironically, it appeared that the greater degree of dependency, the smaller the amount of external help offered.*
>
> *(Equal Opportunities Commission, 1982, pp. 17–18)*

The feminist case was that community care assumes the existence of informal carers who are persuaded to take a larger share of the work involved. Although the public statements make reference to care as 'a responsibility which must be shared by everyone' (Department of Health and Social Security, 1981, para 1.11), feminists argued that the community does not care, and that:

> *In practice, community care equals care by the family, and in practice care by the family equals care by women.*
>
> *(Finch and Groves, 1980, p. 494)*

 These arguments go some way to explaining the emphasis in government policy on supporting carers (the Carers (Recognition and Services) Act 1995, for example). The drive to support carers is a response to the findings of studies like the Equal Opportunities Commission survey quoted above. But, feminists argue, it may not be entirely altruistic! If services are to supplement rather than replace family care, then it is necessary to locate someone who will take responsibility for a relative or, sometimes, friend or neighbour in need of extra care. If the system collapses, it will have to be completely rebuilt. How much better to shore it up by provision of respite care and other services.

Of course, we know that it is not only women's interests that are at stake when family care is under consideration. Forty-two per cent of carers are men, as the figures quoted in Unit 1 show. Moreover, since the 1980s when the feminists referred to here were developing their case, researchers have begun to consider care in relation to race and to income, as well as gender. They found, for example, that different ethnic groups have different perspectives on care, and that this can often limit the ability of services to respond (Ahmad and Atkin, 1996). Short breaks in seaside towns may not hold much appeal for black carers. Co-resident care (where the carer and cared for person live in the same household) is more often associated with people whose income is low. Wealthier people have more options to buy in assistance. So you could argue that not only is it women who are disadvantaged by the move to community care, so are some men, some people from minority ethnic groups, and poorer people.

In addition, in putting forward the feminist perspective on community care, I have omitted the views of some important people – the people who use care services. We'll look at perspectives of service users in Section 5 of this unit, but will pause for a moment here to consider an important aspect of community care – the greater choice and independence it offers to people who need care.

Community care: back to the ideal

Feminists argued that 'community care' is a coded way for the government to withdraw public support for social care and to push more responsibility into the private family realm.

But this is only one side of the story. Community care would have no power if it had no basis in values which are widely shared. The idea has widespread appeal. Who could defend the inhumane institutions Peter Townsend and Maureen Oswin described (and which you will read more about in Blocks 2 and 4)? You'll recall the discussion in Unit 2 of the way people feel helpless and out of control in hospital settings. Who could put their hand on their heart and say that it's better for young children to go into a home rather than stay with their families? Julia Twigg, a sociologist, contrasts care in a public space with care at home:

> Home has particular significance for many older people. In a context of growing physical or mental frailty, it is a familiar environment where the individual has confidence in his or her capacity to manage. Being and feeling at home means behaving as you wish without fear of observation or rebuke. It allows older people to manage as **they** wish, and not according to some professional mode of coping. Home is a private space where visitors come only by invitation. Restricting access allows individuals to control presentation of their lives ...

> The significance of home can be illustrated by looking at the key site of contrast – the hospital ward. Wards are public spaces, even though they are not open to the public as such. The public nature of the space relates to the access of professionals, of non-kin, non-friends – of relationships that have no private quality to them and do not rest on the capacity of the individual to include ... all aspects of the patient's life become subject to its [medicine's] totalising gaze: food becomes nutrition, visits become social support.

> (Twigg, 1997, p. 228)

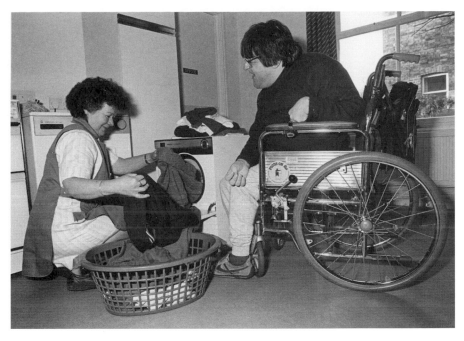

Community care at its best gives people more control over their lives than care delivered in large institutions

In short, Julia Twigg is saying that people, whoever they are, have more control when they are cared for in their own house than they do in a public hospital ward.

Community care, therefore, has flexible meanings. It may be used to contrast with institutional care; it may imply publicly provided services to support caring work which happens in communities; or it may mean, as feminists argue, that responsibility for care is pushed back on to unpaid family members. While bearing in mind the shortfalls of community care *practice*, it is important not to lose sight of the *ideal* that it represents, an ideal that commands widespread support.

Public and private

The concept of 'public versus private' is one you will meet several times in your study of K100. I have used it twice in this section:

- to contrast care in institutions, paid for from public funds, with community care, where responsibility for care is shared between the private world of the family and publicly provided services

- to contrast the *private* space of the home with the *public* space of the ward.

Look out for 'public' and 'private' as you work through K100.

Look at this

Key points

- I have identified three different meanings of the term 'community care': as a contrast to institutional care; as referring to services which supplement rather than replace care by families; and as a way of persuading family members, usually women, to take the major responsibility for care.

- Despite arguments about what it really means, the ideal of community care has widespread appeal, as offering people who need care more control over their lives.

Section 2
Community care: policy into practice

In Section 1 I discussed three different meanings of the term 'community care'. In this section we'll be taking as our focus the community care reforms introduced by the NHS and Community Care Act 1990. You learnt something about its impact on health care in Unit 2. Here I shall explore how the idea of supplementing rather than replacing family care works in practice. The main provisions of the Act are in Care Systems and Structures and you will find it helpful to have this by your side as you work through this section.

I shall be asking three basic questions about how community care works: Who decides? Who pays? Who cares?

2.1 Who decides?

As you will see from Care Systems and Structures, major objectives of the NHS and Community Care Act 1990 were:

to promote the development of services which would enable people to live in their own homes whenever possible

to ensure that practical support for informal carers was a priority

to make a proper assessment of need at an individual level.

(Hughes, 1995, p. 6)

Here we'll be looking at how decisions are made about the services an individual will receive. This will involve introducing some technical terms which, although they may appear mystifying at first, will be important if you are to understand how community care is intended to work. In the box is a glossary of these terms for you to refer to.

Community care: some technical terms

Assessment: the process of determining individual care needs.

Care package: a set of services which will meet the needs of the individual as agreed at the assessment.

Care manager: the person, often a social worker, who manages the package, and has a degree of budgetary responsibility. He or she will contract with those providing the service, and will usually be the major point of co-ordination for everyone involved.

Care plan: a written record of the care that an individual can expect to receive.

In order to be eligible to receive community care services of any kind, it is necessary to have an individual *assessment* to determine 'care needs'. The idea is that, rather than provide blanket services (all adults with learning disabilities should spend their days in the local adult training centre, for example) each person should have an individual *care package* determined by an assessment carried out by the social services department (social work department in Scotland, health and social services board in Northern Ireland). The package is to be managed by a *care manager*, and should be recorded in the form of a *care plan*, a copy of which is to be left with the person whose needs are recorded.

The practitioner's guide, issued following the passage of the NHS and Community Care Act 1990, advised that the following factors should be taken into account in a comprehensive community care assessment:

> *Biographical details, self perceived needs, self care, physical health, mental health, use of medicines, abilities, attitudes, lifestyle, race, culture, personal history, needs of carers, social network and support, care services, housing, transport, risk, finance ...*
>
> (Quoted in Meredith, 1995, pp. 82 3)

Not only this, but assessment should offer choice:

> *Assessment should take account of the wishes of the individual, and his or her carer, and of the carer's ability to continue to provide care ... efforts should be made to offer flexible services which enable individuals and carers to make choices.*
>
> (Department of Health, 1989a, para 3.2.6)

This looks very positive. To place the needs and wishes of the person who uses a service at the centre of the assessment process may look like common sense, but was in fact quite revolutionary compared with much previous practice, which had fitted people to what was available. You might see it referred to as 'needs-led' rather than 'service-led' provision. However, there is no guarantee that all identified needs will be met. Except where a social services authority has a statutory obligation to provide a service – which is rarely the case – it is legally able to refuse to meet the needs identified at assessment if it cannot afford to do so.

To bring this rather abstract discussion of community care policy and practice down to earth, let's try applying some of this information to the Durrants' situation.

The Durrants and community care

When you met him in the drama, Arthur Durrant, following his discharge from hospital, had had an assessment which had resulted in a care package. The assessment was conducted by Dev Sharma, Arthur's social worker, who was acting as the care manager. Services were coming into the Durrants' home from different sources – the community nurse and home carers employed by Care at Home – to supplement the care Lynne was able to supply for her father; the package was paid for by the social services department and managed by Dev Sharma.

The assessment was about determining Arthur's care needs, but what exactly are care needs? A psychologist, Abraham Maslow, developed a model which can help answer this question.

Maslow's model of human needs

Maslow (1970) saw human needs as a hierarchy, that is to say, human beings have many different needs but, until basic needs for food, drink, sleep and security are met, it is impossible to satisfy higher-order needs – social needs, self-esteem, self-actualisation. These needs can be represented as a triangle (Figure 2).

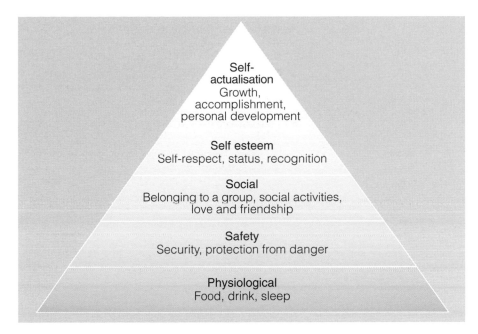

Figure 2
Maslow's hierarchy of needs (adapted from Maslow, 1970)

Maslow wasn't thinking of community care assessments when he drew up his model, but it can be a way to look at care needs.

Activity 2   **Care needs**

Allow about 10 minutes   Think back to Arthur Durrant's situation in the drama. Which needs does his care package seem to supply? Use Maslow's hierarchy to help you consider this question.

Comment   It seems that the care package meets only basic needs – physiological needs for food, drink and, in this case, medical interventions. It is also possible that it contributes to a sense of safety, although we know from the knife incident that Arthur didn't feel entirely safe. What the care package does not meet are any of Arthur's higher-order needs, for example his need for company and things to pass the time other than endless TV. In Arthur's case at least, having his care needs met seems to be another way of saying 'we'll take responsibility for keeping you alive, but the rest is your business'.

The reasons for this minimalist definition of care needs are clear if we remember that social services authorities can legally refuse to meet needs identified at assessment if they cannot afford to do so.

This is a pretty bleak picture. By no means all community care assessments result in this very basic view of what care needs are. But it is important to remember that care needs are a very limited view of human needs. What is provided under the name of community care can too easily be the minimum.

If the Durrants' assessment really had taken 'the wishes of the individual and his or her carer' seriously, a very different package of care might emerge.

The care manager role

Should we blame Dev as care manager for any deficiencies in Arthur's care package? Care managers have a difficult task. Beverley Hughes, in her book about older people and community care (1995) identifies some dilemmas:

- **Resources.** Care managers have budgetary responsibility, but the budget is not infinite. Dev Sharma will have to balance Arthur's needs against competing demands from others.

- **Responsibility without power.** Dev might like the Durrants' home carers to have more training. But they are employed by Care at Home; he is not their line manager. He might also like more input from Arthur's GP but has no authority to demand it.

- **The unwilling client.** Community care ideals assume that clients will want and be able to be involved in determining their needs. But you know enough about Lynne and Arthur to appreciate that conducting an assessment which takes their needs and wishes into account will be a tough proposition.

We probably do not know enough to determine blame, and it would probably not be profitable to do so. What we do know is that community care policies determined that Arthur lives *in* the community rather than an institution, but that, whoever was responsible for deciding his care package, his quality of life is poor indeed.

Key points

- To qualify for social care services, individuals have their needs assessed by social services. This assessment determines the liability of social services to pay for the care package.

- Care needs are the needs someone has for care as identified through assessment. Care needs can be quite a narrow way of looking at human needs.

- Care managers have a difficult job to do in ensuring that care packages meet people's needs without too great a drain on resources. They have responsibility, but do not necessarily have the power to exercise it.

2.2 Who pays?

In Section 2.1 I asked 'who decides?' We now look at who pays for care under the community care system. As discussed in Section 1, feminists among others argued that community care was a way of pushing more of the costs of care on to informal carers, mostly women relatives. Most research on which these arguments were based was undertaken in the 1980s, before the community care reforms. In practice, as the reforms have taken root, the reality of who pays is more complicated than the simple issue of whether care is supplied by paid (or formal) carers or unpaid (informal) carers.

Who pays depends on other factors, for example whether care is defined as 'medical' or 'social', and where you happen to live.

We begin by looking at the significance of defining care as 'medical' or 'social'.

Activity 3

Allow about 20 minutes

Medical care or social care: drawing the line

Turn to the Reader and read Chapter 30 by Julia Twigg, 'The medical/social boundary' as far as the subheading 'Touching'. Then make your own notes on:

(a) why the boundaries between what is medical and what is social care have changed

(b) the significance of these changing definitions for the question of who pays for care.

One way of tackling this is to read through the chapter once to get the general argument, then reread each paragraph in turn. Underline or highlight key words or phrases. Summarise in one phrase or sentence each paragraph's key idea, and then decide which are relevant to the question.

Comment

Twigg makes the following points.

(a) Boundaries between medical and social care:

- The boundary between social and medical care has always varied, in different times, places and individual circumstances.
- As anxiety grew about the increasing proportion of older people in the population there was a tendency to redefine long-term care as semi-social.
- Cost pressures on the NHS led to its retreating into what Julia Twigg calls 'the medical heartlands of acute hospital care', always the highest-status specialisms, as opposed to long-term care where cure is unlikely.
- Campaigns waged by some groups, notably the 'disability lobby', fuelled the trend away from treating disabled people and people with learning disabilities as 'medical' problems. Similar arguments apply to older people. (You'll recognise here more lay challenges to the biomedical model to add to those in Unit 2.)

(b) Significance for who pays:

- The key point is that 'there is a wide acceptance that it [medical care] is something that should be free to the individual free from direct concern about cost'; whereas, Twigg argues, 'social care is part of social life, and as such it represents something that you are primarily expected to pay for yourself'.

The final sentence is a useful summary: 'The division between health and social care is increasingly a division between care that is free to the individual, and that which has to be funded from his or her own purse.'

Study skills: Different ways of taking notes

Did you find you were able to follow the method of taking notes on Twigg's article suggested in Activity 3? Did it get you to the important points? This is another example of 'time investment' (which you read about on pages 115–16 of *The Good Study Guide*). By spending a bit longer, you can often get a lot more out of your reading. But of course your time is limited, so you have to make judgements about what is worth investing time in.

Another way of investing time – which some people find very useful and others don't like at all – is to make notes diagramatically. Below you can see notes on the Twigg article, set out in diagram form. Read them, starting from the middle, and see whether you think they bring out the main points more clearly. Will they be easier to remember? Would it be easier to make use of notes like this when you are planning an essay? Is it worth the time and effort? These are just ideas to think about. You will have to find out what works for you.

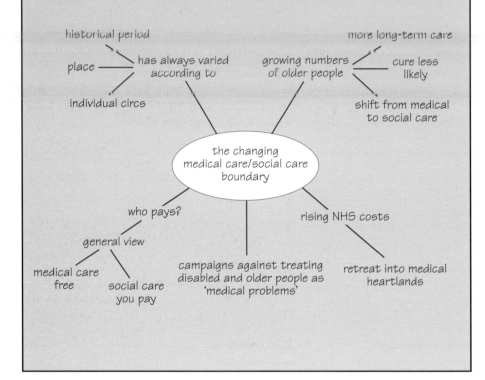

Twigg's explanations of the changing boundaries of medical and social care will be familiar to you from the discussion of the impetus to community care in Section 1 of this unit. But her starting point is slightly different. Rather than asking, as I did, what made institutional care unattractive, she asks why the boundaries between social and medical care have changed. She comes to a similar answer to the one reached in Section 1.

The combined forces of a political agenda and economic drivers led to a clearer articulation of where medical responsibility stops and social responsibility starts. Defining what is medical care also defines what is social care – whatever is not medical becomes social. As Twigg puts it, 'social is the residual category'. And, crucially for our 'who pays' question, she argues that social care, unlike medical care, does not come free. Redefining long-term care as social rather than medical is a way of shifting responsibility for paying for care from the public to the private sphere. In making this case, Twigg has over-simplified a complex set of issues. Her arguments are far less true of services for children, for example, or of social work services. But what she is identifying is part of a trend to make social care a private family responsibility.

How does this affect who pays? One way of answering this question is to say that the decision about whether care is medical or social is an increasingly important determinant of 'who pays'. If, as Twigg argues, health care is free at the point of use while social care is, at least in part, a private responsibility, then the scene is set for arguments to rage. This is behind the debate on continuing care. This question of where to draw the line between medical and social care was addressed by the Royal Commission on Long Term Care (1999) which recommended that some elements of social care should also be free to consumers. Although this was accepted in Scotland, in England, Wales and Northern Ireland, no change resulted.

In order to determine what the National Health Service should pay, local health commissioners draw up clear criteria to determine who is eligible for free continuing (or long-term) care paid for by the NHS. We'll look at an example of these criteria now.

Activity 4

Allow about 10 minutes

Eligibility for long-term health care

Read Offprint 5, which is an extract from a document entitled 'Continuing Health Care: long term health care fully paid for by the NHS' published by Bedfordshire Health Authority.

Using the list headed 'Criteria for eligibility for continuing health care', decide whether the following case scenarios (not their real names) will be eligible for fully funded long-term health care on the NHS. Give reasons for your decision.

Mrs Brown
Mrs Brown has Huntington's chorea, her movements are very fluid, she cannot stand and requires two people plus the hoist to transfer her. She needs help with all personal care, encouragement is required to eat and drink. In the past, there have been frequent urine infections, and a high risk of pressure sores. She lives alone. *yes, total dependency criteria*

Mr Golding
Mr Golding is in the advanced stages of Parkinson's disease. He has recently had a stroke. He needs a wheelchair to move about the home and to go out. His wife is the main carer. *Yes, lever dementia* *No*

Comment   *Mrs Brown* seems to meet the total dependency criteria on at least two counts:

- need for a hoist and two people to move her
- 'complex methods of feeding'.

The danger of pressure sores may also be relevant.

Unless *Mr Golding* is thought to be within six months of death, he is unlikely to meet the criteria, although both Parkinson's disease and a recent stroke are recognised medical conditions.

In fact, I have cheated here in that when I set these cases out, I knew the answers. Mrs Brown has all her care needs fully funded by the NHS. She has three one-hourly, and three half-hourly visits from home carers per day.

Mr Golding is not eligible. He has the services of a home carer one hour every morning, for which he pays a means-tested £35 per week.

What you pay depends on where you live

The document you examined here is one attempt to introduce clarity into the question of who is eligible for long-term fully funded care. These criteria were developed on a local, rather than a national, basis, which means that the idea of universal provision is undermined. Whether you get continuing care free on the NHS may depend on the eligibility criteria established locally – on where you live as well as on your needs.

What you pay if you are not eligible for NHS-funded care will also vary according to where you live. The less that is defined as health care, the more costs fall in other areas. While health care is funded from national taxation, the costs of social care fall on social services budgets (funded locally) and individuals according *both* to their means *and* to where they live. Government guidelines to local authorities issued in 2001 stipulate that councils may 'recover such charges as they consider reasonable' (Department of Health, 2001, Section 1.5). In effect, local authorities have discretion in the amount charged for community care services. A survey conducted by the Labour Party's Research Department in 1996 found that, while Derbyshire residents got all home care services free of charge regardless of income, residents of Surrey were liable to pay up to £320 per week. Eleven local authorities made no charges, while flat rate charges varied from £1.50 per week to £9 per *hour* (Labour Research Department, 1997).

Individuals who need nursing-home care, but fall outside the eligibility criteria for health care, may be forced to sell their homes in order to finance the costs, with knock-on effects on the expectations their children have for inheritance.

In conclusion, the answer to the question 'who pays' for care is complex, depending upon whether long-term care needs are defined as medical (in which case care comes free to the user with the taxpayer ultimately footing the bill) or social. If care needs are deemed to be social some care services may still be delivered free in certain areas of the country. But in most areas the individual will be expected to pay some or all of the costs, according to income, and the rest of the costs will be borne by local, rather than national, revenue.

2.3 Who cares?

We have looked at who decides and who pays. What are the implications of the changes I have outlined on who cares? We will look at this briefly here, as it will be treated in more detail in Section 3.

Paid carers. At one time, help in the home was provided by home helps, whose job it was to provide domestic help, while health professionals (community nurses in particular) undertook health care. Now home helps are increasingly replaced by home carers, whose job is defined as providing personal assistance, including tasks once defined as the domain of health professionals. It means that more care is being delivered by low-paid workers, while higher-paid professionals confine themselves to strictly defined duties. I explore this in more depth in Sections 3 and 4.

Informal carers. The costs of care may increase the pressure on the people termed 'informal carers'. Mrs Golding, whose husband's circumstances were described earlier, said:

> The system is unfair. If I was negligent, if I allowed pressure sores to develop, or if I wasn't so used to helping him move from his wheelchair to the bed or toilet, we might get free care, and a lot more of it. As it is, our charges were put up from £6.85 to £35 a week last October.

In this section, I examined the impact of community care reforms, focusing on three questions – who decides, who pays and who cares. In the next section we look in more detail at a case study of a private agency which sprang up in response to the market created by the NHS and Community Care Act.

Key points

- Health care is free at the point of delivery, while individuals are expected to contribute to the cost of social care.

- Long-term or continuing care is increasingly defined as social rather than medical care. The costs of social care are borne in part by private individuals, while health care is paid for out of public funds.

- Sharper divisions between medical and social care have an impact on who pays for care and who does the caring, and tend to increase pressure on informal carers.

Section 3
Labour or love? Home carers

Sections 1 and 2 dealt with changes in policy. Section 3 examines the changing roles in social care that have been influenced by these policy changes by adopting a case study approach to look in depth at the work of one group – home care assistants. There are numerous groups of workers I could have chosen, and I am not saying that home carers are necessarily more interesting or representative than, say, care managers. But a case study is a helpful way of exploring certain issues. It can give a sharp focus for questioning, as I said in Unit 1, which a more general approach does not supply.

I use the case study to examine some of the propositions that have been set up in Sections 1 and 2 as consequences of the policy changes discussed there: propositions about the changing nature of the social care workforce, issues about paid workers whose work takes them into the private domain of the home, the relationships they build with clients, and the sort of training they may need.

3.1 Home care: what does the job entail?

What do home care assistants actually do?

As more people who need care continue to live in their own homes, the job of home care assistant has become more significant.

The Durrants have 'home cares', as Lynne calls them, coming into the house twice a day, every day. Home care assistants or home carers are essential to community care. They provide one of many services which enable people to stay in their own homes for longer, and which provide much-needed relief or assistance to family carers. In 1993 there were approximately 150,000 home carers in the UK, according to Age Concern (Bell, 1993, p. 10).

Home care is a development of the old home help service. But there are distinct differences. The home helps did housework and domestic tasks in the home. They rarely undertook intimate personal care, except by negotiation with individual clients. The role of home carers, however, is increasingly defined as providing personal care rather than doing housework.

What does the job entail, and what sort of person becomes a home carer? The resource for answering these questions is the audio cassette, where you will hear interviews with employees of a private agency, Independent Nursing Services (INS), which provides home care services in the counties of Bedfordshire, Buckinghamshire and Hertfordshire.

Part 3 of Audio Cassette 1 starts with extracts from two interviews. First, you will hear Mary, a senior home care assistant, speak about herself and her job.

Activity 5   **The job of a home carer**

Allow about 20 minutes

Read Mary's job description which follows. Then listen to part 3 of Audio Cassette 1 (side 2), up to the end of the interview with Mary. Make notes on how Mary describes her job compared with what the job description says. What is the same? What else does she mention?

Job description: Home Nursing Care Assistant

1   To provide a personal care service in clients' own homes, including washing, dressing and associated personal care, and general care/duties required to maintain optimum independence of the client within their own home.

2   Helping clients with their mobility.

3   Serving meals.

4   Supervising any medication (medication must not be given by unqualified staff).

5   Sitting with clients who are terminally ill, frail or disabled.

6   To recognise if the client is deteriorating. Any change should be reported to the client's general practitioner and/or an INS nurse manager.

7   To maintain client records as provided by the Company and to make accurate returns.

8   To maintain the Company philosophy of maintaining clients in a state of well-being in their own homes.

9   To be aware of the Company Health & Safety policy and the employee's own responsibility under the Health & Safety at Work Act.

10   Any other agreed duties that may be required from time to time.

Comment   Although Mary mentions a number of the things on the job description, such as personal care services like washing, dressing and getting people out of bed, her emphasis is elsewhere. What she talks about most is her personal relationship with the people whose homes she goes into, the little extras which make her job, and sometimes their lives, worthwhile – things like popping in as she passes the house, taking someone's dog out for a walk, knowing other members of the family. She also talks about the things her clients do to show their appreciation: they give her cards and Christmas gifts which, she says, 'means a lot'; they send sweets for her children; and one couple make cakes for her.

If you look at how Mary describes her job in the light of Maslow's hierarchy of needs (Section 2), you can see that the job description defines her role as supplying basic physiological needs. But she *talks* about the job as being as much about meeting higher-level needs – social needs, self-esteem – as about meeting basic needs.

For Mary the rewards of the job are social rewards. You heard her on the tape comparing her present job with INS with her previous job in a factory. Although she works as hard, possibly harder (she talks of a 70-to-80-hour week), she says the home care job is 'not like going to work to me any more'. It gives her variety, discretion to use her own judgement, an ability to get her own problems into perspective, greater tolerance and patience. She makes the job sound idyllic.

Mary works to a care plan, the contract that has been agreed between the social services department and the client after an assessment (see

Section 2). In this case, the social services department has commissioned INS to do the work, so the care plan is actually a statement of the services that the social services department is purchasing from INS.

Activity 6

Allow about 20 minutes

Care plans: love or work?

When 'care' was defined in Unit 1, it was referred to as love or work, often a mixture of both. To care about someone is to love or feel affection for them; to care for them is to attend to their physical needs.

Look at Figure 3 below. Alice Foster is one of Mary's clients (although her name has been changed on the form for the sake of confidentiality). Is the care Mary is paid to do for Alice love or work or both?

CARE PLAN

Mrs Alice Foster

If the daughter is there, she will let you in. If not, the back door will be open.

Lunch Visit Saturday and Sunday about 14.00: (2 carers)

The personal care:

To empty the leg bag and to put her on to the commode with the help of the hoist. To make sure she is comfortable back in the armchair.

Please make a hot drink if she requires it.

Evening Visit about 19.00: (2 carers)

The personal care:

With the help of the hoist, to transfer her from the armchair to the wheelchair, to push her into the bedroom and to put her on to the commode if she requires it. To empty the leg bag.

To put an inco. sheet on to the bed.

To transfer her with the hoist on to the bed and to undress her.

To give her a wash, to get her in her night clothes, to put on her night boots, to remove her teeth.

To treat the pressure sores, if necessary.

To connect the night bag (check that the bottom of the bag is closed).

To give her a sachet of Fibrogel. To leave an orange squash on the bedside cabinet.

Others:

To switch the television on and make sure she has her glasses handy.

Figure 3

Comment

Your answer to the previous activity should have made answering this one easier. Mary is actually paid to do the things specified on the care plan. Although the care plan specifies tasks, such as connecting the night bag and moving Alice about, you know from Mary's interview that that is not what the job is about for her. If she did not do what was specified, she might well be disciplined or sacked, but it is what is *not* specified that is important for Mary. It is also one of the things clients value, as you will see later.

While love and work are, or can be, intertwined, it is much easier to cost care as labour than care as love. It is very much care work (or tasks) that INS are expected to provide. No one can legislate for the love side of care. Imagine how difficult it would be to write that into a care plan.

A potential difficulty for home carers is that the extras, the love side of care, are not costed. Mary says, apologetically perhaps, 'I'm afraid I'm a bit of a softy' to get round the problem of people needing more than she is paid to do. She says it is because she gets to like most of the people she cares for. This 'emotional labour' is rarely costed when care packages are calculated.

Good practice?

To do what Mary does, squeeze in extra duties, is not considered to be good practice. *CareFully*, a guide for home care assistants prepared for Age Concern, is a publication I draw on in this section because it represents what is considered good practice in a job which is only just becoming recognised as needing training and codes of conduct. The author states:

The tasks you do should have been agreed and clarified in advance between the person needing care, their personal or family carer and the person putting together the care plan or care package. If when you arrive you find there is any difference in opinion or expectation about the work you will do, this should be reported immediately to your line manager, who may be in a position to advise who could undertake those tasks that you are either not allowed or not required to do yourself.

(Bell, 1993, p. 41)

3.2 Relationships with clients: family, friend or paid carer?

I said in Section 1 that community care should support care in the family, not replace it. Yet many people attribute the need for home care to a breakdown in the capacity of the family to provide care. Chris Field, a director of INS, described home carers' jobs in an interview which you will hear later in the unit as 'a replacement for a member of the family'. Not only are they supplementing family care, sometimes, he implies, they almost become that family.

There are some references to this in Mary's interview. In describing how she came to do the work, she refers to her experience of caring for her father as the reason she decided to find a job as a home carer. She says at one point that she tries harder with people who don't have families nearby, because she is the only contact they have from one day to the next. It is also significant that she lives locally and knows members of the family. But the analogy cannot be carried too far. She herself says that caring for 'other people' is obviously different from caring for family. In fact, the idea she uses most is that of a 'friend'.

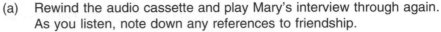

Activity 7   **Home carer or friend?**

Allow about 15 minutes   (a)   Rewind the audio cassette and play Mary's interview through again. As you listen, note down any references to friendship.

(b)   Then, with your list in front of you, compare the sort of friendship she describes with your own experiences of friendship. How similar are they?

Comment   (a)   References to friendship:
- Mary says, 'You become friends with 99% of the people.'
- She gets Christmas cards and gifts, and sometimes a cake.
- She does people favours in her own time.
- She goes to funerals.

(b)   How does this compare with friendships outside a paid carer's relationship with her client? There are clearly similarities with ordinary friendships, things like give and take, affection. There are also differences:
- Choice. Friends choose one another. There is no choice for Mary in who she visits, nor do the clients have a choice of home carer.
- Payment. Mary is paid, friends come free!
- Physical intimacy. The technical words on the care plan – washing, dressing, toileting – hide some complex and intimate interactions which are unusual (although not unknown) in relationships between same-sex friends. It is even less usual for such intimacy to be part of a friendship between a man and a woman.
- Records. Home carers have to record what they do – it was part of the job description.
- Easy to replace. Mary's clients are replaceable; there's always a new one coming along when one dies. As she put it, 'you go to the funeral and you say goodbye and it's one of those jobs where you get another one on your books and you ... make friends with them, I'm afraid.'

It may seem natural that Mary tries to be a friend to her clients, but you should by now be wary when things seem 'natural'. It is a consequence of providing care in the home that people bring certain expectations into the situation. As it says in *CareFully*:

> *You must always remember that when you enter the home of a person who needs care, you do so at their invitation. An invitation that they have a right to withdraw at any time ... You must always be aware that you are working in someone else's home – not your own – and treat it accordingly.*

(Bell, 1993, p. 40)

It is probably helpful to Mary to use the idea of friendship to remind her, and us, that she is a guest in someone else's home. The clients who give her gifts play their part in this modelling of a friendship. However, these are *not* friendships, and it is important for home carers to draw boundaries around their relationships with clients.

Limitations to friendship: the importance of boundaries

What are boundaries? In the sense used here they are the rules set up by people to decide what is and what is not acceptable in a particular relationship.

Sometimes boundaries are written down or made explicit in some way. Some professionals manage this by creating structures in which to work. For example, a psychotherapist makes a one-hour appointment with a client, the client is seen in the therapist's consulting room, and all contact between the two is confined to that hour. Such boundaries have the useful function of determining the duration of the contact, and individuals do not need to feel personally responsible for ending a meeting or a relationship and apparently rejecting a person in need.

Because home carers are working in someone else's home, it can be difficult for them to set such hard and fast boundaries. Their *professional* responsibilities are limited, but Mary's interview indicates that their sense of *personal* responsibility for their clients is less easy to limit.

In these situations it is important to be clear about boundaries, especially because home carers are managed from the office at a distance, unlike workers in a residential home, hospital or day centre.

To consider boundaries further, we will return to the drama you heard in Unit 1. Imagine that Doreen, the home carer, has gone on a course to learn more about care. One session is about discrimination. She decides that she has been discriminating against Lynne and that she will change her attitude. She sets time aside at weekends to chat with Lynne about things and feels that she can really see a change in Lynne. Then, two months later, her course complete, she tells Lynne she has another job, and won't be seeing her again.

Pete, a young man, replaces Doreen. It's the first time he has done this sort of work. Doreen tells him on his induction shift how she is trying to treat Lynne as a human being. Pete follows Doreen's advice and asks Lynne to join him in McDonald's for a coke when he has finished his shift. From then on, Lynne hangs around Pete at finishing time and asks him if he fancies a coke. She asks him for his home phone number and begins ringing at least once a day. For three weeks he and she go to McDonald's on a Saturday after he has finished his shift. Pete pays. Lynne tells Eddie she has a new rich boyfriend and stops seeing him. But in the fourth week Pete decides he has had enough, and tells her he has to get home and not to phone except in emergencies. She bursts into tears.

Activity 8   **Unwritten rules**

Allow about 10 minutes   Try to write the unwritten 'rules' about care workers' relationships with clients that Pete broke on his first few weeks.

Comment   These are the 'rules' the course testers suggested:

- Care workers do not socialise with clients out of hours.
- Care workers do not encourage clients to see them as potential lovers.
- Care workers do not pay out of their own money for things clients might need or want.
- Care workers do not give their personal home phone numbers to clients – all contact must be through the care agency.

The activity shows that, although home carers may think of themselves as friends or family, their relationships with clients need to be carefully managed if misunderstandings are not to arise. This requires a degree of skill which is more than just common sense.

3.3 Skilled work?

INDEPENDENT NURSING SERVICES

Ideas about being a replacement member of the family or a friend suggest that home care is something anyone can do – particularly, perhaps, if they are women like Mary with experience of caring for her father and bringing up children.

In fact, there are mixed messages about this. On the one hand, Mary and other home carers talk about themselves as ordinary people coming into the home to lend a helping hand. On the other hand, the company is called Independent *Nursing* Services and the publicity leaflet shows a woman wearing a uniform not unlike a nurse's uniform – and we usually think of nurses as skilled workers.

So is this skilled work or are home carers just ordinary women who transfer the skills they have learnt in the private capacity of their own family duties to the public world of paid work? I have noted that home carers need some skills in keeping boundaries. Is there *more* skill involved? This is the subject of the next activity.

Blankshire County Council	SOCIAL SERVICES DEPARTMENT CARE PLAN	CM09 PRN

NAME: Mr D. Soames	ADDRESS:	
D.O.B. 19.11.1922	GP: Dr Chapman	
N.o.K. Wife		

OBJECTIVES:

Mr Soames has Parkinson's disease, and his balance is poor. Mrs Soames also recently had a fall and has a hernia. She can no longer help her husband to get up, or in and out of bed. Mrs Soames can manage to get all meals. Assistance with some local shopping may also be needed. In the main, Mr Soames will require help with personal, i.e. washing, dressing, toileting.

TWO CARERS INITIALLY. Hoist should be delivered on 4.6.96.

Care/Services provided	Start date	Frequency	Agency and carer	Contact person	Tel. no.
Approx. 7.30–8.00 am for 1 hour to get up, washed, toileted and dressed, and transferred to chair.	4 June 96	x 7	Care at Home B. Carpenter		
Approx. 5.30–6.00 pm for ½ hour Assist with getting to and from the toilet.	4 June 96	x 7	Care at Home B. Carpenter		
Approx. 10.00–10.30 pm for 1 hour. Assist with washing, undressing, toileting and putting to bed.			Care at Home Gill Hall		

DATE OF REVIEW:

Ongoing as we need to clarify situation once hoist is being used as to whether or not two carers are required.

CONTINGENCY:

This will be dependent on Mr Soames's ability to participate and his confidence. No changes towards carers being used without consultation with Social Worker.

TELEPHONE NUMBER: ADDRESS:

CARE MANAGER – NAME AND TITLE: B. Mills

I AGREE TO THE CARE PLAN

CUSTOMER: .... CARER: ....

TICK BOX TO INDICATE COPY GIVEN TO CUSTOMER ❏ FILE
                                                  D. NURSE
                                                  CARE AT HOME
                                                  B. MILLS

Figure 4
Example of a social services department care plan

Activity 9 **What anyone does?**

Allow about 10 minutes

Using the information you have about Mary's job, including the interview on the audio cassette, the job description, and the care plans in Figures 3 and 4, make a list of what she does.

Then divide the list into two using these headings:

- things she does which almost anyone does in their daily life
- things she does which require specialist skills.

Comment   You probably put many of the tasks under the 'what anyone does' heading. Making a hot drink, switching on the TV, or shopping are tasks many people do in their day-to-day lives at home. Most people are not called upon to wash adults, or take them to the toilet, but such activities are routine where young children are concerned.

However, the job also requires some specialist skills – using a hoist, lifting and handling, treating pressure sores, and emptying a leg bag. How many people even know what a leg bag is if they are not involved in care work?

As you can see from this activity, there are limitations to seeing the job as something anyone can do. Home carers need skills in keeping boundaries and they need some technical know-how. But, other than a compulsory course on moving and handling, and following the boss around for a couple of days, Mary had no formal training; she just started from day one. You wouldn't like to think your doctor or your bus driver had this little training, but it seems to be acceptable for care workers.

Who decides what is a skilled occupation? Is it necessarily more difficult to write software than it is to follow a care plan? Does the community nurse's job of administering Arthur's drugs actually require more skill than moving and toileting him? Is it more important to be in charge of a lathe or to be in charge of a vulnerable person's well-being? The answers to these questions are a matter of opinion. But in assessing the work paid carers do it is useful to bear in mind this idea:

> Far from being an economic fact skill is often an ideological category imposed on certain types of work by virtue of the sex and power of the workers who perform it.
>
> (Phillips and Taylor, 1980, p. 82)

In other words, some people have the power to decide what is and what is not a valued skill.

Care work is a classic example of socially important work being accorded little economic value because it is defined as unskilled or semi-skilled, a job someone can do with minimal training; and it is perhaps no accident that it is work usually done by women who are presumed to have learnt how to do it through their work in the home as wives, mothers and daughters. There is more about how skills are defined in Unit 5 and in Block 7.

Training and induction

As you have seen, it is not uncommon to believe that home carers need no training because the work they are expected to do is just like they would do in their own home.

In her recorded interview Mary described her initial training at INS like this:

> I went out training with the boss as it was because he'd just started [providing services] in my area, and I went out on me own within two days which I was quite nervous about and I took it from there.

Activity 10 **Training for home care**

Allow about 5 minutes

Now listen to the next sequence in part 3 of Audio Cassette 1, in which Sue describes her training as a home carer with INS. In your opinion, is the training adequate?

Comment

The training appears to have improved since Mary's day. The National Vocational Qualification (NVQ) Sue refers to provides a systematic framework for assessing her work and, as she indicates, gives her pause for reflection on what she is doing. However, she identifies a major gap in the preparation she has been given for working with clients from ethnic minorities. She feels ill-equipped to provide care in a way that is sensitive to cultures which are different from her own, and would have liked a lot more information. As it is, she is feeling her way, through using children as interpreters, and being guided by the clients themselves.

Elements of good practice in work with people from minority ethnic groups

Ideally, a client from a minority ethnic group should be able to request a home carer from the same ethnic background. If that is not available – and it frequently is not – the author of *CareFully: A handbook for home care assistants* (Bell, 1999) identifies the following issues for home carers working with people from ethnic minority groups.

Language. The client should have information about the care plan, the organisation and the complaints procedure in their own language.

If the home carer does not speak the client's language, an interpreter should be present at the first meeting and should be available whenever difficulties arise.

Food. The home carer should be aware of religious and cultural practices *vis-à-vis* diet, and food hygiene. For example, Muslims wash plates and crockery under running water, orthodox Jews use separate cooking utensils for meat and dairy products.

Clothing. Knowledge is needed about how to assist clients with clothing like saris or turbans, and what is seen as appropriate for particular occasions and times of day.

Although the author of CareFully does not say this, it is just as important that a home carer from a Jewish or Sikh background has the opportunity to learn about the cultural preferences of people from the majority culture.

The need for home care assistants to have training for their contact with a wide range of people in their own homes does not stop with the need for information about different cultural preferences and practices. The drama about the Durrants, for example, suggested that it might be desirable for Doreen to know more about people with learning disabilities. As a result of community care policies, more people with learning disabilities now live in their own homes, so more home care assistants will find that their jobs entail working with them. Julia Twigg and Karl Atkins, in a book entitled *Carers Perceived* (1994), argue that the dominant model of carers, paid or unpaid, as people who care for older people is unhelpful. It is important to recognise that caring for a frail older person will be rather different from caring for younger disabled adults.

This discussion of the diversity of clients who need home care services has brought us a long way from the idea of home carer as replacement member of the family or friend. These 'common sense' ideas are not enough to ensure good-quality care for every client. A lot more is involved, and training for the home carer matters. As you will hear in Section 4, however, improving the quality is something that is constrained by the way care is managed, organised and financed.

The General Social Care Council and the Code of Practice for Social Care Workers

In 2002, well after we made the recordings, the General Social Care Council has been established and has issued the first ever nationally agreed standards for social care professionals in the form of a code of conduct for social care staff. The purpose of the code is to set down the conduct expected of social care workers so they know what is expected of them, and the public knows what to expect.

The code of conduct states that social care workers must:

- Protect the rights and promote the interests of service users and carers.

- Strive to establish and maintain the trust and confidence of service users and carers.

- Promote the independence of service users while protecting them as far as possible from danger or harm.

- Respect the rights of service users whilst seeking to ensure that their behaviour does not harm themselves or other people.

- Uphold public trust and confidence in social care services.

- Be accountable for the quality of their work and take responsibility for maintaining and improving their knowledge and skills.

You'll find the employer's side of this code in the next section of the unit, and more about the GSCC in Unit 26.

The full code is available on websites for each country in the UK – www.gscc.org.uk, www.ccwales.org.uk, www.ccetsw.org.uk and www.niscc.info [all accessed 1.10.02].

Study skills: Learning from audio cassettes

In K100 you use audio cassettes often. How are you getting along with the Block 1 cassette? Do you just listen at the times we suggest in the text or do you, like some students, listen while you are doing other things – driving, ironing, lawn mowing? Do you listen just once or several times? Do you find it easy to remember what you hear or do you have to take notes to keep track? Do you feel that you are learning important things and, if so, what? Are they different from what you learn from the printed text? How important was it to be able to hear Mary being interviewed rather than just read her words in print? Did hearing her make her more of a 'real person'? Was it easier to understand her circumstances and her concerns? If so, what did that help you to learn?

I can't answer these questions for you. But next time you are writing your study diary you could note down some answers for yourself. Since you will be investing a lot of your time on the audio cassettes, it is important to think about whether you are allowing the right amount of time and getting the most from your use of them. If you want some more ideas on what audio-visual media can teach you, have a look at Section 7.4.2 of Chapter 7 of *The Good Study Guide* (pp. 188–90).

3.4 Home care: listening to clients

So far I have discussed home care from the point of view of two workers, Mary and Sue. But you know from the Unit 1 case study that Arthur and Lynne have a much less positive experience of home care than the one presented to us by Mary on the audio cassette. What do clients actually expect of home care?

There are several possible approaches to answering this question, but a good starting point is listening to what people say. That is your next activity.

Activity 11   **Listening to Reg Martin**

Allow about 15 minutes   Read Offprint 6 'Excerpt from an interview with Reg Martin' by Wendy Rickard. Reg has HIV/AIDS and lives at home alone.

(a)   Note down the main points Reg is making about good practice in home care.

(b)   When you have done so, ask yourself what this account has to say in the light of your reading so far in this unit. Does it confirm some of the points that have been made? Does it tell us any more about the challenges for paid workers in providing care in people's homes?

(c)   How far would the GSCC code of conduct help ensure that Reg got the sort of care he wanted?

Comment   (a)   Here is my summary of Reg's account of good practice:
- *sensitivity* – to what he needs when he needs it
- *competence* – at household tasks, at knowing what to do
- *affection* – doing little extras which show affection for him as an individual
- *time* – willingness to stop and chat, to pop in with some extra shopping
- *continuity* – someone who gets to know his ways, and what he likes to eat.

(b)   Relevance to the unit:
- Caring is *women's* work – Reg expects Glenda to do as she would in her own home.
- Good-quality care depends on *personal* as well as *professional* qualities.
- Being in his *own home* gives Reg more sense of his own power – to decide not to continue with the home help service, for example.

- Paid carers who go into the privacy of someone's home need to *adjust their approach* to each individual, develop trust, rapport and compatibility.
- Paid carers need to be *skilled* in building personal relationships as well as proficient in the basic tasks.

(c) The draft code of conduct might help. For example, 'strive to maintain the trust and confidence of service users and carers' would, if interpreted sensitively, lead to a home carer working hard to ascertain what Reg wants, and respond.

However, they are framed of necessity in very broad terms, needing to cover many different situations, and they will do little to address problems to do with lack of time for the little extras, and high staff turnover leading to lack of continuity.

Overall, Reg's account reiterates the point that good care depends on the worker's ability to both care *for* and care *about* their clients.

Establishing a relationship

Reg's is only one point of view, but he makes some useful observations about the importance of an individual's approach to each person which can offer some general guidelines. It shows the importance of establishing a feedback loop from clients to workers, care managers and employers if quality is to be a hallmark of care at home.

3.5 Home care: a changing division of labour

Mary and Sue are paid workers and, despite talk about friendship and 'replacement member of the family', there is no real confusion as to their status. However, they are not highly paid for what they do. In 1996 their hourly rate was £4.10, exactly the wage that was being canvassed as the legal minimum at that time.

The fact that home carers are paid low wages, and often do more than they are paid for, reflects a belief that it is somehow undesirable for carers to be motivated by cash. Clare Ungerson, a feminist sociologist who has written extensively about care, put it like this:

The assumption is that nominally paid workers will provide better quality care, since they are doing the work for love rather than money.

(Ungerson, 1990, p. 20)

There is plenty of evidence of the belief that care is more about love than money in the way Mary describes her job – her emphasis on friendship and the extra things she does for her clients. Certain consequences flow from this belief.

- Carers should not 'watch the clock' or 'be in it for the money' – an idea which finds clear expression when nurses or paramedical staff strike for better wages, and are criticised for putting themselves before those they care for.

- Carers should know how to do their job without extensive training.

- Care plans may specify a certain minimum of care work but some home carers provide for clients' social needs too, and this emotional labour is not reflected in their contracts of employment or wages.

- The sheer hard labour involved in some types of care work is hidden behind a rosy glow of love and goodwill.

However, as more care is delivered 'back home' and the role of health personnel is more narrowly defined, the work home carers do appears to require more technical skill. Jobs once done by health personnel such as community nurses are now routinely done by home carers. It is evidence that in the changing world of care the trend is to devolve more responsibility to lower-paid, semi-skilled workers, most of whom are women.

Key points

- Home carers work to job descriptions and care plans which specify care *work* as their main function. However, many home carers see their jobs as providing for clients' social needs as well as their basic physical needs. This emotional labour is not formally recognised or remunerated.

- Because home care is delivered in the client's home, there can be confusion over the type of relationship that home carers develop with clients. It can be hard for home carers to limit their sense of personal responsibility for clients, even though their professional responsibilities are limited.

- Some aspects of the work of home carers require specialist skills, but training is largely on the job, and the belief that good home care is a natural extension of women's roles in the private sphere of the family often means that formal training is neglected.

- The General Social Care Council, established in 2001, for the first time issued codes of conduct intended to apply to all UK social care staff in 2002.

- The division of labour in home care is changing as the role of health professionals is more strictly confined to health-related tasks. While home help roles were largely domestic, home carers increasingly are responsible for personal care.

Section 4
Managing and organising home care

In this section, we continue to look at the work of Independent Nursing Services, this time examining how it is managed and organised.

4.1 Introducing the market model to social care

One of the major changes introduced by the community care reforms was the establishment of a market model.

Rather than have all services provided by what are called 'statutory services', that is health authorities, social services departments, social work departments (Scotland) and health and social services boards (Northern Ireland) which are funded from taxation, both local and national, the NHS and Community Care Act 1990 sought to promote a 'mixed economy' where private companies and voluntary agencies could flourish as well. This involved creating *purchasers* and *providers*. (You will find further information about the NHS and Community Care Act 1990 in Care Systems and Structures.)

Under the Act a distinction is drawn between organisations which *purchase* health and social care services, and organisations which *provide* them. Before the Act health authorities and social services were responsible for both funding and providing many services. Now there is a 'purchaser/provider split', where statutory services retain responsibility for purchasing but not necessarily for providing.

This is modelled on the market economy. The purchaser contracts with providers to provide precisely defined and costed goods. Providers (which can be from the statutory, voluntary or private sectors) compete for contracts to provide what purchasers commission. A host of consequences stem from this split, which will become clearer as you work through Section 4.

Features of the market in health and social care are therefore:

- the establishment of purchasers (like social services departments) who commission services, and providers (like INS) who tender to provide the services in competition with other providers

- the requirement, as a result of the purchaser/provider split, that the costs of services are precisely stated; hence the emphasis on developing care plans as a contract stating what services are being supplied, how often, and to what quality

- the view of people who use services as 'customers' or 'consumers' who can exercise choice (I noted in Section 2 that one task of assessment is to take account of individual wishes and to offer choices to individuals and their carers).

The purpose of introducing a market model into health and social care services can be summarised as to:

- promote competition
- drive down costs
- promote choice for clients/customers.

The aim was to move away from monolithic, publicly funded providers of services like social services departments to a situation where purchasers, and consumers, could have a choice of suppliers.

One of the reasons we chose INS as a case study was that it is a private company which is, in many ways, the very model of what the government intended when trying to promote a mixed economy of providers from the statutory, private and voluntary sectors. Examining INS as a provider in the mixed economy gives us an opportunity to assess how this market model transfers to health and social care.

4.2 Managing for quality

The box below gives some facts and figures about INS.

Independent Nursing Services – facts and figures (in 1996)

- INS was established in 1993, at the time the NHS and Community Care Act came into operation.

- It was one of two private agencies licensed to supply home care in Bedfordshire.

- Its services were purchased by three social services departments and one health commission.

- It had five directors and employed 121 staff.

- Of its total business 80% was publicly funded, via purchasers, and 20% was paid for directly by individuals.

- Its turnover was £1.25m per annum.

- Its business with Bedfordshire Social Services Department was worth £800,000 per annum.

- It conducted between 400 and 1,000 home visits per day.

- Profit per visit was approximately £1.

- It had 400 clients.

- It charged purchasers £6.50–£7.00 per hour for its services: statutory services, by comparison, cost up to £15 per hour.

INS is at the delivery end of the process which starts with a community care assessment of an individual's needs, resulting in a care package. This in turn results in a care plan which, as you saw in Section 3, constitutes a contract describing what services a client can expect. INS may provide some or all of the services specified on the care plan. INS is paid through 'spot contracts', that is, each contract is individually costed. Spot contracts, however, are not universal (see the box overleaf).

Now you have some background information about INS, it's time to hear more about it on the audio cassette. The last sequence opens with a short snippet of a conversation between Mary, the home carer whom you heard earlier, and Ann, one of INS's directors, discussing contracts and accounts. You don't need to understand it in detail. I have included it to give you a flavour of some of the consequences of making delivery of care a business. Care becomes a commodity, like anything else, to be bought and sold. Costing care and keeping track of contracts, payments and so on become important activities for purchasers and providers alike. One point you will note from the discussion is that there is a lot of potential for confusion.

Spot contracts and block contracts

Purchasers can buy services from providers through spot or block contracts. Spot contracts are issued on a case-by-case basis. The package is drawn up and suitable providers are individually selected from a list determined by commissioners.

Block contracts, as the name implies, are issued when a provider is paid to supply a block of services to a large number of people. An example of a block contract is when a social services department contracts with one provider to provide all residential services in its area. This gives advantages to both purchasers and providers in that the purchasers have fewer decisions to make – all frail older people who need residential care, for example, go to establishments run by a particular provider – and the providers have a steady flow of business. But block contracting usually means less individual choice and less competition.

The rest of the audio cassette is an interview with Chris Field, a director of INS.

Activity 12

Allow about 10 minutes

Managing for quality

Listen to the next sequence in part 3 of Audio Cassette 1 as far as the point where the narrator says, 'It requires a particular sort of person ...' As you listen, make some notes for yourself on what provision is made for ensuring quality.

Comment

Chris mentions:

- staff are employed on regular contracts
- there is 24-hour back up in the office
- there are qualified nursing staff on hand
- clients have the opportunity to comment on the services they receive
- the company is busy – people come back for more
- there is a formal complaints procedure.

INS's management claim to provide a quality service – but it is important to note that as a provider they serve two customers:

- the purchasers on whom they rely for more business
- the clients.

Activity 13   **Problems in managing for quality**

Allow about 10 minutes

Now consider what *problems* Chris mentions in managing for quality. Listen to the same section of Audio Cassette 1 again, this time making notes on any problems Chris mentions. Once you have made your notes, divide them into two lists:

(a)   problems in relation to purchasers

(b)   problems in relation to clients.

Comment   (a)   Purchasers:

- INS is expected to supply 'Marks and Spencer's quality for Woolworth's prices'.
- INS competes with other agencies which do not have regular employees and do not have back-up services.
- INS can report any shortfall in services to the social services department but it is not INS's responsibility to supply them. The purchaser controls the purse strings and has the last say on the amount of resource to allocate.

(b)   Clients:

- Clients are often confused and vulnerable and, Chris implies, are unlikely to use complaints procedures or complete questionnaires.
- Staff are managed at a distance – the system relies very much on the integrity of staff and their willingness to bring problems to the attention of managers.
- INS are not in a position to supply extra resources unless the purchaser can be persuaded to agree.

The message is that it is a struggle to maintain quality in the face of unfair competition and demands to drive down costs in order to obtain contracts. At the time we recorded the audio cassette (in 1996) statutory regulation on home care was very weak. There was then no obligation on purchasers to set up independent inspection procedures for home care. Chris claimed on the audio cassette that it was the *providers* who persuaded Bedfordshire Social Services Department to introduce a scheme to accredit agencies with minimum standards; independent providers of home care were not obliged to establish complaints procedures. INS's quality procedures for clients were not perfect, but they were much better than they might have been. It was not until 2001 that draft National Minimum Standards Regulations for Domiciliary (home) Care were issued for consultation (see the section on the development of the Care Standards Commission and National Minimum Standards in Unit 8).

Activity 14   **Meeting the aims of the market model?**

Allow about 10 minutes

From what you have read and heard so far, estimate how far the introduction of a market model into home care services has met its aims. You'll recall that I summarised these as to:

(a)   promote competition

(b)   drive down costs

(c)   promote choice for clients/customers (use as your yardstick one of the clients from an ethnic minority described by Sue in her interview).

Comment   (a)   Promote competition. This does seem to have happened. There are a number of providers, so that the purchasers have a choice about whom to issue with contracts.

           (b)   Drive down costs. From what we heard, providers are under heavy pressure to cut costs in order to obtain contracts. You will also remember that INS's charges are up to 50% lower per hour than the costs of statutory home care providers.

           (c)   Promote choice for clients/customers. There is more choice than when local authorities were the only providers, *but* Sue's description of her work with people from minority ethnic groups who do not speak English suggests that not everyone will be able to exercise choice. What might one of those clients need in order to make effective use of a complaints procedure? Access to information, in his or her own language, an interpreter, knowledge of how the system works, telephone numbers, confidence that the home carer would not hear of the complaint before action was taken, and so on.

INS's clients, like most users of social care services, pay for their care. In that sense they are genuine customers. However, their strength as paying customers is mitigated by several factors.

- They do not necessarily pay the full costs.

- They do not negotiate directly with the provider – it is the purchaser who makes the assessment, draws up the care package and writes the care plan. The system is therefore more bureaucratic and less immediately responsive to customer demands than if the contract were directly between the provider and the client.

- Payment is normally made, not to the provider, but to the purchaser, who then pays the provider for the work done. Again, this means that the purchaser's role gets in the way of a direct contractual relationship between client and provider.

- Clients need information about alternative suppliers if there is to be a real choice.

You have seen that, while the principle of a mixed economy of care does to some extent meet its aims, the idea that it gives clients real choice may be idealistic.

In Section 5 we'll be looking at alternative ways of providing services which, their proponents claim, offer real power to people who use home care services.

4.3 Managing for flexibility

This section is based on the second part of Chris's interview on the audio cassette where he talks about staff employment and training. Some of this will already be familiar to you from Section 3, and it will be a useful opportunity to recap and to consider how far Chris's perspective matches what we heard from the home carers themselves. You will hear him say, for example, that 95% of the job is 'common sense', a view which coincides with ideas expressed both by home carers, like Mary, and clients, like Reg.

A key concept Chris uses in this part of the interview is flexibility. Flexibility is also something that Mary and Reg see as important. Both of them value the opportunities for flexibility that home care offers. But Chris uses the idea in other ways.

Activity 15   **Flexibility**

Allow about 10 minutes   Listen again to the interview with Chris in part 3 of Audio Cassette 1. This
    time play it to the end. Note any references he makes to flexibility. He
doesn't always use the word, but it is implied at several points.

Comment   Flexibility is implied in the following:

- the need for staff to have a flexible approach by acting towards
  clients as they would towards a mother, father, aunt or sister

- the need for staff to be flexible by responding to demands, 'the
  person on the ground has to determine what is actually necessary at
  the particular point of visiting'

- the need for staff who are flexible because they do not bring with
  them expectations from the public sector where people 'tend to have
  very hard and fast rules as to what they will and will not do'

- the need for staff to be flexible enough to work evenings, nights and
  weekends, because it is a 24-hour service.

You probably noticed that flexibility is mainly demanded of staff.
'Flexibility' is one of those words that sounds very positive, but hides as
much as it says. It is hard to argue that staff who have a flexible approach
to their work are not good staff, but if you pause to consider its practical
implications for INS's employees, you might notice that it means:

- being prepared to work unsocial hours

- an individual approach to every client

- being prepared to make up the gap between what care plans state
  and what a member of the family might do – extra shopping, time to
  sit and talk, take the dog out

- having a good deal of autonomy and discretion in your work but, in
  the case of home carers at least, being paid at rates which many an
  unskilled male labourer would reject

- relying on staff to do a responsible job without necessarily offering
  them the training to back that up.

Some course testers found Chris's approach quite offensive. One said
'You shouldn't give voice to someone with such views'. Chris hasn't
been given his space because we necessarily agree with all he says. But
what he says does neatly encapsulate some of the consequences of
making 'care' a market commodity, to be bought and sold.

> **The GSCC's Code of Practice for Employers**
>
> In 2002 the newly created GSCC issued a Code of Practice for
> Social Care Employers. Like the National Minimum Standards for
> Domiciliary Care, these will in time impact upon people like
> Chris Field. The code says employers must:
>
> - Make sure that people are suitable to enter the social care
>   workforce and understand their roles and responsibilities.
>
> - Have written policies and procedures in place to enable
>   social care workers to meet the codes of practice for workers.
>
> - Provide training and development opportunities to enable
>   social care workers to strengthen and develop their skills
>   and knowledge.

- Put in place and implement written policies and procedures to deal with dangerous, discriminatory or exploitative behaviour and practice.

- Promote the codes of practice to social care workers, service users and carers and cooperate with the care councils' proceedings.

The new codes of practice for staff and employers and the introduction of regulation of home care agencies will make a difference. However, what they do not address is the low pay and resourcing issues that characterise the social care sector. In the new health and social care market, finding staff who are willing to be flexible in the way Chris describes is essential. INS's success as a provider depends on its being able to supply a flexible, low-paid workforce ready and able to do work that the social services department, which may well employ unionised staff, will not take on. There are positive aspects to this. It's a more enjoyable job because of it, as Mary points out in comparing home care with her previous job in a factory. But it also highlights the truth of Gillian Pascall's view, quoted in Section 1, that community care is built upon the work of low-paid women.

4.4 Summing up

In this section, we have looked at INS as an example of how the market operates in health and social care. You have seen that the market offers some distinct advantages to purchasers, providers and, in some respects, clients, and that it appears to meet at least two of its three aims, to promote competition and drive down costs. However, there are few guarantees of quality for users of home care, and the purchaser/ provider model is not always effective in promoting consumer choice. Finally, you saw that the rhetoric of a 'flexible' workforce may hide the fact that the 'success' of the market depends upon the exploitation of a low-paid, predominantly female, workforce.

Key points

- Providers of home care operate in the context of a market.

- To be successful in the home care market, providers need to drive down costs to satisfy purchasers. This may make it hard to maintain the quality of the care provided to clients.

- The market does offer more choice to clients, but their power to exercise choice is limited by the way the purchaser/ provider system works.

- Providers of home care need a flexible workforce, but this may have a negative impact on the pay and conditions of employees, most of whom are women.

Section 5

Changing the perspective: independent living

This section explores challenges to the whole idea of social care as a means of meeting the needs of people who are perceived as having 'care needs'. To do this, it examines 'user' perspectives. You have spent a fair amount of time in this unit on 'user' or client views of existing services. You read Reg Martin's account and you considered how much choice users of home care services actually have.

Now we will take a more radical look at care from a user perspective, and examine the case for independent living.

5.1 Making a case for independent living

The reading for this section is Chapter 19 in the Reader by Jenny Morris, 'Creating a space for absent voices'. Jenny Morris is a freelance writer and researcher who was thrust into the role of a user by an accident in adulthood which means she now uses a wheelchair. She is also a feminist but, as you will see, her position differs from that of the feminists you have met so far in this unit; indeed, she is explicitly critical of them. As I said in the box on feminist perspectives in Unit 1, there is more than one feminist perspective. As you read the chapter you will see evidence of this.

Activity 16 **Re-examining feminist research on community care**

Allow about 15 minutes

Read the section entitled 'Silencing our voices' in Chapter 19 in the Reader now. Some of the issues raised will be familiar to you from Unit 1. As you make notes, concentrate on the criticisms Morris makes of 'feminist research on community care'.

Comment   The main criticism Morris makes of feminist research on community care is that it failed to take into account the perspective of older women and disabled women. Feminists claimed to be speaking for *women*, but somehow failed to notice that not only are unpaid carers usually women but many older and disabled people are also women. Morris argues that feminists portrayed them as 'dependent people' who 'burden' women within the family. This failure to take account of the views of older women and disabled women led some feminists to campaign for a return to institutional care, which, Morris says, demonstrates 'patronising, cavalier, discriminatory attitudes' to disabled people. The absent voices of the title are those 'dependent' women whose views feminists had *not* considered.

She makes other criticisms.

- Feminist research suggests that carers and cared for are always easy to distinguish, but in some cases these roles are not so clearly defined. (This was discussed in relation to Lynne and Arthur in Unit 1.)

- Some women are denied the chance to care for families and actually want the opportunity to care. This is true of black working-class women and women with learning disabilities.

This is a good example of the way ideas develop by one argument challenging another. Morris has added a new dimension to the arguments of feminist critics of community care – the views and experiences of disabled people, many of whom are women. In a way she is saying, 'see what happens to the argument if we add another factor into the equation'. You will see that adding this new factor not only changes the argument but also has practical applications for the way care services are structured.

Activity 17   **Challenging concepts of dependence and independence**

Allow about 15 minutes   Now read the section of Chapter 19 entitled 'Challenging concepts of dependence and independence'. Make notes on:

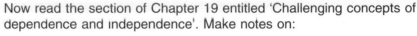

(a)   the competing definitions of 'independent living' by:

    (i)   professionals

    (ii)   the Independent Living Movement

(b)   the arguments disabled people use to challenge the idea that physical impairment means dependence

(c)   why Morris objects to the word 'care' when applied to the assistance needed by disabled people.

Comment   (a)   (i)   Morris says professionals define 'independent living' as initiatives developed within the context of community care policies, based on people's 'functional ability or inability'; in other words, it is to do with whether they can manage their day-to-day life without outside help.

        (ii)   The Independent Living Movement's definition is more about human and civil rights and exercise of choice – to have personal relationships, to be a parent, to have equal access to education, etc. Brisenden describes it as 'simply being able to achieve our goals'.

    (b)   Disabled people challenge the idea that physical impairment means dependence by challenging the common definition of its opposite, 'independence'. The Independent Living Movement's definition of independence is more about being able to make choices and achieve personal goals than it is about 'the ability to do something for oneself, to be self supporting, self reliant' which, Morris says, is the traditional interpretation of the word in Western societies.

    (c)   Morris objects to the use of the term 'care' when it refers to the 'need for personal assistance'. She argues that to call someone 'a carer', whether paid or unpaid, is to put them in charge, to give them power over the person they are caring for. The use of the term 'carer' implies dependence on the part of the other person.

In Unit 1 you were warned that the use of the term 'care' is, in some instances, controversial. Morris's use of it is an example. She only uses 'care' to criticise it. When she wants to refer to the sort of tasks we have called 'care work' she uses 'help' or 'assistance' instead.

If you have followed this argument so far, you can see that Morris is, on behalf of 'disabled people', challenging a whole set of assumptions upon which community care is based. If you stop seeing disabled people as having 'care needs' and think of them instead as having 'rights', then the task is not to assess needs in a narrow way, but to promote people's rights to choice, to put them in control, to open opportunities to pursue goals they choose – which may or may not include being able to do their own shopping or tie their shoelaces. I'll come back to this idea shortly, but first complete your reading of the chapter.

Activity 18   **Hearing absent voices**

Allow about 15 minutes   Read the final section of Chapter 19 in the Reader, entitled 'The experience of statutory services'. Here Morris is quoting what she has called the 'absent voices', the people who experience care at the receiving end. For the purpose of this chapter, Morris has selected only women's voices, as the chapter is about women in particular. Read the pages and then make notes on the evidence that being in receipt of care actually promotes dependence.

Comment   Morris argues that care services, far from relieving dependence, actually create it.

- Moira did not get help with being a mother because she was provided only with personal care, and it seemed the providers were reluctant to respond flexibly to what she saw as the support she required to be a parent.

- Elizabeth could not get services which would support her in keeping paid employment.

The idea behind care services is of passive people who need only basic maintenance. As Valerie is quoted as saying:

> *They think that community care is about someone being cosy and comfortable, being kept clean.*

This brings us back to Maslow's basic needs, but the women Morris interviewed wanted services to meet a greater variety of needs.

Services should be able to support disabled people in employment

Morris concluded from her research that:

- physical impairment – the limitations on what people can do imposed by a condition – does not create dependence in itself; rather, it is the context, the way help is provided, which is important
- the quality of someone's life is determined by the nature and quality of assistance provided to enable them to go about their daily lives
- the categories of 'carer' and 'dependant' are created by the way we conventionally look at the world with traditional notions of independence in mind.

I have included this discussion because it enables us to identify some general assumptions about care and dependence on which the structure of care services are based. To sum up, people who are not able to be independent in the way it is normally defined are seen as helpless and to need 'care'; but 'care' is provided in such a way as to sustain helplessness, deny opportunities to make choices and prevent people from fulfilling roles other than that of 'dependant'.

In the rest of this section I consider how Morris's arguments translate into practice in two ways: changing the language, and changing the system.

Study skills: Linking the course to your own interests and experiences

Jenny Morris puts some challenging arguments. Do they relate to your own experiences in any way? As you were reading did you make any notes of connections in the margin? In K100 we make a point of focusing on specific people's circumstances and ideas but often, because it is a broad course, their particular concerns will be a little removed from your own interests and experiences. Yet in most cases there will be very fruitful connections you can make, if you stop to think. One way of 'personalising' K100 – of shaping it to your own concerns – is to note down links to your own experience as you go along. You can then accumulate these notes in a folder marked 'Personal File'. By the end of the course you will have a collection of your reflections on your own experiences and concerns.

5.2 Changing the language: from needs to rights

The Independent Living Movement employs the language of civil rights in its challenge to traditional definitions of independence, which are about ability to manage daily life without assistance from others. The language of rights gives an alternative framework in which to examine what people should be able to expect from services.

Rights and citizenship

The notion of civil rights stems from debates on citizenship. It is argued that everyone living in a country is a citizen and should have rights. A citizen is seen as someone able to participate in society on an equal basis. Citizenship rights are often divided into three: legal rights, for example the right to free speech; political rights, for example the right to vote; and social rights, for example the right to a minimum income (Marshall, 1981). However, many demands that are often called 'rights', for example 'the right to work', are not rights in our society in that they are unenforceable in law. So the language of rights can be confusing. In arguing for citizenship rights, disabled people are demanding the wherewithal to participate in society as equals. And to be able to participate as equals, disabled people argue for *more* resources to establish that equality.

Arguments about rights are often accompanied by arguments about responsibilities or duties. If people are to have rights, then they should accept responsibilities too, to contribute to society as well as to take from it.

Campaigning for civil rights

I considered care needs as an approach to defining what community care should be delivering. What happens if I change the framework, and use rights instead?

Activity 19   **From needs to rights**

Allow about 5 minutes   Imagine what Lynne Durrant would say if she were asked what she wants from life from a rights perspective. Write a list, beginning each sentence with 'I have a right to ...'

Comment   I imagine Lynne saying:

- I have a right to a home of my own.
- I have a right to some freedom.
- I have a right, as an adult woman, to go out without accounting for my actions.
- I have a right to spend what I earn on what I choose.

Incidentally, I could *not* imagine her saying 'I have a right to an assessment of my needs as a carer'. Lynne wants to be free of caring altogether.

Changing 'needs' to 'rights' changes the way we look at a problem. It is an illustration of the importance of language, and the connection between the words that are used and attitudes that was the subject of Unit 1, Section 2. None of the rights suggested is actually a legal right, but looking at someone as a person with rights, rather than in a 'care' category, can make a difference to the way their problems are seen, and confirms Morris's argument that care and dependence are in part created by the way care services are framed.

5.3 Changing the system: a case for direct payments?

It is hard to see a system designed to deliver care on a large scale, such as Independent Nursing Services, being able to deliver the sort of flexibility Morris's respondents wanted. Although Chris Field valued flexibility too, it was primarily flexibility for the employer, not for the client to decide what she wants, when she wants it. That is not compatible with delivering 1,000 visits a day to clients who, if they complain about little else, are likely to pick up the phone if their home carer is late or does not turn up at all.

One widely canvassed solution to the difficulties of providing flexible care, which reflects what people really want rather than what they are deemed to need, is to change the system so that those who receive the service become the direct employers of their own care workers or personal assistants (see the box opposite). This idea is known as 'direct payments'. The Direct Payments Act, introduced in 1996, permitted local authorities to make direct payments to some users of services. The campaign for direct payments was led by organisations of disabled people such as the British Council of Disabled People, on behalf of anyone who uses care services. It represents a development of the market model discussed in Section 4 in that it makes the relationship between service user and provider a direct one, uncomplicated by the role of the purchaser.

Activity 20   **Direct payments for the Durrants?**

Allow about 5 minutes   If the Durrants directly employed their care workers, what additional powers might they have? Make a list.

Comment   They could:

- choose the people who work for them
- determine their hours
- decide what duties should be carried out
- negotiate rates of pay or conditions of work, within the limits of existing employment legislation.

If they were wealthy enough, they might well have opted for a private arrangement – employing a housekeeper, perhaps, or an agency nurse.

Here is a summary of the arguments in favour of direct payments (*Personal Assistance Users' Newsletter*, July 1996) based on research into what users want:

- direct payments offered users more choice and control
- they were more flexible
- assistance was more frequently delivered in the manner users wanted
- costs were on average 30–40% less than equivalent service-based support – direct payment users' average hourly cost was £5.18; service-based support average hourly cost was £8.52
- users were more satisfied.

Personal assistants

Personal assistants are directly employed by a disabled person to help with personal and domestic tasks, work, social and leisure activities. The extent and type of help is determined by the person who needs help.

The use of the term 'personal assistant' is a deliberate strategy to move away from the dependence-creating ideas of a 'carer'. Jenny Morris's chapter in the Reader explained why some disabled adults object to the idea that they need 'care'. The term 'personal assistant' is drawn from the business world, where executives have personal assistants to answer the phone, keep diaries, etc. They are usually women.

Critics of this shift in terminology argue:

- it diminishes the 'emotional labour' and 'love' dimension of care because the personal assistant image implies that the work is to do with tasks, rather than a mixture of work and care
- it may give power to service users, but it may well take power away from workers
- personal assistant jobs are dead-end jobs
- users of services may be vulnerable to exploitation unless safeguards are in place
- users may not be equal opportunity employers.

Activity 21   **Direct payments: advantages and disadvantages**

Allow about 10 minutes   Use what you know of users of services from the block so far, or your own experience, to summarise the advantages and disadvantages of moving to a direct payments system for all service users.

Comment   Advantages:

- People could choose exactly what services they wanted rather than accept what's on offer.
- People could choose exactly whom they wanted to employ. Jenny Morris's research suggests that most disabled people actually prefer assistance from people without previous experience because their approach is more flexible. (Remember that Chris Field too had this preference.)
- People from black or other minority ethnic groups could choose workers who know about and respect their culture; men could choose male assistants, women could choose women ...
- There might be more continuity.
- Workers would be more likely to respect people as employers, rather than users.
- On the evidence we have, direct payments would be cheaper.

Disadvantages:

- Users might be vulnerable to unscrupulous people.
- There would need to be a system of inspection for agencies who supply personal assistants.
- Who would be in charge? In the Durrant household, for example, would Arthur or Lynne be the employer? Would it be a recipe for greater conflict?
- Employees might be exploited or discriminated against. We know that Lynne has racist views, so it's unlikely she would be an equal opportunities employer.
- Personal assistants are likely to be trapped in dead-end jobs with few training or promotion opportunities.
- Provision would need to be made for back-up services for sickness or holidays.
- Where there are complex care needs there might still need to be input from specialists who are not directly employed by the users.
- Not everyone has the skills to be an employer.

Initially, most users of direct payments were disabled adults, like the people Jenny Morris interviewed for her research. Direct payments spread only slowly to other groups, such as older people and people with learning difficulties or mental health problems. When direct payments were extended to older people in a pilot scheme run in Portsmouth during 1999, it was found that the few people who did take it up received a high quality service. However, take up was limited because of the difficulty of finding suitable applicants for personal assistant jobs and the lack of a designated worker to support the scheme. It did emerge that in some cases carers 'used the scheme to extend their own choice and control' – not that of the 'users'! (Clark and Spufford, 2001). Direct payments schemes do have an important role to play in increasing people's choice of the type of care or support they want, but when they are being used by people who are confused or have little speech additional safeguards are needed to avoid exploitation.

There is an important difference in being seen as someone who employs personal assistants rather than as someone who needs care. It moves the argument away from a person's individual limitations to a framework which all can comprehend. Everyone needs personal assistance, whether from a car, a word processor, a washing machine or a person. The change of language brings disabled people into the mainstream rather than confining them to the marginal status of dependants.

Key points

- Advocates of independent living challenge conventional notions of independence, and argue that the way care services are structured actually creates dependence.

- Changing the perspective from care needs to rights changes the framework for looking at what users of care services want.

- It is argued that changing to a system of direct payments so that users can directly employ personal assistants rather than receive care from home care services will enhance users' power and offer them services which are more flexible and responsive to their needs.

- Most research into independent living and direct payments is based on the experiences of disabled adults. The appropriateness of the system for other groups is less well proven.

- Changing from the present system to a system of direct payments may not enhance the status or working conditions of employees.

Study skills: Reading

You have done three weeks' worth of intensive reading now – and we hope you have found it stimulating and informative. But how effective a reader do you feel you are? Since reading takes up by far the largest part of your studies, it is very important to reflect on what you are supposed to be achieving from it, and whether you are going about it the best way. To help you reflect on your reading technique, I suggest you read Chapter 5 of *The Good Study Guide*. It asks you to read a three-page article about whether rising levels of income are making us happier. It is important to do this exercise properly because the rest of the book keeps referring back to the article.

Afterwards, try to find a few more minutes for your study diary. This week you could make a feature of comparing your experiences of studying by reading with learning from the audio cassette.

Conclusion

This unit has looked at the effect of the reforms introduced by the 1990 NHS and Community Care Act, focusing on one particularly significant service, home care. It has also examined the idea of a market in health and social care, and finally discussed the challenges to traditional ideas about how care services should operate developed by the Independent Living Movement. Look back now at the core questions for the unit and, if you have the time, jot down your answers to them in the light of the work you have done.

References

Ahmad and Atkin, 1996

Bell, L. (1993) *CareFully*, Age Concern, London. (2nd edition 1999)

Clark, H. and Spufford, J. (2001) *Piloting Choice and Control for Older People: an evaluation*, London, York Policy Press / Joseph Rowntree Foundation.

Department of Health (1989a) *Caring for People* (White Paper), HMSO, London.

Department of Health (1989b) *An Introduction to the Children Act 1989*, HMSO, London.

Department of Health (2001) *Fairer Charging Policies for Home Care and Other Non-residential Social Services – Guidance for councils with social service responsibilities* (LAC(2001)32) Department of Health, London, www.doh.gov.uk/scg/homecarecharges (accessed 1/5/2002).

Department of Health (2001) *Domiciliary Care National Minimum Standards Regulations Consultation Document*, Department of Health, London.

Department of Health and Social Security (1981) *Growing Older* (Cmnd 8173), HMSO, London.

Equal Opportunities Commission (1982) *Who Cares for the Carers?*, EOC, Manchester.

Finch, J. and Groves, D. (1980) 'Community care and the family: a case for Equal Opportunities', *Journal of Social Policy*, Vol. 9, No. 4, pp. 487–511.

Hughes, B. (1995) *Community Care and Older People*, Open University Press, Buckingham.

Joseph Rowntree Foundation (1997) *Foundation*, January, p. 3.

Kings Fund (1980) *An Ordinary Life*, Kings Fund, London.

Labour Research Department (1997) 'The home help lottery', *Labour Research*, January, pp. 23–5.

Marshall, T.H. (1981) *The Rights to Welfare and Other Essays*, Heinemann, London.

Maslow, A. (1970) *Motivation and Personality*, Harper & Row, New York.

Means, R. and Smith, R. (1994) *Community Care: Policy and Practice*, Macmillan, London.

Meredith, B. (1995) *The Community Care Handbook*, Age Concern, London.

Oswin, M. (1971) *The Empty Hours*, Penguin, Harmondsworth.

Pascall, G. (1986) *Social Policy: A Feminist Analysis*, Routledge, London.

Phillips, A. and Taylor, B. (1980) 'Sex and skill: notes towards a feminist economics', *Feminist Review*, Vol. 6, pp. 79–88.

Townsend, P. (1962) *The Last Refuge*, Routledge & Kegan Paul, London.

Twigg, J. (1997) 'Deconstructing the "Social Bath": help with bathing at home for older and disabled people', *Journal of Social Policy*, Vol. 26, No. 2, pp. 211–32.

Twigg, J. and Atkins, K. (1994) *Carers Perceived: Policy and Practice in Informed Care*, Open University Press, Buckingham.

Ungerson, C. (ed.) (1990) *Gender and Caring*, Harvester Wheatsheaf, Hemel Hempstead.

Walmsley, J. (1990) 'Provision for the non able-bodied poor in the eighteenth and early nineteenth centuries', *The Local Historian*, Vol. 20, No. 1, pp. 9–19.

http://www.gscc.org.uk [accessed 1.10.02]
http://www.ccwales.org.uk [accessed 1.10.02]
http://www.ccetsw.org.uk [accessed 1.10.02]
http://www.niscc.info [accessed 1.10.02]

Acknowledgements

Grateful acknowledgement is made to the following sources for permission to reproduce material in this unit:

Illustrations

Figure 1: Foundations Booklet. Meeting the Costs of Continuing Care, January 1997, Joseph Rowntree Foundation; *pp. 131 (left two), 141, 164, 176*: John Birdsall Photography; *p. 131 (right two)*: Michael Austen; *p. 133*: Rural Media Company; *p. 134*: Mencap; *pp. 152, 177 (bottom left)*: John Harris; *p. 158*: courtesy of Independent Nursing Services, Bedford; *p. 177 (top left and right)*: Brenda Prince/Format.

We would also like to thank Independent Nursing Services for their assistance in providing information for this unit.

Unit 4
Understanding Care Relationships

Prepared for the course team by Andrew Northedge
Updated by the author

While you are working on Unit 4, you will need:

- Course Reader
- Offprints Book
- *The Good Study Guide*
- Audio Cassette 1, side 1
- Wallchart

Contents

Introduction

To set up a care relationship that works well is a delicate matter, whether you are at the giving or the receiving end. You have met plenty of examples in Block 1 where care relationships have been very demanding – physically, emotionally and personally – and where one side or the other has felt unhappy about the position in which they find themselves. But the reasons for dissatisfaction vary.

In Activity 18 of Unit 3 you met Elizabeth, a disabled woman quoted by Jenny Morris, who described her care assistants as 'very patronising ... overbearing ... dictating ... smothering a person's sense of independence'. And Morris herself says:

> *Disabled women often try to assert their independence ... only to be confronted by the assumption commonly held by professionals and care workers that they have the right to define what is needed and how help should be given.*
>
> *(Morris, in the Reader)*

Morris objects to the way disabled people find themselves *positioned* within relationships – the tendency to assume, because a person needs assistance with some activities, that they must be generally helpless and dependent, and that it is up to others to take a strong lead in relationships.

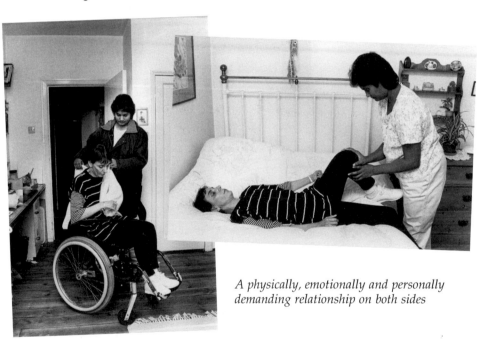

A physically, emotionally and personally demanding relationship on both sides

On the other hand, the response to home helps by Reg Martin, whom you also met in Unit 3, was very different. He hated it when they asked what he wanted them to do for him. He felt overwhelmed by having to think what to tell them. He was only too happy when a new home help, Glenda, took to deciding what food to buy him, and came to her own conclusions about what to clean and wash. Apparently, what meant being patronised and smothered to Elizabeth meant welcome relief to Reg.

In Unit 4 we explore the very varied *meanings* of care relationships and how these meanings arise. Millions of care relationships are going on as you read this, and each carries its own particular meanings for those involved. But where have all those people picked up their ideas of how to relate to each other? How does any of us know where to begin?

Core questions

- Why is negotiating the meaning of care relationships important?

- How do people work out how to play the roles of 'carer' and 'receiver of care'?

- What makes care involving intimate bodily contact particularly difficult?

- Why can it be difficult for an individual person to challenge the meanings imposed upon them in care contexts?

- What happens when care roles conflict?

- Can care relationships be equal?

Section 1
Playing roles together

Care relationships are seldom just a matter of 'doing what comes naturally'. For one thing, you may be caring for, or being cared for, by someone you would not otherwise get on with. And a care relationship has to adapt to circumstances: it may be brief, as in an acute hospital ward, or it may be very long lasting; it may be flexible according to need or, as you saw with the home care plans in Unit 3, it may involve a high degree of regularity. Also some of the things you and the other person have to do together are very different from what goes on within other relationships. What is more, you need to be able to conduct a care relationship in a calm and consistent way, without the fallings out and reconciliations that can occur in many other kinds of relationship.

In other words, a care relationship has to be specially 'constructed'. This is true even when the care relationship is built on an existing family relationship. You are not simply relating to someone according to your personal inclination. You have a particular kind of *role* to play. Moreover, the other person has a role too. In fact, your two roles go together as a matching pair – carer and receiver of care. The one role implies the other. A care relationship involves both parties enacting their roles together in a co-ordinated way.

But this role-playing is not necessarily harmonious. Take Reg Martin and his home helps, for example. According to him, a new person would come in and say something like, 'I'm your home help. Now what do you want me to clean?' This might seem a very reasonable question to ask but Reg did not like it at all. He said, 'I could never understand a home help asking such a question ... you shouldn't need to ask. But they insisted and I couldn't cope ... I decided that this was a bad no go.' Reg seems to have developed such a hostility to this question that he was about to give up the home help service. How can we make any sense of such a strong reaction to an apparently polite and helpful question?

1.1 Defining the scene

I shall approach this puzzle by asking what kind of 'scene' the home help was proposing that she and Reg should play out together.

Activity 1 **Defining a scene**

Allow about 5 minutes   When the home help asked, 'What do you want me to clean?', she was, in effect, proposing a 'definition' of the 'scene' that was opening up between herself and Reg.

(a)   What kind of 'scene' was she suggesting?

(b)   What role was she giving herself in this 'scene'? What role was she giving Reg?

Quickly jot down your thoughts.

Comment   (a)   It seems to me that the home help was proposing a 'scene' in which one person organises the work of another and tells them what to do.

           (b)   She would have the role of being told what to do and Reg would have the role of organising and telling. Perhaps you described it as a 'servant and master' relationship, or 'employee and manager'.

It seems that in his state of sickness Reg did not feel up to playing a role as 'manager'. He felt weighed down by having to remember what needed cleaning and having to write out shopping lists. It seems he experienced the home help's question as oppressive, because it thrust him into a role he did not feel comfortable playing.

How can one person push another person into playing a role? The home help did not say, 'I want you to act as my manager', so why did Reg feel under pressure? In fact she did something more subtle. She started to act out a scene in which she was a person needing to be told what to do. In such a scene the matching role is clearly someone who tells that person what to do. Since the scene was already beginning and Reg was the only other person there, what else could he do but play that matching role? He found himself absorbed into the action of the scene the home help had initiated. Through her opening question she had both 'defined the scene' and begun to act her role in it, and Reg then found himself drawn in.

Glenda, however, presented herself to Reg quite differently.

Activity 2   **A different definition**

Allow about 10 minutes

How was Glenda's presentation of herself different from the previous home helps? Look back at the interview with Reg (Offprint 6) and answer these questions.

(a)   Glenda began by announcing her name rather than her job title. What difference would that make to the way the scene between the two is defined?

(b)   What were the next things Glenda said and did? How did they create a different kind of relationship with Reg?

(c)   How would you describe the scene she presented for herself and Reg to play? What was her role and what was Reg's role?

Comment   Here is my interpretation.

(a)   By opening with her name, Glenda presented herself to Reg as a person first and a home help second. She opened up a line of ordinary person-to-person communication, rather than speaking to him only through her formal role. The 'great big smile' backed up this invitation.

(b)   Glenda said such things as 'I've come to do some shopping', rather than asking, 'What do you want me to buy for you?' This is a more flexible way of defining the scene, because it leaves open who should decide what to buy. It offers scope to Reg to take on the 'deciding' role if he wants to, or pass it over to Glenda. Reg's first reaction was that he ought to make a list, so she let him get on with it. But when he started getting into difficulties she offered to 'have a look'. Then she made a few suggestions and Reg felt tremendously relieved. Gradually, after that, she took over a lot of the decision making about shopping, although she made a point of buying him 'special' things, which made Reg feel she was including him. Broadly, she defined a scene in which she and Reg would sort out Reg's needs together.

(c)   Subsequently, she played her role according to how well Reg was feeling. She did not define their relationship as purely functional – with the roles fixed and formal. She left scope for Reg to change the definition of the scene according to his mood. Yet she was far from passive within the relationship. She took an active role in judging his needs. Beyond her helping work she also took time to sit down and chat at times. This extended the definition of the scenes they played out together, giving Reg a role as a person with a life and interests beyond his immediate illness and disabilities.

Key points

- Your opening remarks tend to manoeuvre another person into a particular way of relating to you.

- You can play a role either in a way that leaves the other person's options open, or in a way that 'closes them off'.

Activity 3   **Openings to everyday scenes**

Allow about 5 minutes   I am sure you can think of examples of everyday scenes, at home or at work, which could be radically reshaped by an opening remark.

(a)   For example, say you surprised a guest snacking from your fridge.
- You could take any tension out of the situation by saying, 'While you're there could you pass the milk', and then chat about something else.
- You could ask, 'Are you hungry? Can I get you anything?' hinting that you don't mind, but you would rather she asked first.
- You could say, 'I'm so sorry there wasn't enough to go round at lunch' – to make her feel guilty at slighting your generosity as a host.
- Or you could raise the emotional temperature by asking, 'Do you normally help yourself in other people's houses?'

How does each of these ways of opening the scene define you? How does each define your guest?

(Notice the significance of questions. Asking a question puts pressure on the other person to answer – to join in the scene with you, on the terms you have set up in your question.)

(b)   You are sitting with family, or friends. The TV is on and you say, 'Is anyone watching this rubbish?' How does this question define you and how does it define the others present? What pressure does it exert on them? What alternative questions could you ask, which would define the scene differently and have a very different impact on your companions?

(c)   Stop and think of one or two other examples from your everyday life, where you could 'change the scene' by what you choose to say.

Defining yourself within the scene

A social interaction is any kind of situation in which people communicate with each other or do things together.

The sociologist Erving Goffman studied how people relate to each other across a wide range of situations. According to him, each of us enters into 'social interactions' with an interest in trying to control what goes on. After all, much of what we do in life, we do through dealings with other people. We negotiate the routine business of daily life through interactions with family members, friends, shop assistants, work colleagues, clients, carers, and so on. In order to handle these various social interactions we need to have ways of influencing how other people behave towards us. We do this by trying to influence how situations are defined.

> ... *it will be in ... [the individual's] interests to control the conduct of the others ... This control is achieved largely by influencing the definition of the situation which the others come to formulate ...*
>
> *(Goffman, 1971, p. 15)*

Goffman says the main way you can influence the definition of a situation is through the way you present yourself within it. You are capable of presenting yourself in many different ways. But within a given situation you have to choose just one way. Interactions do not work unless everyone 'agrees' to play a specific part within the scene and stick to it. You have to opt for a version of yourself which will (you hope) be effective within that situation. Goffman allows that there is scope for shifting the definition of a scene while it is playing and for modifying the roles of participants. But he says that such changes have to be consistent with what has gone before. This strictly limits the scope for change. Consequently, it is in the opening 'projection' of yourself that you have most opportunity for influencing the way others treat you.

 Turn to Offprint 7 which contains extracts from Goffman's *The Presentation of Self in Everyday Life*, and read the first paragraph.

Study skills: Coping with challenging reading

Goffman's language and way of arguing can seem quite difficult at first. But that is true of a lot of interesting and original writing. Somehow you have to find ways of pushing on through the difficult passages. Obviously, the first thing is to try to concentrate hard and see whether you can make sense of it. If that doesn't work, try jotting down a few notes of what you *think* is being said. This may help to focus your thoughts. But if you are still confused, just move on and try the sections that follow. Sometimes 'the penny drops' a while later.

Activity 4   **Unsuccessful presentations**

Allow about 5 minutes   Can you think of a recent situation where you felt uncomfortable because you did not manage to 'project' yourself as you would have liked (too shy, say, or too loud, or just stupid)? Can you think of how you got stuck with that definition of yourself? Did you try to change it? How could you have presented yourself differently at the outset?

Comment   I thought of when I was sitting in the living room while my teenage daughters watched TV with their friends. I would like to have seemed less old and boring – to have joined in, commenting on the programmes, without seeming to be trying too hard; to have been seen as having a worthwhile point of view, and not just lack of insight into today's popular culture. Perhaps I shouldn't have opened with a quip about the hackneyed plot.

Key points

Goffman's argument runs like this:

- Each of us has an interest in exerting some control over what goes on within social interactions we are involved in.

- We try to achieve this control through influencing the 'definition of the situation'.

- A key way of influencing the 'definition of a situation' is through the way you present yourself within the situation.

- Your greatest opportunity for influence lies in your opening 'projection' of yourself, since after that you have to maintain a consistent 'front'.

Erving Goffman

Erving Goffman (1922–1982) appears in several places in K100. He made a major contribution to the way we understand relationships within the medical and caring worlds. He was Canadian, but was based at Edinburgh University from 1949 to 1951 when he carried out research in the Shetland Islands, exploring the way islanders related to each other. After returning to the USA he was involved, as a 'participant observer', in detailed studies of relationships within mental hospitals. Goffman wrote several influential books. Three of particular relevance to K100 are: *Asylums: Essays on the Social Situation of Mental Patients and other Inmates*, a study of relationships and institutions; *Stigma: Notes on the Management of Spoiled Identity* (concerning the way people cope with physical impairments which mark them out as 'not normal'); and *The Presentation of Self In Everyday Life*, his first book, which is very relevant here in Unit 4.

1960 and 1962

Playing to the 'script'

You can only succeed with a projection of yourself which other people are prepared to accept. And you then have to play out the scene the way others in the situation *expect* it to be played. Reg and Glenda did not start their opening scene from nothing. They were working within a widely shared understanding of home help work, which views it as a version of 'housework'. Cleaning and shopping are seen as traditional 'women's work' – low in status, poorly paid and weakly defined in terms of what has to be done and to what standards. It would be difficult for Glenda to project herself to Reg as, for example, a high-powered, career-oriented woman. And Reg would probably feel uncomfortable if she tried. It fits much more comfortably if Glenda projects herself as a homely woman, who enjoys putting the house straight. If she accepts 'housework' as the broad frame of reference, she can draw on traditions of everyday relationships between 'housewives' and 'menfolk', knowing that Reg will be familiar with playing the other side. It is as though they have a 'script' to guide them.

Since their relationship is acted out within Reg's own home, where he has a sense of being 'in charge', and since Glenda's work is of relatively low status, they are on a fairly even footing. (On her side, she has the authority of a paid role for the social services department and the advantage of being the physically able member of the relationship.) Neither of them is in a clearly passive or subordinate role. Both sides have a basis from which to negotiate the terms of the relationship. The 'script' they are playing to is not very tightly defined. (In this context, the term 'script' does not refer to something written down, but rather the kind of language to be used and the general lines along which participants will expect a scene to develop.)

However, some care relationships are more tightly defined and more hierarchical, for example a doctor's relationship with a patient. Within the biomedical model, the doctor's role is to focus on the patient's body and its functioning. The patient's role is to report clearly and accurately on the body's functions and the feelings it transmits. There is relatively little scope for the patient to influence the definition of this scene. The doctor generally makes the opening moves, while the patient waits to be asked questions.

Activity 5

Allow about 5 minutes

Departing from the script

Think ahead to your next consultation with your GP. Are there opening moves you could make which would change the definition of the scene?

What would happen if you sat down with a pad and said, 'Doctor, before starting on me, there are some details I'd like about your training and experience'? Or what if you breezed in and said, 'I'm going to tell you exactly what's wrong with me and what medicines I need you to prescribe'?

Comment

Doctors might vary in the manner of their response, but I find it hard to imagine any doctor conceding much ground to you. If you cut across their projection of themselves as 'in control' of the consultation, I imagine that most would refuse to proceed. One person I know, who tried, simply found the consultation terminated and was invited to return in a different frame of mind.

Doctors cannot let patients take the lead in defining the scene. They are invested with *responsibility*. They are professionally and legally accountable. It is important that they stay close to accepted practice in conducting their consultations, or they could find themselves in trouble. When you enter your doctor's surgery, the scene you enact is not played ad lib. The 'script' is fairly tightly prescribed.

In many respects the 'script' for consultations does its job well. With its well-defined roles for doctor and patient, it gets people through the surgery at a steady rate. It enables doctors to diagnose and prescribe. It gives patients an impression of confidence and knowledge on the part of the doctor. And it gives doctors some protection against the doubts and ambiguities of their work.

However, it can also give rise to difficulties. You have already seen an example of this in Unit 2 in Ruth Pinder's study of patients with Parkinson's disease. If the doctor is projected as the person who has the expert knowledge, the matching role is a patient who knows nothing. Yet Pinder shows that it is vital to sufferers from Parkinson's disease that they know as much as they can about the implications of the disease, so that they can be 'in control' of the illness. Within the traditional doctor–patient relationship this transfer of information can be difficult, as you heard from Mrs P:

> *I would like to discuss a lot of things with him [Dr X] ... I've never had the opportunity to discuss the symptoms. And what to expect. I'd like to ask him. It's hard isn't it.*

> (Quoted in Pinder, in the Reader)

When a well-defined scene is already rolling, it is hard to find the right moment and the form of words to shift its direction. So the doctor–patient 'script' both provides a very useful framework and also constrains the relationship in ways which may sometimes be detrimental.

Structures that both enable and constrain

Life within a society is made possible by structures. They operate at many levels, from the details of daily life (e.g. the routines of getting up in the morning, or the ritual greetings we use when we meet people) to the broader organisation of society (e.g. the channels through which mass media 'news' is generated, or the rules under which benefit payments are made). Even the language through which I am communicating now is a structured system of written symbols. But structures not only enable things to be done, they also impose constraints.

The doctor–patient relationship is a good example. This highly structured relationship gives you access to advice drawn from the large knowledge base and the long-developed practices of the medical profession. However, the very structures of the relationship which make it possible to supply the advice – the polite formality, the assumption of authority by the doctor, the diagnostic procedures, the understood confidentiality of information you give, the rapid decision making – also place tight limits on what can go on within the relationship. Much of the time we are unaware of the limits because we are very used to them. But if, for example, you want to challenge the doctor's interpretation of your illness and bring knowledge to bear from a different source, it can be very hard to do this within the established structuring of the relationship.

> **Key points**
>
> According to Goffman:
>
> - Our room for manoeuvre in negotiating the 'definition of a scene' varies.
>
> - Some situations are fairly evenly balanced and open-ended. Others are tightly defined and have well-established 'scripts' – or power is very much stacked on one side.
>
> - The term 'script' means the conventional ways of speaking and acting in a particular kind of situation.
>
> - 'Scripts' provide a form of structuring within social situations. Like any structures they simultaneously *enable* things to happen and *constrain* what can happen.

1.2 Teamwork

So far I have focused on one-to-one interactions. Yet 'defining a scene' is often a group effort. Goffman says this involves teamwork, with all participants, in effect, agreeing to act and speak within an overall frame of reference. He suggests that it works like a theatrical play in which everyone has taken on a part within the scene. To play your part means setting aside all those aspects of yourself which are not relevant to your role. The scene works only because everyone plays their part properly and avoids acting in ways which undermine or contradict other people's performances. If anyone messes up their role-playing then it is embarrassing for everyone, because it threatens to break up the scene. This would expose the fact that *everyone* is acting and make it difficult to continue the scene.

But how can this work? How do people work out who is playing what? Goffman suggests that it happens through a process of people speaking (or doing) in turn and thereby projecting definitions of the situation and of themselves. But they do this in ways that avoid contradicting people's projections that have preceded theirs.

Activity 6

Allow about 15 minutes

Agreeing who to be

Now read the rest of 'Extracts from *The Presentation of Self in Everyday Life*', Offprint 7. Underline what you see as the key points.

When you get to the end, look back at what you have underlined and jot down brief notes for yourself of the main things the passage says.

Comment

Here is my version.

- Every participant contributes by projecting a <u>definition of the situation</u>, even if mainly by their response to other people's projections.

- Normally participants' definitions are sufficiently '<u>attuned' to each other</u> so that contradictions do not arise.

- This means '<u>putting on a front</u>' – suppressing your 'real' feelings (e.g. don't yawn while someone is telling a story) and acting in a way which suggests that you share common values with the other participants.

- Usually you are allowed responsibility for defining aspects of the situation which are relevant mainly to your own role, on the general understanding that you <u>respect other people's definitions</u> of themselves and do not undermine them. In other words, if someone makes a claim which seems to you improbable – for example, that they are twenty years younger than they look – so long as it doesn't affect your own role, you say nothing.

- In this way the group achieves and maintains a '<u>working consensus</u>' <u>as to what is going on and who is playing what role.</u>

Study skills: Group study

If you attend K100 tutorials you have had an excellent opportunity to see these processes happening and to be involved in them yourself. When you arrive at your first tutorial you can never be sure what the tutor and the other students will be like, and it often takes a meeting or two before people really establish themselves in consistent roles within the group, so that you can begin to form a proper impression of them.

But the development of relationships within a study group is more than an intriguing spectator sport. It affects what you can learn from your tutorials. Constructive, open relationships will give you much more opportunity to share in the 'making of sense'. You also need to find a way to present yourself within the group, so that you feel comfortable speaking. Read Section 7.2.2 of Chapter 7 of *The Good Study Guide* (pp. 160–2). Try Activity 7.1 (pp. 165–6). Then read sections 7.2.5 and 7.2.6 (pp. 170–6).

Playing doctors, nurses and patients

You met an example of this kind of team playing in Unit 2 in Lesley Mackay's research on doctors and nurses.

Activity 7   **The doctor role**

Allow about 5 minutes   Go back and reread the quotations in Section 5.1 of Unit 2. Notice how strongly the idea comes across of the doctor playing a role, with white coat flying and stethoscope dangling. Look particularly at the quotation preceding Activity 14. Do you see elements of a theatrical play?

Comment   Mackay is talking in terms of a little play being enacted in the presence of the patient, in which the doctor is omniscient and everyone else awaits his wisdom. (If you don't know the meaning of a word like omniscient and can't glean it from its context, look it up in a dictionary, but remember the warning in the box on page 107 of *The Good Study Guide* about specialist terms.)

In reality, however, the nurse spends much more time with patients and often knows a lot that the doctor does not. Somehow the nurse needs to be able to communicate essential knowledge to the doctor, in the patient's presence, without appearing to undermine the doctor's 'omniscient' status. According to Leonard Stein's research in America, they achieve this through playing 'the doctor–nurse game'.

> *The cardinal rule of the game is that open disagreement must be avoided at all cost. Thus, the nurse can communicate her recommendation without appearing to be making a recommendation statement. The physician, in requesting a recommendation from a nurse, must do so without appearing to ask for it.*
>
> *(Stein, 1978)*

The doctor–nurse game

Nurse to patient:	This is Dr Jones.	*An open and direct communication.*
Nurse to doctor:	Dr Jones, this is Mrs Brown, who learned today of her father's death. She is unable to fall asleep.	*This message has two levels. Openly it describes a set of circumstances: a woman who is unable to fall asleep and who that morning received word of her father's death. Less openly, but just as directly, it is a diagnostic and recommendation statement: Mrs Brown is unable to sleep because of her grief, and she should be given a sedative.*
Doctor to nurse:	What sleeping medication has been helpful to Mrs Brown in the past?	*Dr Jones has accepted the diagnostic and recommendation statements but, not knowing the patient, is asking for a further recommendation from Nurse Smith, who does know the patient, about what medication should be prescribed. Note, however, that his question does not appear to be asking her for a recommendation.*
Nurse to doctor:	Pentobarbital mg 100 was quite effective the night before last.	*Nurse Smith makes a disguised recommendation statement.*
Doctor to nurse:	Pentobarbital mg 100 before bedtime as needed for sleep, got it?	*Dr Jones replies with a note of authority in his voice.*
Nurse to doctor:	Yes I have, and thank you very much, doctor.	*Nurse Smith ends the conversation with the tone of the grateful supplicant.*

(Source: adapted from Stein, 1978)

Through subtle teamwork, doctor and nurse together sustain the presentation of an 'omniscient' doctor.

Activity 8   **The passive actor**

Allow about 5 minutes   The patient is entirely passive in this scene. Does that mean that she has no role and is unimportant to the scene? Does her silence contribute anything?

Comment   The patient is actually essential to the scene. It would be unnecessary to play the doctor–nurse game without the patient. But the patient also contributes, simply by accepting her passive role. Her contribution is to defer to both doctor and nurse. Her silence accentuates the busy and assured professional performance going on beside her. Perhaps Mrs Brown did not want to be sedated, but in the presence of an 'expert' nurse, who defers to an even more 'expert' doctor, she does not voice an opinion. She seems to understand her role and plays it faithfully.

However, things have been changing since Stein outlined the doctor–nurse game. A more recent study in Sweden reported that:

> *In our investigation, the nurses who had been working for 15–20 years often emphasised that it was during the past 8–10 years that marked changes had occurred in their interplay with doctors. Relations in former times are described in terms such as: 'one had to stand on tiptoe', 'the doctors were kings', or 'no questioning was allowed'. By contrast today's relationships are portrayed as collegial; discussion together is common, 'they respect our job', and 'they listen and take our views into account'.*
>
> (Svensson, 1996, p. 383)

But even if the 'script' has changed, that does not mean the show has stopped running. It cannot. Nor does this talk of 'play acting' imply that what goes on is not serious. Far from it. The central point is that we human beings cannot function together in any other way. We are dependent on 'making sense of the world' together. Without *shared meanings* we cannot act together.

Key points

- Goffman argues that playing the scenes of life involves teamwork, such that participants accept a 'shared definition' of what is going on.

- Participants also accept that they should speak and act in ways which are consistent with this definition.

- This means suppressing aspects of themselves which are not consistent with their role in the 'scene'.

- It also means not undermining other people's playing of their roles within the scene.

- One example of team playing is the enacting of hierarchical doctor–nurse–patient relationships on hospital wards.

Section 2
Difficult situations

I have been discussing scenes played out in the highly structured settings of hospitals and doctors' surgeries. However, a lot of care takes place in settings where structures are much less clear – where the meaning of a scene can be highly *ambiguous*, and where any working consensus between participants is fragile.

2.1 Working in ambiguous situations

When a social worker goes into a family home, for example, the members of the household may not agree at all with the social worker's definition of what the visit is about, or what should take place during it. Far from co-operating, they may vigorously resist the 'script' the social worker is trying to work to. In fact, a frequent requirement of a social worker's job is to work with clients to try to arrive at a *redefinition* of their situation.

For example, where parents' beliefs and practices regarding child rearing appear to be damaging to their children, the social worker cannot simply play along with the parents' definition of their behaviour as 'normal' and 'proper'. Instead, the social worker has the very difficult task of entering into a relationship with the parents in which their presentation of themselves is open to question – where their claims to competence as parents are not taken for granted. Since this is potentially undermining of the parents, an obvious tactic for them is to try to undermine the social worker first – to shore up their own definition of the situation by discrediting the social worker's claims to understanding and authority.

Working with 'definitions of situations' and 'self-presentations' is a critically important aspect of a social worker's job, but it is a far cry from the clear role structures and well-established 'scripts' of the medical world. Coping with ambiguity, with contested definitions, and with weakly established 'scripts' is in the nature of the work.

Assessing risk

Dev Sharma's arrival at the Durrants' home, following the incident involving a knife, is an example of an ambiguous situation. The morning after the incident he has to visit the Durrants, having received a telephone call from the home carer, reporting a claim by Arthur that his daughter has threatened him with a knife. Dev has to initiate a *risk assessment*. But what exactly happened and how should he set about his duties?

As a social worker Dev Sharma is expected to follow guidelines. The General Social Care Council's Code of Conduct for workers will need to guide Dev's actions. For your convenience they are reproduced here.

- *Protect the rights and promote the interests of service users and carers.*
- *Strive to establish and maintain the trust and confidence of service users and carers.*
- *Promote the independence of service users while protecting them as far as possible from danger or harm.*
- *Respect the rights of service users whilst seeking to ensure that their behaviour does not harm themselves or other people.*
- *Uphold public trust and confidence in social care services.*
- *Be accountable for the quality of their work and take responsibility for maintaining and improving their knowledge and skills.*

You can see that Dev is not required simply to arrive at his own personal interpretation of events in the Durrants' home. He is expected to work within a code of practice, and also within a partnership of service users, carers and other professionals. Nevertheless, he has to begin by trying to establish the facts of the knife incident and to gather relevant opinions as to its meaning. Was there a genuine threat to attack, or was it just an angry gesture when Lynne happened to have a knife in her hand? Was this an early incident in a cycle of escalating abuse against a frail older person? Or was it a 'normal' dispute in a family where relationships are difficult – a brief moment of assertiveness by Lynne within a lifetime of oppression by Arthur? However, before he can find out anything, Dev's first challenge on entering the Durrants' home is to 'communicate and engage' (another core competency).

Activity 9

Allow about 10 minutes

Communicating and engaging

Rewind side 1 of Audio Cassette 1 to the final sequence in the Durrant case study. Arthur is talking to Dev on the morning after the knife incident. Listen again to this sequence, then answer these questions.

(a)   What kind of 'scene' is Dev playing out with Arthur? Do you have any worries about how he should relate to Arthur?

(b)   How well is Dev establishing the facts of the knife incident?

(c)   Is Dev 'working in partnership'?

Comment

(a)   It seems to me that Dev is playing a scene with Arthur in which he is an efficient investigator of facts and circumstances, and a seeker of solutions. At the same time he is being a sympathiser and reassurer when he says, 'Of course it must have been very upsetting'. This is probably helpful in encouraging Arthur to open up to him, but is Dev running the risk of becoming absorbed into Arthur's definition of the situation? If he plays 'supporter' to Arthur does he compromise his relationship with Lynne? Is he allowing Arthur to blame everything on Lynne, instead of steering him towards accepting shared responsibility for what goes on in the family?

(b)   Dev has obviously already asked Arthur some questions before we join them, and we hear him checking whether similar events have happened before. But he will obviously need to hear Lynne's side of the story too – which seems to be a problem.

(c)   At the stage we join them Dev is having difficulty engaging Lynne in a working partnership. There seems to be some danger that he is being drawn into Arthur's view that Lynne is 'the problem'. To reach a balanced assessment he will need to consult with Rita and Doreen and talk to Lynne. After that, an effective working partnership will need to involve the three of them, as well as Arthur.

Activity 10   **Difficult communications**

Allow about 5 minutes

Dev tries twice to speak to Lynne through the door. But what 'script' can you work from when someone is not even prepared to be in the same room? Listen to the sequence again.

(a)   In his first attempt to speak to Lynne what kind of scene between them does Dev project? What kind of reply from Lynne does this script 'expect'?

(b)   He adopts a different 'script' the second time. What kind of scene does Dev project this time? What kind of reply from Lynne does this new script 'expect'?

Comment   (a)   It seems to me that in his first attempt Dev is projecting a scene in which Lynne is frightened, confused and looking for a way out. He's saying, 'You are frightened – it's all OK – not very serious – we can sort it all out with a talk'. He seems to be inviting Lynne to reply along the lines, 'Oh, all right, I lost my temper. I didn't mean it. I'm sorry and I won't do it again.'

(b)   The second time he seems to be raising the stakes, projecting a scene where Lynne is in trouble and had better co-operate: 'You have done something bad – you need to join in sorting out what we are going to do about it, or things will get bad for you.' He seems to be inviting a reply along the lines, 'Please don't send me away – I'm really sorry – I can't think what came over me – I'll do whatever you suggest, if it keeps me out of trouble.'

Dev's second 'script' seems to backfire when Lynne storms out. Her parting insult suggests that she does *not* see Dev as a potential partner in working out a resolution to the situation. Did this second 'script' sound too much as though Dev was on Arthur's side? Obviously, Dev will have to find another approach. Working in partnership with Rita might be a way forward. In such an ambiguous situation assessing risk is going to be very difficult and Dev will need all the support he can draw from the other care workers involved.

'Care values' in relationships

In his dealings with Lynne and Arthur, Dev is expected to speak and act in accordance with the basic values of the social work profession. Going back again to the former CCETSW guidelines, these include the requirement that he should:

> *Identify, analyse and take action to counter discrimination, racism, disadvantage, inequality, and injustice, using strategies appropriate to role and context; and*

Practise in a manner that does not stigmatise or disadvantage either individuals, groups or communities.

(CCETSW, 1995, Part 2, p. 18)

Activity 11 Promoting care values

Allow about 5 minutes In the light of these requirements, what is Dev's responsibility when Arthur says, 'She's not really all there' and 'She should have been put away years ago'? What should he identify and analyse? What actions might he take?

Comment

- If he is to comply with the values base, Dev ought to *identify* that Arthur is displaying a discriminatory attitude towards Lynne's learning disability. He is speaking from a well-established 'script' which defines people with learning disabilities as not proper people – less than full members of adult society. He is positioning Lynne as someone whose actions are not rational, whose interests do not need to be taken into account, who should be 'put away' from the society of 'normal' people.

- Dev should also *analyse* the situation in the Durrants' home and recognise the impact on Lynne of Arthur's attitudes, since the two of them are cooped up together in their small flat.

- Taking action to counter Arthur's attitudes could involve working with Rita, Lynne and Arthur to discuss Lynne's needs, give recognition to her contribution to Arthur's welfare, and encourage Arthur to see Lynne's point of view. (It would not include talk along the lines of 'sending Lynne away'.)

- Although his attention is focused on the risk of violence to Arthur, Dev should be careful not to *practise in a manner which stigmatises* Lynne.

Lynne's disability raises one set of difficult values issues. Her final cry to Dev raises another – there is no difficulty here in *identifying racism*. However, having *analysed* the situation, Dev may feel inclined to make allowances for Lynne's learning disability. And when it comes to *taking action to counter* it, Dev will be very accustomed to racism; it is a hazard many care workers encounter regularly. To assume he has an obligation to take action himself is actually adding to his burden. He might well regard combating racism towards himself as a responsibility shared with his colleagues and supervisors, and choose to ignore Lynne's taunt.

> **Key points**
>
> - Some care situations are highly ambiguous.
>
> - Care workers' interpretations of them may be actively contested by clients.
>
> - Care work may require renegotiating the meaning of a care situation in partnership with clients and other care workers.
>
> - Care workers are responsible for trying to 'define situations' in ways which uphold their professional value base.

2.2 When meanings fall apart

We have explored the challenges of entering into situations which are ambiguous and open to competing interpretations. But what happens in a situation where nobody knows what is going on, where established meanings have collapsed altogether? Tom Heller gives a graphic account of such a situation in his description of his experience of the Hillsborough football stadium disaster.

Activity 12 | **The experience of Hillsborough**

Allow about 20 minutes

Find Offprint 8 by Tom Heller and read through it once. Then go through it again looking for answers to these questions.

(a) Why did Tom Heller feel so helpless?

(b) How did he manage to define a role for himself?

(c) What made the situation begin to seem more under control?

(d) What was the impact of returning to his children playing in the garden?

Comment | (a) In spite of his years as a doctor, Heller found himself stranded without any working definition of the scene. He says:

Nothing could have prepared me for the scenes inside.

He had no guidelines as to what to do – what role to play:

My God, what could I do? Who was going to tell me what to do?

(b) Desperate to do something, he took out his stethoscope:

... grateful to have the time at last to do something that I knew how to do. I often use 'stethoscope on the chest time' to think during consultations. It's a good ploy really; the patient thinks that I am being ever so thoughtful and thorough, and I have time to think about what the hell to do next. Panic overtook me on this occasion.

He was still unable to work out a useful role:

If only someone would arrive who knew what to do.

Then at last equipment began to arrive:

... and we started working together, putting up drips on everyone.

Then later:

I decided to use my newly refound skills to put up drips on everybody who was going to be transferred to hospital ... It was ... a sign to the hospital doctors that we general practitioners could do something right after all ...

(c) Towards the end there is a sense of 'meaningfulness' being gradually restored:

By this time the routines were more established. Someone was writing down the obvious major damage to each person and what he or she had received in the way of drugs, etc.

A kind of pattern had been constructed. Collective action became possible again. Roles could be allocated. The horror of the deaths remained, but the blind panic of the total collapse of collective meaning receded a little.

(d) There was a further shock when Heller returned home. Having experienced normality totally shattered, he found himself stepping back into a domestic normality which had continued completely undisturbed. How do you play 'normal', when you have just been exposed to the insubstantiality of normality's foundations?

Heller leaves no doubt about the horror and panic produced by a situation where action was urgently called for, yet there was no framework within which to construct action. He found himself desperately casting around for things to do, falling back on his trusty stethoscope as a way to 'play doctor', but finding it inadequate for the circumstances. He was clearly relieved when the drip equipment arrived, giving him a structured role. And even in this desperate situation he was concerned to be seen to put on a good performance. He cared what the hospital doctors thought.

This account shows how helpless we can feel without the 'social meanings' which we normally project on to the world around us. It also shows how hard we work to put meaning back together when it has collapsed. Normality is not allowed to be out of service for long.

Key points

- Some of the clearest demonstrations of the central role of 'shared meaning' in making daily life possible occur when for some reason that meaning collapses.

- If meaning does collapse, we can no longer act purposefully – we know neither who we are supposed to be within the situation, nor what we should do.

> **'Props' to support a performance**
>
> Heller casts light, in passing, on the 'play acting' which goes on within the normal work of being a doctor. Goffman says that we add credibility to the roles we play by dressing the part and using 'props' (as they are called in the theatre). The doctor's stethoscope is a good example. Unambiguously associated with medical examination, it gives authenticity to a doctor's performance. Heller says he uses his stethoscope so that he can pretend to be 'thoughtful and thorough', when actually he is racking his brains about what to do next. Doctors are meant to appear knowledgeable and decisive. So, instead of sitting scratching his head, Heller goes through a few examination routines.

In Sections 1 and 2 you have seen the importance of the shared meanings that we construct together – how they enable us to act collectively within social situations. In particular, you have explored Goffman's ideas about how those meanings are constructed through:

- the way we present ourselves within social situations
- the way we respond to other people's presentation of themselves and help to shore up their performances.

It is particularly important in a care context to understand the way meanings are negotiated within relationships. Caring activities often cut across the ordinary everyday meanings we project into relationships. So awkward situations can arise, where there is confusion about who is supposed to be doing what, and for what reason. A very obvious case is where care activities involve the body. This is the subject of Section 3.

Section 3
Working with people's bodies

In Activity 2 in Unit 1 we established that Lynne Durrant will not take on caring tasks for her father if they involve physical closeness and touching. We commented that, 'If Lynne were to ... wash Arthur it would be deviating from the normal rules which govern social behaviour.' But what are the rules for touching?

3.1 Norms of body touching

Before exploring the 'rules' for touching, we can start by asking what the 'facts' of touching are.

Study skills: Questioning the facts (Part 1)

Gathering facts is not as simple as it sounds. It is labour-intensive and expensive. And in the case of touching we cannot establish the 'real' facts. We cannot actually *watch* how much people touch. Even secret cameras would be of limited use. How long would they have to run for, and in how many different types of situation? The whole exercise would be extremely elaborate, expensive and ethically dubious.

A more practical approach is simply to ask people about their experiences of touching and being touched. But then you have to rely on what they say. Are people telling you what *actually* happens, or what they have *noticed* happens, distorted by their perceptions (e.g. you are more likely to remember an unwanted touch than a casual handshake)? Or are they telling you what they would *like you to think* happens? Then again, how many people should you ask? And what kinds of people – from how many different age groups, classes and ethnic backgrounds? How many questions should you include? How can you word the questions so that the meaning of the answers is clear?

Because these are difficult questions to answer, we seldom end up in the social sciences with pure, simple, unchallengeable facts. Yet that does not mean giving up the attempt. Data gathered by research are usually valuable, even though imperfect, but we must always remember to treat them with caution. They are never more than 'the best facts available'.

Some well-known studies of touching were carried out in the 1960s by Sidney Jourard. In one study he asked 300 American college students about whom they touched and were touched by and on what parts of the body (using an anonymous questionnaire). Some of the results are shown in Figure 1 (overleaf). The heavily shaded areas are where over 75% of the group reported having been touched *at some time* by the person identified below the figure. The clear areas are those where fewer than 25% reported having been touched at some time by that person.

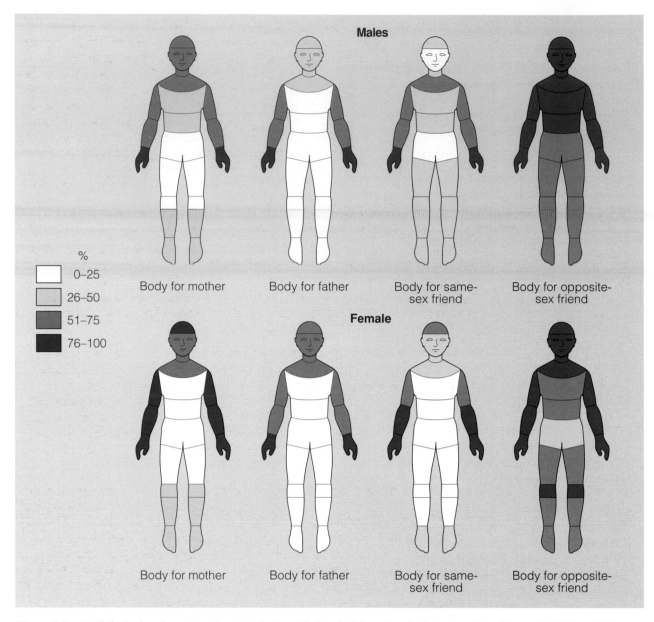

Figure 1 Parts of the body where American students said they had been touched at some time (Jourard, 1966, p. 229)

Activity 13   **Patterns of touching**

Allow about 10 minutes   Study Figure 1 and note down your conclusions. On what body areas is most touching done? Where is least touching done? Who gets touched most and by whom? Who does most touching?

To help you get started, the figure at the top left shows that over three-quarters of the men had been touched on their hands by their mothers. But fewer than 25% had been touched anywhere between the waist and the lower leg by their mothers. More than half had been touched on their arms, shoulders and head by their mothers.

Comment   What struck me first was that in this group of American students everybody reported having experienced a lot of touching of hands. Second, there was scarcely any touching of the genital areas except by an opposite-sex friend. Fathers touched a good deal less than mothers. When male friends touched each other, only the genital area and face seemed to be ruled out, whereas women had seldom been touched by female friends anywhere between the shoulders and the feet. When it came to the opposite-sex friends, I found myself wondering whether in the 1960s some college women might have been reticent about reporting being touched by men friends, whereas some men might be particularly keen to report being touched all over by women friends. I also remembered that this was before gay liberation, when same-sex friendship would be taken for granted as being non-sexual. I wondered what effect that would have had on the reporting (although the questionnaire was anonymous). Whatever the case, it is pretty clear that the most extensive body touching (as reported) was by friends of the opposite sex.

In other studies Jourard found variations in reported patterns of touch in different countries and concluded that some cultures are more touch-oriented than others. In American culture, he argued, people touch very little except in the context of contact sports or sexual intimacy. The norm is to touch only occasionally and then only hand-to-hand. (The 'norm' is what people in general do – a kind of average.) Obviously, caring activities often involve departing from the norm.

Jourard found a lot of reciprocity in patterns of touching. So, for example, those people who touch you on the arms are people you too touch on the arms. This represents a kind of symmetry in the relationship – an equality of intimacy. Again care work breaks the rule here. When a person is touched in 'norm-breaking' areas during caring activities, they do not usually reciprocate by touching the carer in the same places. The intimacy is one-sided, creating an awkward imbalance in the relationship.

Study skills: Questioning the facts (Part 2)

As well as some interesting diagrams, Jourard leaves us with plenty of questions about the 'facts' he reports. For example, there is something odd about having been 'touched at some time'. That must mean since they were adults; otherwise touch by their mothers would surely cover all parts. And how relevant are facts from American colleges in the 1960s to us now? Students of that time and place were mainly in their late teens and early twenties, mainly better off, mainly white. So why doesn't K100 quote a recent British study? The reason is that we don't know of one. Research funding seems to have been spent on other things than re-running Jourard's study. It is often impossible to get information about exactly the people, places and times you want. You have to make the best use you can of what is available.

Although we need to be careful about making sweeping generalisations from these data, what they do suggest is that touching activity is 'patterned'. And by showing us one particular pattern they help us to think how patterns for other groups in other places might differ.

3.2 Meanings of touching

Jourard's findings emphasise the sexual meanings of touch. But according to Julia Twigg, touch carries other meanings too.

Activity 14   **Understanding touching**

Allow about 15 minutes   Read the section headed 'Touching' in Chapter 30 in the Reader. Then write brief notes of your conclusions about the meanings of touch.

Comment   I noted that Twigg begins from the Jourard research and sexuality. Then I wrote:

- Touch as expression of authority and power – superiors touch inferiors.

- Women are more often touched than men (lower status?) and brought up within a more tactile culture. Do men interpret touch as inferiority?

- Decline in touching in impersonal modern society (though became fashionable again in 70s) – now mainly restricted to sexual intimacy.

- Accepted importance for the young, but older people are deprived of touch.

- Touching work has 'servant' status. In care professional hierarchy, the higher the level the less body touching.

- Ambiguity. Touch can mean both power and low status – carer can both dominate and lose status through touching.

Study skills: Making generalisations

In her chapter Twigg makes a lot of generalisations about trends in patterns of touching and about meanings attached to touch. This makes the chapter interesting but also risky. Certainly, course testers found plenty to question here. For example, one argued that high-status doctors such as surgeons and gynaecologists do a great deal of touching. Another provided examples where modern societies do more touching than some earlier societies. Another pointed out that Jourard's findings seem to contradict the idea that women are more often touched than men. And yet another doubted that patterns of touch were something you could successfully generalise about in such a broad way, because cultures are so variable. We decided the article was still useful for you to read, because of the questions it raises and the arguments it develops about the patterns and meanings of touch in social care. But it is important to recognise that it represents just one line of argument.

Twigg is arguing that, although touching is seen as a 'good thing', especially for children, it can be difficult to do because of the messages it gives. It carries hints of power and authority, although it is associated at the same time with low-status work. Most unnerving for care workers, it carries connotations of sexual intimacy, especially when it involves that most untouched area of all, the genital area.

Physical contact in a care situation

How can you conduct a 'routine' care activity when it involves forms of contact which normally signal sexual intimacy? Jocalyn Lawler studied Australian nurses' reactions to such challenges. Here one of the male nurses she interviewed remembers a student experience:

> *I was working on the ante-natal ward roaming around conducting breast checks for reasons that I was unsure. Now I found that situation highly embarrassing ... because I didn't know why the hell I was looking at them. (Laughter) I had to ask all these women all the time 'can I see your breasts?' and I must have been a bright shade of red ... I think it made them feel embarrassed. After a few tortured days ... I finally sought to find out why I was looking at breasts, and [I found that] there were breast abscesses and cracked nipples and redness. ... I was certainly relieved to know why I was looking at breasts ... So long as I can establish a logical reason for being there and doing what I'm doing, then I can apply the reason to my action and establish a logical framework and do it. If the individual has a problem with me doing it then I can say 'look, this is why I'm doing it'.*

> *(Quoted in Lawler, 1991, p. 143)*

The nurse found that he needed to be able to 'establish a logical framework'. Until he understood what he was doing, he could not project a convincing definition of the situation, to override the potential sexual reading of it. His visible embarrassment served only to draw attention to the sexual connotations, which made the situation all the more embarrassing for the women. But once he had a good solid 'medical' definition to project on to the situation, he was able to exclude sexual interpretations. Lawler says it is important that nurses develop an ability to take the lead – defining situations in ways that exclude embarrassing meanings:

> *Managing embarrassment has an element of teaching and coaching whereby the nurse leads the patient in defining situations that may be novel for the patient. If nurses are not embarrassed, it gives permission for the patient also to feel no embarrassment.*

> *(Lawler, 1991, p. 142)*

> **Key points**
>
> * We touch according to cultural rules about who can touch whom on what parts of the body and under what circumstances.
>
> * Touching that departs from everyday norms is strongly associated with sexual intimacy.
>
> * Touching also has ambiguous connotations of power and status.
>
> * When care work involves touching, especially of the genital areas, a non-sexual frame of reference has to be confidently projected in order to keep sexual meanings at bay.

3.3 Meanings of nakedness

Caring also involves breaking rules about seeing people naked. In times past the taboos against seeing members of the opposite sex naked were so strong that doctors sometimes had to work 'blind':

> *... it was only at the end of the eighteenth century in Britain that childbirth could benefit from obstetric examination, an undarkened operating room, and delivered – if a male physician was to do it – unencumbered by its having to be performed under covers. The gynaecological examination is even today a matter of some concern, special effort being taken to infuse the procedure with terms and actions that keep sexual readings in check.*
>
> *(Goffman, 1975, pp. 35–6)*

Until 200 years ago, sexual meanings of nakedness were so threatening that male doctors had to deliver babies in darkened rooms, with the mother under covers. And even now a gynaecologist has to observe rituals which emphasise the *medical* interpretation of the situation.

In a nursing context Lawler says there are rules about what parts of the body can be exposed when. The basic rule is '... that unnecessary exposure of the body ... is to be avoided'. However, mistakes can occur:

> *It was on a night that we had a lot of ... cystoscopies [urethra and bladder examination], ... and – I will never forget this night! There were two of us [nurses] and we went into the room and pulled down the patient's bedclothes and (laughter) – I will never forget – he was only young and what we realised after that he'd had a menisectomy [knee surgery] (laughter) and he turned round and said 'My God, you're so thorough!' I walked out of that room and never went back in there again ... we went and just pulled down the entire covers and lifted the gown up! You know still to this day I don't know who was more shocked.*
>
> *(Quoted in Lawler, 1991, p. 141)*

Nakedness, however, is not associated only with sexuality. Look back at the first photograph on page 30 of Unit 1. The nakedness of this person sends a signal of helplessness and need. There is also a sense of exposure to the view of others who are not naked – a sense perhaps of humiliation. How can you project your normal 'self' to the world when you are deprived of the clothes and props which you use to support your act? As Twigg says in the longer article from which the Reader chapter is taken:

> ... to be naked is to divest oneself of protection and disguise. Nakedness creates vulnerability, and this takes on a particular character when the experience is asymmetrical. To be without your clothes in the context of those who are clothed is to be at a disadvantage. Denying prisoners or patients their clothes, interrogating people naked, are common techniques for undermining individuals and creating vulnerability. It is in order to mitigate such effects that doctors are taught how to examine patients in ways that limit their exposure.
>
> (Twigg, 1997, p. 224)

Twigg's article is about giving and receiving baths. This, of course, involves nakedness in the presence of others – a potential sense of vulnerability. But older people, she says, face a further sense of being at

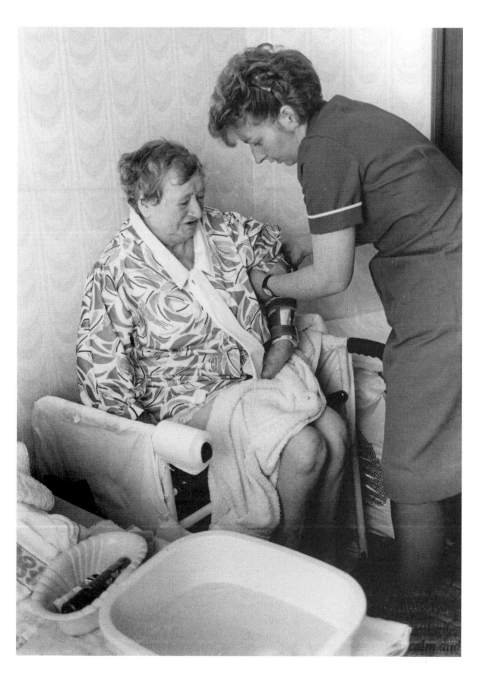

Breaking normal rules of personal privacy

a disadvantage in 'being naked in front of someone who is young. Nearly all the representations of nakedness in modern culture are of youthful bodies. There are very few unclothed depictions of ageing' (p. 225).

Key points

- Like touch, nakedness is associated with sexual intimacy.

- Nakedness in a context where other people are clothed is also associated with vulnerability and humiliation.

3.4 Managing the meanings of a bath

How can you help someone to bath in a way that maintains a positive, constructive frame of reference? Sexuality, vulnerability and shame lurk in the wings, waiting for any slip-ups. To combat them you can strive for the other meanings of bathing outlined in the section of Twigg's Reader chapter that you read in Unit 3 – luxury, relaxation, invigoration, health, hygiene and cleanliness.

To illustrate one way of constructing a positive framework for a bath, here are some guidelines for helping a person with learning disabilities to have a bath:

> *Assisting a client with bathing is something that can be done with dignity as well as something which can provide an opportunity for empowerment. You can make a mundane event a meaningful one if you:*
>
> 1 *Know the task properly, so you do it competently as well as considerately.*
>
> 2 *If possible give the person choice.*
>
> 3 *Explain what is happening as you go along.*
>
> 4 *Be gentle.*
>
> 5 *Be respectful.*
>
> 6 *Involve the person even if this is only through eye-contact or a smile.*
>
> 7 *Provide opportunities for learning and growth. For example one person might learn to let you know if they like the temperature of the water or learn to wash their face separately, or eventually gain independence in bathing.*
>
> 8 *If it is safe to do so, allow the person to be totally alone in the bathroom for a while. This can be a very special time.*
>
> 9 *Bath-time can be made into an enjoyable and sensuous experience if perfumes, talc, soft towels, pleasant music and so on, are used at this time.*
>
> *(O'Rourke, 1994, pp. 27–8)*

Activity 15   **'Constructing' a bath**

Allow about 5 minutes   In these guidelines what is the frame of reference within which bathing is placed? How are positive meanings of bathing promoted?

Comment   The overall frame of reference here is bathing as an opportunity for learning and for pleasure. There is also a strong emphasis on respect and choice – giving priority to the experience of the person having the bath as opposed to the convenience of the bath giver. And there is an emphasis on talking to, and having eye contact with, the person having the bath. It is interesting that the very first recommendation is to be competent and know what you are doing. As in the case of the male nurse doing the breast examinations, attempts to define the scene are difficult to sustain if you are unsure of yourself.

Bathing is one of many ways in which a carer can be involved with a person's body. Others include helping with movement, feeding, dressing and undressing, and going to the toilet. All of these require the carer to have 'access' to the body of the cared for in ways which go well beyond everyday boundaries. Both carer and cared-for need to learn to manage the meanings of these unconventional situations, working out positive definitions, developing suitable 'scripts', and learning to enact their roles skilfully.

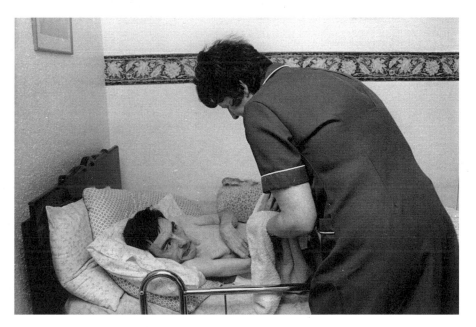

Managing the meaning of intimate care

Activity 16   **Intimate care within the family**

Allow about 10 minutes   Finally we return to Lynne. Has what I have said about:

(a)   norms for touching

(b)   meanings of touching and nakedness and

(c)   techniques for managing meanings in intimate care situations

clarified why she was reluctant to undertake care tasks that involved seeing and touching her father's body?

Look at the points above in turn and write down the implications for Lynne.

Comment   The difficulty of Lynne's position became much clearer to me as I thought about what I have been discussing in this section.

(a)   The first point is that she would be deviating from the norms of her culture, as to who touches whom and where. At the same time, she would be breaking deeply ingrained rules of privacy within family life.

(b)   In doing so, she would have to cope with connotations of intimacy – even incestuous sexuality – with a father with whom she had long had hostile relations.

(c)   In order to ward off such meanings she would have to be able to impose her own alternative definitions on sensitive situations. But how could she do so with a father who has always dominated her? Indeed, he imposes a framework on their relationship which positions her as a person with learning disabilities – a clumsy and incompetent worker about the house and poor company for an adult. Unless she could rise up and impose a definition of herself as a competent carer, assisting with routine 'body maintenance' work, she would constantly feel under threat of exposure to embarrassing sexual interpretations. Lynne shows in her factory job that she can undertake adult work involving routine tasks. But it is not the physical tasks in intimate care she would find difficult, it is controlling the meanings of situations which are ambiguous and potentially disturbing.

Key points

As Twigg and others have pointed out:

- When one adult is bathed by another (who is not a sexual partner), associations of sexuality, vulnerability and humiliation need to be kept out of the frame.

- This means looking to the other available meanings of bathing and finding ways of emphasising them.

- Bathing is just one example of the significance of 'the body' in care work – of the importance of understanding and being able to control the frameworks of meaning within which intimate care activities are undertaken.

Section 4
Different realities

4.1   What is reality?

I have been looking at how we share with others in constructing the meanings of our interactions. We seldom do it consciously. Yet simply by getting on with the business of doing things with other people, we participate in creating and sustaining frameworks of meaning. This is one aspect of what is called 'the social construction of social reality'.

You grasp a person's arm. That is *physical reality* – an action which can be proved to have happened (witnessed by observers or recorded on video). But that physical reality is not what either your mind, or the mind of the person you are grasping, is focused on. Both minds attend instead to the *meaning* of the grasp. Is it a part of a friendly greeting, an urgent request for attention, a threatening gesture, or a sexual advance? In choosing between the possible interpretations, you look at the context. What kind of scene is being enacted here? What role are you presenting yourself in? What role is the other person projecting for himself or herself?

For both of you the 'reality' you are aware of is the 'greeting' or the 'threat', or whatever else you take the grasp to mean. This 'greeting' or 'threat' is the *social reality* to which your subsequent actions and words will be addressed.

However, it is a made-up or *constructed* reality. You cannot *prove* that a greeting or a threat has taken place, simply by video recording. You still have to interpret the actions you have recorded, and to make that interpretation you need to know the context – the flow of meaning that led up to the event. So this *social reality* is less clear, firm and unambiguous than physical reality, yet it is no less real. What happens next – a returned greeting, or a cry for help, or a struggle to get free – will depend entirely on the *interpretations* you and the other person have placed on the act of grasping. Your subsequent physical behaviour will be driven by the social reality of the event as you and the other person experience it.

I am dwelling on the distinction between physical reality and social reality because both are important but their implications are different. Social reality, being socially constructed, can and does change, as people's ideas, words and actions change; whereas physical reality just is. Often when we are talking about reality as it affects care services we are actually talking about social reality; for example care being seen as women's work, or budgets being very limited. These are powerful elements of social reality and they have many consequences. But they can be changed by changing the way people think. On the other hand, the many physical realities that affect care, such as the limitations imposed by impairments, or the increasing age to which people live, cannot be defined away by changes in our ideas – although they can be tackled in various ways to alter their impact.

We take both physical and social reality for granted as we go about our daily lives. We seldom pause to consider that the social part of reality might change – or even collapse. Yet you saw that for Tom Heller the surface reality of daily life disintegrated dramatically at the Hillsborough disaster. While a normal day was being enacted by his children in the garden, an unimaginable collapse of normality was happening a few miles away. A celebratory football gathering became transformed into a horrific turning point in many people's lives. The physical reality of the deaths was only part of the horror. It was the meaning of the event which was traumatic. The physical reality of dead bodies may now have been dealt with, but the emotional impact – the personal meaning – of being involved in such an event can only be addressed through talking, thinking, comforting, and 'coming to terms'. This social reality lives on long after the physical event.

The daily construction of social reality goes on at many levels throughout society. In Unit 1 you saw, for example, that patterns of motherhood and family life, which are often assumed to be 'natural', are based on ideas and ways of thinking over which there has been much debate and conflict. I could discuss the role of television and the newspapers, or of government legislation, in this process of *social construction* of the social world we live in. However, we do not need to consider all these issues here; this discussion is simply an introduction to the general idea of social construction. It is just concerned with how social reality is constructed at the local level as people interact with each other.

We are now going to explore how a group of people developed their own separate version of social reality. You will see that in some care institutions certain groups of care staff may come to understand their work quite differently from other groups. We shall be looking at how, in this way, alternative versions of social reality can exist alongside each other.

4.2 Frontstage and backstage

We are going to examine an account of research carried out in a nursing home by Geraldine Lee-Treweek. She sketches a picture of an institution which is, in effect, divided into two 'worlds'. One I shall call the 'lounge world'. This is the public part of the nursing home which visitors see, and where the staff on view are mainly trained nurses. The other is the 'bedroom world' – hidden from public view – where unqualified care assistants (called auxiliaries here) work at cleaning and dressing the patients, emptying leg bags and assisting with toileting. Lee-Treweek draws on Goffman in describing the bedrooms as a 'backstage' area, where all the work is done to prepare the patients for display in the

Watching TV in the lounge of a home for older people

'frontstage' public area. Her research concentrates on the 'bedroom world', and reveals a distinctly different culture from that of the 'lounge world': a different understanding of what the work of the home is about, different attitudes to the patients, and different ideas of how to treat them.

A cautionary note about the article

The piece you are about to read is called 'Bedroom abuse: the hidden work in a nursing home'. Abuse is a disturbing and difficult topic which is dealt with more fully in Block 5. I shall not go into the ethical, legal and regulatory sides of it here. I am simply approaching abuse as an aspect of the care world in which sharply discrepant accounts of reality get generated. The article is quite short and, although it presents a vivid account and a thought-provoking analysis, it leaves out a lot of the detail that would be needed to draw clear conclusions about how abusive practices in the home are. For example, Lee-Treweek does not tell us how frequently the events she describes occur. Also she uses the term 'mistreatment' without explaining where she draws the line in regarding incidents as mistreatment. Since she is talking of mental rather than physical abuse, a lot rests on her interpretation of what is oppressive or abusive. The care staff involved would, no doubt, differ in their interpretation. So, as you read, remember that Lee-Treweek's is one particular interpretation, and try to think what the care staff's interpretation might be.

Two other points:

- This home is not presented here as 'typical' (although Lee-Treweek suggests there are parallels in other homes).

- The article does not set out to 'blame' the staff involved. Its purpose is to understand the circumstances under which groups of staff develop particular values and modes of practice.

Activity 17   **Examining bedroom care**

Allow about 45 minutes

Look at questions (a)–(e) below and then read Chapter 25 by Lee-Treweek in the Reader.

(a)   What kind of work do the auxiliaries do (not the actual tasks, but the general *type* of work)?

(b)   What are the main pressures the auxiliaries experience?

(c)   What do the auxiliaries see as the key priorities of their work?

(d)   What techniques do the auxiliaries use to maintain order in an environment which is prone to disorder?

(e)   What are the main elements of the auxiliaries' subculture?

Try writing 'type of work', 'pressures', 'priorities', 'imposing order' and 'subculture' as headings down the side of a sheet of paper and then make notes under the headings as you read.

(f)   When you reach the end, summarise the differences between the lounge world and the bedroom world.

This is quite a demanding activity, so don't rush it.

Comment   My answers are below.

(a)   The auxiliaries' work is hard physical labour. It is dirty, poorly paid, low-status work. Qualifications are not required and little training is offered.

(b)   They work under intense time pressure. They also have to cope with a lot of disorder – physical mess, spitting, sobbing, confusion and, at times, violence.

(c)   The auxiliaries see their key priorities as getting through the work, producing well-ordered, well-presented bodies, and maintaining order in the bedroom (not, for example, chatting to the patients, or helping them with emotional crises.)

(d)   Lee-Treweek says auxiliaries maintain order by dominating patients – depersonalising them (not greeting them, not saying goodbye, talking about them in their presence), treating them as objects, ignoring their requests, ignoring their personal space. She also says that patients who resist this treatment are 'punished' in various ways.

(e)   The auxiliaries' subculture prizes 'hardness'. They have a tough job and pride themselves on their toughness – their ability to cope and to get through the work quickly regardless. They make light of violence, showing off bruises and making jokes. They see themselves as able to handle aggression. They regard the medical staff as 'soft'.

(f)   The lounge world is a place where patients are visibly 'cared for', where they are clean and tidy and well behaved, whereas, in the bedroom world, order is constantly having to be created out of disorder and patients are seen mainly as bodies to be 'serviced', ready to be put on display. It is an environment of restrictions, tight discipline and, says Lee-Treweek, humiliations and punishment. Within this social world, ideas and values such as respect are 'soft', a luxury for those who don't have to do 'real' work.

Did you get the gist of what is meant by a subculture? It is a set of shared values, ideas and ways of talking and behaving. The auxiliaries have their own subculture in that they know, for example, that they can get tough with patients when other auxiliaries are present, but not when the nurses are present. They can trust other auxiliaries to share their values, but they know the nurses have 'soft' values.

Why has this kind of subculture developed? Lee-Treweek makes some suggestions. The auxiliaries are employed to 'service' patients' bodies at speed, day after day. If they don't work fast they don't get through the work in time. But the patients they are attending to can be very difficult, which threatens to impede progress unless the auxiliaries force the pace regardless. Since they have little time to stop to attend to the emotional needs of their patients, the auxiliaries have to 'toughen up' and not get emotionally involved. As a group they support each other in making these tough attitudes and beliefs seem legitimate. (Many groups involved in socially difficult work – undertakers, referees, debt collectors, personnel managers – develop mutually supportive subcultures of some kind.) The auxiliaries have had little training to discourage the development of self-serving values and practices. Since they operate out of sight of the world at large, it is difficult to find out about their practices let alone regulate them.

Lee-Treweek says that the auxiliaries' subculture of efficient body servicing, discipline and punishment dominates the bedroom world. The patients who try to resist are 'punished' by being ignored or humiliated. Most simply get absorbed into it. Meanwhile the trained nurses are unaware of questionable practices within the bedroom world culture because they are kept hidden. The auxiliaries know all about the lounge world because it is the 'official' public one, which they have to defer to. But in the hidden bedroom world they see themselves as the real workers, who keep the place going. For patients the conventional sense of a bedroom as a haven is reversed. Instead of being an area of privacy, personal control and safety, it is one of abrupt and brusque body handling, control by others and, apparently, exposure to abuse.

At Cedar Court we see two parallel versions of social reality co-existing within the same building. The auxiliaries' understanding of care in the bedroom world is distinctly different from values and ideas about care discussed in the public world (such as you might expect to see espoused in the lounge world and in the home's publicity leaflets). Each version of reality carries force within its own world. For patients it is a matter of transferring from one social reality to the other several times a day, although, as Lee-Treweek points out, it is the bedroom version in which they spend the most time.

So what *is* reality in the case of the bedrooms of Cedar Court Nursing Home?

- The *physical reality* is patients being handled briskly and sometimes forcibly, at times not being spoken to, or being left out of reach of their buzzers.

- *Social reality* as constructed by the auxiliaries is a well-run, well-disciplined, efficient bedroom care service, in a context of very difficult and demanding patients.

- *Social reality* as constructed by the trained staff probably agrees regarding the efficiency, but without recognising the element of force and discipline – playing up the quality of the care instead. (We are not given details.)

- Lee-Treweek, from her social base in the academic community of care researchers, constructs the *social reality* of the bedrooms as unacceptably insensitive treatment, regularly spilling over into abuse.

Where a community is isolated, and where there is a clear dividing line between the powerful and the weak, a culture of pervasive and arbitrary discipline, with humiliating punishments established as routine, springs up rather easily. Cases come to light from time to time in boarding schools, residential homes, the armed forces, and so on. I must also include families, as we know from examples such as that of Fred and Rosemary West (the Gloucester serial killers). From outside it is scarcely believable that such abnormal 'realities' can be sustained for years without being exposed to public condemnation. Yet, from inside, these oppressive worlds are simply 'normality'.

So can we say that there is a 'proper normality', a 'true reality' from which these oppressive versions deviate? Not really. Where would you look for it? Rather, there is a *public world* of speeches, sermons, pronouncements, commissions of inquiry – a reality, as publicly espoused – together with a multitude of *private worlds* whose constructions of reality are known only to those involved. Maintaining active channels of communication between public and private worlds is the only way in which any kind of general 'normality' can be aspired to.

Key points

- 'Social realities' are meanings constructed through people interacting with each other (i.e. they are social constructions).

- These constructed social realities nevertheless have real consequences.

- Lee-Treweek's study shows that, where a community functions in relative isolation, social reality may come to be constructed in a way which deviates markedly from 'official' public ideas.

- Where there are also sharp power differences (as between auxiliary nurses and frail, confused older people) a separate 'world' can develop in which routine oppression of the weak becomes 'normal', 'necessary' – even a source of pride.

- This is not a matter of individual people starting out with a desire to harm. Rather it is a social process of constructing a version of reality which consolidates the power of the strong and makes their lives as convenient and satisfying as possible, while systematically ignoring the needs of the powerless.

Before leaving Cedar Court, I must emphasise that the auxiliaries did a very important job, on which the well-being of their patients depended. As individuals, each no doubt felt they were carrying out their duties responsibly and appropriately. The important questions are not about the motivation and attitudes of individual care workers but about the circumstances under which unacceptable subcultures develop. The course returns to these matters later. For now we return to less extreme situations.

Study skills: Study shock

You are now three-quarters of the way through Unit 4. How are you coping? Perhaps you have never done as much reading as in the last four weeks? Does it feel like a tidal wave washing over you? Many people find the first impact of OU study quite unnerving. When else in adult life are you expected to think so rigorously and concentrate for so long – and in your leisure time too? Can you keep this up? Well, most people *do* get accustomed to the pace after a few weeks. Somehow they find a second wind. Until *you* do, the main thing is just to take what you can from each unit, and keep moving on to the next unit at the end of the week.

At least next week brings a break in the flow, when you switch to skills work instead and you also have half the week for your assignment. Whatever else you might miss, try not to fall behind on the assignment. If you haven't done so already, have a look at the essay title now, or when you've finished Unit 4. Then you can start mulling ideas over before getting down to serious work on it. Don't wait until the end of Unit 5 to look, because essays often take longer than you think. Make sure you allow time to do yourself justice.

Section 5
Meanings shaped within the wider society

Goffman draws attention to the meanings negotiated between people during interactions. But this approach can draw attention away from some other meanings which are imposed by the wider society. When you enter a situation it makes a difference, for example, whether you are a woman or a man, whether you are rich and privileged or poor and marginalised, whether you appear to belong to a minority ethnic group, whether you are old or young and whether or not you are disabled. You may be very effective at negotiating meanings, but the position you start your negotiations from often depends on factors beyond your control.

5.1 Defined by disability

People with disabilities, for example, often say they suffer as much from *social* disadvantages and exclusions as from the disability itself. This is not simply a matter of insensitivity on the part of individual people, but of attitudes within society at large. Take Anne McFarlane's experience at a craft class for disabled people:

> *discontent set in amongst us all because basically the place was so dirty ... It was cold and there was no carpet on the floor and there was a filthy path to walk up with holes that people used to fall into. After weeks and weeks of moaning I said 'Well shouldn't we do something about it? Why shouldn't we have some luxury when we know that the doctor who sits in the office next door is knee deep in carpet?' So they all said 'Oh what a good idea, you can organise it and write the letter and we'll all agree.' So I wrote the letter and sent it and that was my first big mistake. Because ... the next week I got called in to see this doctor. He said 'What was the problem?' and I said, sitting there with my wheelchair on his carpet, 'Well you know you're sitting here in luxury and we haven't got anything and we all think that we should have some decent surroundings and some decent stuff – tables and things, and we need the path made up.' And he said he thought we were very ungrateful because we hadn't had anything before and now we've got this room and we had somewhere to come. And he came out of his room and he asked everybody what they thought because they were all sitting round this great big table. And they all said 'Oh no we're very happy here. We really like coming here. It's perfectly all right.'*

> (Quoted in Campbell and Oliver, 1996, p. 41)

Activity 18

Allow about 5 minutes

Claiming equality

(a) When she had been provided with a place for a craft class, why do you think Anne McFarlane was so 'ungrateful'?

(b) Why do you think the others backed down when the doctor came out to speak to them?

Comment

(a) Anne McFarlane seemed to be fed up with the assumption that because she was disabled she should be happy to put up with a dirty, badly maintained environment. Why should 'luxury' be inappropriate for her? Why should a non-disabled person be sitting in one room with a thick carpet, while disabled people sat in the next room in filth? Why should disabled people be treated as socially inferior?

(b)   As they talked amongst themselves the class members began to redefine themselves as people with a legitimate grievance about the standard of accommodation. As the representative of the class, Anne McFarlane spoke to the doctor in these terms but was quickly defined by him as 'ungrateful'. And when the doctor came to speak to the class they switched immediately into a 'grateful' mode. Disabled people are very used to playing the role of 'being extremely grateful'. It is the dominant mode in which they relate to society at large – as lucky recipients of whatever they get. When the doctor spoke, this dominant definition snapped into place, leaving Anne McFarlane isolated. However much she might wish to renegotiate the scene, the dominant definition was too strong – particularly as she now was defined as a 'trouble-maker'. She left the class after that meeting.

Similar experiences have been reported by other disabled people when they tried to resist being defined as 'happy to accept less than other groups in society'. Nasa Begum is black, disabled and a woman:

I know what happens with disabled people and with black people if you start saying critical things. It's all the chip on your shoulder stuff and that you are a real militant.

(*Quoted in Campbell and Oliver, 1996, p. 116*)

Me and this other guy were both 'mega-hated' in this sheltered housing because we were seen as obnoxious, young radical disabled people. We were only radical because we didn't want to go to the church service and I didn't want to go to Yately Industries, which was an industrial workshop. But it was seen to be completely out of order.

(*p. 43*)

As you explore the ways meanings are negotiated between people, you need to be aware that there are meanings which cannot easily be negotiated – definitions which are so widespread, so built into the way things work and are spoken about, that it is extremely difficult for an individual person to negotiate a way past them. Indeed, if you go against the grain of dominant definitions, you are as likely to isolate yourself as to improve your position.

Gender definitions provide another example. You saw in Unit 1 that women enter care situations already identified as appropriate carers, expected to be sympathetic, gentle, and well attuned to long hours of giving support. Men are written into 'scripts' which prioritise career demands. But when women try to speak from the same 'scripts' they are often heard as selfish, uncaring and 'unwomanly'.

Key points

- It is important not to over-emphasise Goffman's approach. Meanings are not created *only* out of negotiations between individual people. Some are shaped by the structures of the wider society.

- When individuals try to resist dominant society-wide definitions of themselves, they risk becoming isolated as trouble-makers or misfits.

Section 6
Pressures of role-playing

In the final section I look briefly at some of the challenges of playing caring roles.

6.1 Role conflict

Growing up as carer for a brother

Remember the children in Unit 1 who cared for their disabled parents. They find themselves simultaneously positioned within two very different frameworks:

- as children being brought up by their parents
- as carers taking responsibility for their parents' welfare.

Consequently, for these children the meaning of interactions with their parents is often ambiguous. Should they play the dependent, deferential child, or the responsible and skilled carer? In fact, they have to be prepared to switch the way they present themselves according to circumstances. Katrina's mother 'expected her to be an adult in the privacy of their own home, but a child in public' (Unit 1, Section 1.4).

Similarly, Lynne Durrant finds herself locked in contradictory role relationships with her father. She is an adult daughter, who has had to switch to a caring role, but she is also a person with learning disabilities, who has always been treated as less than a full adult. Lynne applies herself (albeit reluctantly) to her care duties, yet her father continues to talk to her as a person who is incapable of doing things properly. However much she tries to project herself as a responsible adult, her father's words and actions reassert the past definition of their relationship. It is not hard to imagine Lynne's frustrations. There she is, trying to shift the definition of family 'scenes' to take account of her new tasks and responsibilities, only to find herself being pushed back into the old demeaning definitions by the more forceful verbal skills of her father. It was in just such a situation – with Lynne carrying out her caring responsibilities by peeling potatoes, while Arthur treated her as a child – that Lynne waved her knife at him – thereby threatening to redefine the situation by deeds instead of words.

You can also see role conflict in Rita's relationship with Lynne. In one role Rita is Lynne's friend and supporter, speaking on her behalf at her workplace (and in the interview). But in another role she is a representative of the local care services, whose community care policies require her to support Lynne in continuing to keep house for her father (even though she is plainly unhappy doing so). In the extract below, taken from a research interview with Lynne, Rita is supposed to be helping Lynne to present her views to the interviewer. However, she has slipped into her other role, as being 'in charge' of Lynne and encouraging her to keep caring for her father. Rita:

> *I think dad sometimes gets cross 'cos you aren't doing the things you really should do. 'Cos you just want to go out. Am I right? It's not always dad's fault he gets cross is it? It's sometimes your fault ... Well I say to Lynne sometimes that hard as it is for her to have to have someone like dad dependent on her to a certain extent – he took care of her when she was young and helpless and needed someone – and now she is grown up and able to cope in life she should help if she can.*

Activity 19   **Rita's conflicting roles**

Allow about 5 minutes   Do you think Rita is talking to Lynne as an adult here? How is she defining the scene? What relationship is she projecting between the interviewer, Lynne and herself?

Comment   I feel Rita is 'talking down' to Lynne here – telling her off 'in public'. She uses the language of *duty* and *blame* – 'doing the things you really should', 'it's sometimes your fault'. The way she says, 'you just want to go out', makes it sound as though there is something wrong with wanting to go out when you are in your forties and unhappy at home. Then she says, 'Am I right?', which implies that Lynne needs to be cajoled to accept the 'true' situation. I also feel that the way Rita draws the interviewer in, saying 'Well I say to Lynne', is as if Lynne were a wayward child in the presence of two adults.

Obviously, Rita is in a difficult position, trying to play two roles. Equally, it must be uncomfortable for Lynne to rely on Rita for support, but also to find her sometimes taking the other side. It must have been particularly uncomfortable to find herself cast in a child-like role in front of a stranger.

I was struck by the way Rita vigorously promotes a particular definition of reality, at this point in the interview. Her account of Lynne's circumstances places great emphasis on her daughterhood. Yet Lynne has a sister unaffected by disability. Why is the responsibility Lynne's, not her sister's? Rita also makes questionable assumptions about Arthur's role in caring for Lynne when she was young. What about the alternative definition of Lynne, as a woman in her mid-forties with a right to an independent life, free from her oppressive relationship with her father? Why define her father as the person in need? What about Lynne's needs? Does Rita's definition of reality here conflict with her role as Lynne's supporter?

Role reversal: a son feeds his mother

> **Key points**
>
> • When two different frames of reference apply to a care situation, role conflict will arise.
>
> • Role conflict creates ongoing tension for both carer and care receiver as their relationship gets pushed in different directions by the demands of the competing frames of reference.

6.2 Power

You have seen an extreme example of the exercise of power in the hidden bedrooms of Cedar Court. However, power differences arise in most care relationships. As you saw in Unit 2, even 'public' hospital wards exert an impressive level of discipline on patients. Here is one of the nurses from Lawler's study:

> *Basically nurses have an incredible amount of power ... Most of them don't realise that. They are very powerful people. You get somebody who is an executive or up-market business person, or anybody – doesn't matter who they are – come into hospital and all of a sudden they're subservient, you know. No matter who they are. It's the way you treat them. You bring them into hospital, strip them of all their clothes, put them in pyjamas and shove them in bed and tell them to behave. And people take it!*
>
> *(Quoted in Lawler, 1991, p. 148)*

Power is also exerted in such humdrum situations as waiting-rooms, as you will remember from the Reader chapter by Lesley Doyal (Unit 2). The women in the antenatal clinic waiting-room were kept waiting for up to three hours for a three-minute consultation, and were told 'not to worry' if they asked questions. This forcefully projected a demeaning definition of reality: 'We know you will be worrying your little head over all kinds of things, but you don't need to, because we will tell you anything you need to know. Just sit there and be well-behaved. Your

The powerlessness of the waiting room

time is not important – ours is very precious.' Similarly, women giving birth felt the role assigned to them within the labour process was peripheral. They felt powerless, and lost confidence in their own bodies, as they became caught up in the drama going on around them, of doctors and nurses and high-tech equipment. A service, ostensibly centred on them and their needs, was played out as a scene in which they felt they had scarcely any significance or influence.

Pregnancy and childbirth involve only a temporary subjection to medical definitions and practices. However, people with disabilities can find such definitions and practices dominate their whole lives, as we hear from Anne McFarlane (whom you met earlier in her craft class).

> *I was perceived to be ill by everybody including the professional people and other people that visited me ... The predominant feature throughout my institutional life was the fact that I was left in bed a lot of the time when I could have been up. Because I couldn't dress and wash myself, the staff did for me what they felt was adequate and sometimes it was totally inadequate. I was very much kept where they wanted me to be kept.*
>
> (Quoted in Campbell and Oliver, 1996, p. 37)

Sometimes it is very clearly the role of care workers to exercise power. For example, patients in residential care may have to be restrained to protect themselves or other patients. Social workers have an explicit duty to exercise power at appropriate times. They are expected to be able to:

> *Take action to contribute to the care, protection and control of people who are a risk to themselves or others.*
>
> (CCETSW, 1995, Part 2, p. 30)

Even in the case of informal care in the family home, power issues can loom large. Kate Cooney, the woman with rheumatoid arthritis quoted in Unit 1 (Section 3.4) talked of the problems of always having to ask for things and having to accept them done the way others choose, instead of just doing them when and as you want. Ruth Pinder (Reader Chapter 13, Unit 2) talked of similar problems for Parkinson's disease patients, and the frustration of not being able to reciprocate, leaving them feeling permanently in debt to their carers.

Having the upper hand sometimes leads to an impulse to exercise this power. Carers have many ways of doing this, for example delaying attending to needs, or withholding 'treats'. Over time this can develop into patterns of systematic domination, spilling over into abuse. Remember Vicky, quoted by Morris, whose carer/lover almost suffocated her (Unit 1, Section 3.4). We should remember, though, that 'power play' is a two-sided game and cared-for people can also exert power. We don't know what pressures Vicky herself may have been imposing.

Key points

- Care relationships tend to involve an imbalance of power.
- Playing unbalanced roles over a long time very easily leads to 'power play'.

6.3 Authenticity and emotional labour

One problem with playing roles is the implication of artificiality and insincerity. Can carer and cared-for be 'real people' to each other at the same time as playing properly structured roles? How much of 'yourself' should you let into a care situation? It seems to depend, to some extent, on the type of care work and the situation.

Mary, the senior home care assistant you heard on the cassette in Unit 3, talked about 'her personal relationship with the people whose homes she goes into, the little extras which make her job, and sometimes their lives, worthwhile' (Unit 3, Section 3.1). Glenda seemed to take the same attitude in her visits to Reg, with the result that he felt very comfortable having her in his home.

For nurses there has been a change of emphasis (outlined by David Armstrong (1983) and summarised here by Linda Jones).

> ... manuals of nursing up to the 1970s, whilst identifying the patient as 'an individual human being and not a case', emphasised the need for formality and detachment. The main focus was on the patient's physical needs ... By the end of the 1970s nursing theorists ... were emphasising that 'helping the patient to communicate', establishing an atmosphere of trust and intimacy and being aware of one's own emotional needs and anxieties were essential elements in nursing.
>
> (Jones, 1994, pp. 472–3)

However, if care workers in domestic homes, hospitals and elsewhere are to become more involved with those they care for, this implies a willingness to cope with the personal emotions that involvement brings:

> Sitting with a distressed person ... listening to someone when they are angry, courageous, resentful or sad, and acquiring the ability just to 'be' with someone who is lonely, frightened or in pain, is taxing and requires an appropriate response.
>
> (James, 1989, p. 27)

As you may remember from Unit 2, the term 'emotional labour' is used to describe this draining and effortful responsiveness. Nicky James argues strongly that the emotional side of care relationships is as important and as demanding as the physical side:

> Emotional labour is hard work and can be sorrowful and difficult. It demands that the labourer gives personal attention which means they must give something of themselves, not just a formulaic response.
>
> (James, 1989, p. 18)

Jones presents a more formal version of emotional labour, which includes *not* showing emotion and 'putting on a show' of positive emotions:

> The term emotional labour highlights the way in which much of the work of servicing and caring for people in human service organisations involves formal and ritualised intimacy, which is not 'natural' but socially constructed ... Human service workers – from supermarket cashiers and lawyers to residential care workers – have to manage both their own emotions and those of their customers, clients and patients. For example, health workers (except perhaps doctors) are expected to be polite, calm and

Managing emotions

relaxed; however harassed they feel inwardly, they are taught to make time for the patient and respond cheerfully to his/her needs. They may need to work, therefore, both to conceal their own 'real' feelings, to suppress those feelings and to stimulate positive feelings in themselves. For example ... forcing themselves to be cheerful and attentive to particularly irritating or demanding patients ...

(Jones, 1994, p. 467)

Sometimes getting involved with patients means getting involved with other relationships too. Here is an account from James of a nurse visiting a patient at her home.

A battle royal started. The older one hit the younger one across the face, and the father wanted to get the police to evict the elder daughter because she wouldn't go. And while all this was going on the little lady upstairs was breaking her heart because she could hear the row. In the end I had to go downstairs and really shout, because they didn't listen to me talking quietly. I said 'Your mother is dying upstairs, and you really ought to get your priorities right'. And I was there about an hour and a half trying to placate them ... I came out absolutely emotionally drained. I really didn't feel I had anything much left to offer anybody else.

(Quoted in James, 1989, p. 34)

Key points

- There is always a question in formal care work about how far carer and cared-for should relate to each other 'as people'.

- The requirement that a carer copes with and manages emotions is known as 'emotional labour'. It is now seen as a major component of a carer's work.

6.4 Finding the right level of involvement

How best to play the roles of 'carer' and 'cared-for' depends a lot on the individuals involved and the setting. Even within a single hospital the degree of personal involvement in nurse–patient relationships can vary widely according to research by J. M. Morse, summarised as follows by Jones:

A recent large-scale research study in eight clinical areas of a city hospital in Canada indicated that 'the relationship that is established between the nurse and the patient is the result of interplay or covert negotiations until a mutually satisfying relationship is reached' (Morse, 1991). It concluded that ... building relationships is a matter of establishing trust, which may be time consuming and difficult ... [The] findings suggested four main types of relationships, ranging from a 'clinical relationship', where the patient has a minor illness and contact is brief, to 'over-involved relationship', where 'the nurse is committed to the patient as a person, and this over-rides the nurse's commitment to the treatment regime, the physician, the institution and its need, and her nursing responsibilities toward other patients. She is a confidant of the patient and is treated as a member of the patient's family.' (Morse 1991). In between lie the 'therapeutic nurse–patient relationship,' a fairly short term interaction in which the nurse views the patient within the 'patient role' first and only secondly as a 'person', and the 'connected relationship', in which this order is reversed, largely because a longer term interaction takes place.

(Jones, 1994, p. 467)

You can see Morse's four types of relationship in Table 1. Morse sees short-term treatments as involving mainly formal role-playing, whereas at the other end of the scale some nurses get so involved in relating to the patient as a person that they lose their grip on the nurse–patient role. (Does that mean they are no longer playing roles? One of the two has long-term care needs, the other has nurse training, and the relationship began from a nurse–patient basis, so it seems unlikely that it will become completely egalitarian and undifferentiated. Rather it is role-playing that has moved beyond the medical frame of reference, becoming more informal and open to shifting definitions.)

Table 1   Four types of nurse–patient relationship

Characteristics	*Types of relationship*			
	Clinical	*Therapeutic*	*Connected*	*Over-involved*
Time	Short/transitory	Short/average	Lengthy	Long-term
Interaction	Perfunctory/rote	Professional	Intensive/close	Intensive/intimate
Patient's needs	Minor treatment-oriented	Minor–moderate	Extensive/crisis 'Goes the extra mile'	Enormous needs
Nurse's perspective of the patient	Only in patient role	First: in patient role Second: as a person	First: as a person Second: in patient role	Only as a person
Nursing commitment	Professional commitment	Professional commitment Patient's concerns secondary	Patient's concerns primary Treatment concerns secondary	Committed to patient only as a person Treatment goals discarded

(Source: Morse, 1991, in Jones, 1994, p. 496)

Jones continues:

> *... the throughput of patients is now so great in many British hospitals that many relationships will necessarily remain at the clinical level. The second type of relationship ... Morse suggests is seen as 'ideal' by Canadian managers and educators ... Yet it seems that nursing theories are encouraging nurses to move beyond ... toward the connected relationship, seeing the patient first and foremost as a person.*

(Jones, 1994, p. 495)

Care relationships, then, are not rigidly fixed, but open to negotiation between carer and cared-for. They are also influenced by the pressures of the times. On one hand, the 'ideal' has shifted towards greater levels of involvement. On the other, financial and administrative pressures often limit opportunities for involvement. Caught in these cross-currents, individual carers and care receivers between them make sense of their relationships as best they can.

Key points

- The extent to which carer and cared-for become personally involved in the care relationship is a matter of negotiation.

- It is also influenced by the context and by prevailing ideals.

Conclusion

You have seen that meanings are central to care relationships. What goes on between carer and care receiver can be made mutually rewarding or unbearable by the frame of reference within which it is conducted and by the way roles are negotiated within that frame. Opening moves are often critical in getting a relationship on to a good footing. You saw, for example, how Glenda transformed Reg's view of home helps by presenting an open-ended definition of her role, which left room for manoeuvre as Reg's needs and inclinations became clearer. At the other end of the scale you saw auxiliaries in a nursing home making their work manageable by seizing firm control of relationships in the bedroom areas.

Following Goffman's lead, we have explored how meanings are negotiated. In some care situations there are well-established frameworks and 'scripts', as illustrated by the doctor–nurse game. In others, what is an appropriate framework and 'script' is very uncertain, as when Dev Sharma was trying to investigate the knife incident. One key area of difficult meanings in care work is bodily contact. Lawler sees working with people's bodies as central to the meaning of a nurse's role:

> *The identity of 'nurse' ... has multiple meanings ... However, they all centre around the intimacy which nurses have with other people's bodies, sexuality, and the problematic nature of the body in western culture. Within the context of the hospital, the nurse's identity helps to provide access to people's bodies and define otherwise awkward situations as socially permissible ...*

> (Lawler, 1991, p. 217)

Care work gives rise to many debates – how it should be practised, the values it assumes, the safeguards it requires, the terms on which it should be offered. To understand these debates often requires a recognition of the 'constructedness' of care relationships and an understanding of the complexities of the meanings surrounding them. I hope that studying this unit has helped you towards that.

Activity 20

Allow about 15 minutes

Consolidating

As a final consolidation of your work on Unit 4, go back to the core questions on page 192. Spend a few minutes on each question, thinking back over what I have discussed and writing down a few answers as they come to you.

Study skills: Consolidating what you have learned

When you come back to Unit 4 in the future, you will find any thoughts you manage to jot down now extremely useful. They will put you back in touch with what you have just learnt.

Looking ahead to the assignment

Don't forget to have a look at next week's assignment. Writing essays is part of the process of learning what is in the course. Starting your thinking early gives ideas time to mature in your head before you write them out on paper. Also you don't want to be lulled into thinking your week's work finishes at the end of the Unit 5 text.

Making notes

Your final study task for this week is to read Sections 6.1 and 6.2.1 of Chapter 6 of *The Good Study Guide* (pp. 128–136).

References

Armstrong, D. (1983) 'The fabrication of nurse–patient relationships', *Social Science and Medicine*, Vol. 17, No. 8, pp. 457–60.

Campbell, J. and Oliver, M. (1996) *Disability Politics*, Routledge, London.

CCETSW (1995) *Assuring Quality in the Diploma in Social Work – 1, Rules and Requirements for the Diploma in Social Work*, Central Council for Education and Training in Social Work, London.

Goffman, E. (1971) (first published 1959) *The Presentation of Self in Everyday Life*, Penguin, Harmondsworth.

Goffman, E. (1975) *Frame Analysis: An Essay on the Organization of Experience*, Penguin, Harmondsworth.

James, N. (1989) 'Emotional labour: skill and work in the social regulation of feelings', *Sociological Review*, Vol. 37, No. 1, pp. 15–42.

Jones, L.J. (1994) *The Social Context of Health and Health Work*, Macmillan, London.

Jourard, S.M. (1966) 'An exploratory study of body accessibility', *British Journal of Social and Clinical Psychology*, Vol. 5, pp. 221–31.

Lawler, J. (1991) *Behind the Screens: Nursing Somology, and the Problem of Body*, Churchill Livingstone, Edinburgh.

Morse, J.M. (1991) 'Negotiating commitment and involvement in the nurse–patient relationship', *Journal of Advanced Nursing*, Vol. 16, pp. 455–68.

O'Rourke, S. (1994) 'The caring relationship', in Brown, H. and Benson, S. (eds) *A Practical Guide to Working with People with Learning Disabilities: A Handbook for Care Assistants and Support Workers*, Hawker Publications, London.

Stein, L. (1978) *Readings in Sociology of Nursing*, Churchill Livingstone, Edinburgh.

Svensson, R. (1996) 'The interplay between doctors and nurses – a negotiated order perspective', *Sociology of Health and Illness*, Vol. 18, No. 3, pp. 379–98.

Twigg, J. (1997) 'Deconstructing the "Social Bath": help with bathing at home for older and disabled people', *Journal of Social Policy*, Vol. 26, No. 2, pp. 211–32.

Acknowledgements

Grateful acknowledgement is made to the following sources for permission to reproduce material in this unit:

Text

Stein, L. (1978) *Readings in Sociology of Nursing*, Churchill Livingstone.

Illustrations

Figure 1: Jourard, S.M. (1966) 'An exploratory study of body accessibility', *British Journal of Social and Clinical Psychology*, Vol. 5, p. 229, The British Psychological Society; *pp. 189 (left), 213, 217, 229, 232*: Sally Greenhill; *pp. 189 (right), 215, 220, 227, 228*: Sally and Richard Greenhill.

Table

Table 1: Morse, J.M. (1991) 'Negotiating commitment and involvement in the nurse–patient relationship', *Journal of Advanced Nursing*, Vol. 16, Blackwell Science Ltd.

Unit 5
Building Better Relationships

Prepared for the course team by Jan Walmsley
Updated by the author

While you are working on Unit 5, you will need:
- *The Good Study Guide*
- Skills video
- Getting a Vocational Qualification

Contents

Introduction

Unit 5 focuses on:

- introducing the K100 skills video
- relationships
- working with guidelines
- learning from experience
- working with numbers
- writing assignments
- open learning.

You have now reached the last unit in Block 1 and the first of the skills units. Before focusing on what is specific to this unit, I shall explain the purpose of the skills units as a whole and how they relate to the rest of the course.

There is a skills unit in all the blocks, except Block 7. They are rather different from the other units. For one thing, they require less reading and ask you to do more activities. For another, they are about applying what you have already learnt in the block, rather than acquiring more information.

The skills units should take you about six hours to complete, roughly half the time you are expected to spend on the regular units. The rest of your study time in this week is for work on your assignment. Of course, the work you do in the skills unit will contribute to that too.

In what other ways are the skills units different from the other units in K100? They are different because they take practice skills as their focus and allow you to try out some practice skills in simulated situations. They also introduce you to some ideas about good practice and invite you to analyse what goes on in care settings in the light of those ideas.

To consider this in more detail it is useful to introduce the idea of 'competence'.

Someone who does their job well can be called competent. What makes a person really competent in caring? I suggest that there are three elements which, when combined, can make someone competent in caring:

- knowledge
- experience
- values.

Knowledge

Units 1 to 4 have covered some of the *knowledge* about relationships that underpins practice in care settings:

- knowledge about *theories and ideas*, for example Bowlby's ideas on the sorts of relationship which enable young children to thrive, Goffman's theories about how people relate to one another

- knowledge about *policy*, for example how community care policies impact on relationships, what community care assessments are intended to do

- knowledge about *practice*, for example the sort of support informal carers might need, how staff in hospitals work together, how home care assistants actually relate to clients.

Experience

But knowledge alone is not enough. To be competent you also need practical skill, which comes from *experience*. You will know as well as anyone that being in relationships is very different from reading about them. Any student nurse will tell you that theory is one thing but, faced with your first patient, the books do not seem to help at all. In constructing skills, practical experience is as important as knowledge.

Combining knowledge and experience should lead to an ability to think through the challenge of the situation and act accordingly. It should also lead to an ability to learn from experience – reflect on what has gone on and to evaluate – and to use that learning next time you are confronted with a similar situation.

Competence in care, therefore, requires practical skills developed through experience informed or underpinned by knowledge.

Values

However, you know from your work on Block 1 that more than knowledge and experience is necessary. It is also important to have a grounding in the sorts of *values* appropriate to working in health and social care. Think back to Dev Sharma's predicament when confronting Lynne and Arthur after the knife incident (Unit 4, Section 2). As a social worker he needed to bear in mind the social work *value base* to guide his actions. This includes countering discrimination and practising in a manner that does not stigmatise or disadvantage individuals, groups and communities. You read in Unit 4 that this was by no means easy to put into practice in his situation. But without values to guide them, workers can all too easily slide into the sort of behaviour Geraldine Lee-Treweek observed at Cedar Court. As Lee-Treweek's Reader chapter shows, workers can have both the knowledge and the skills, but without values to guide them they may forget that they are dealing with people, not bags of potatoes.

> **Values in professional and vocational training**
>
> The central importance of values alongside practical skill and underpinning knowledge is emphasised in all types of formal training for health and social care workers. To take Vocational Qualifications (VQs) as an example:
>
> *... the value base ... details in clear criteria the principles of good practice on which all interactions with individuals (not only clients but other workers, colleagues, managers etc.) are to be based ... The value base unit ... is an integral part of every qualification ... Every time the candidate undertakes a new qualification s/he will need to demonstrate competence for the value base unit within that particular qualification. (Care Sector Consortium, 1992, p. 1)*

Put more simply, values are at the heart of all care work. It is values which differentiate competence in work with people in care from competence in work with inanimate objects. As VQs have been reviewed and the standard setting bodies have changed, the 'value-base' unit has been replaced by 'value-focused' units. However the initial importance of values has remained with the national occupational standards continuing to be built on principles of good practice.

Competence, therefore, requires a combination of knowledge, practical skills gained through experience, and the ability to work according to a set of values.

Obviously, the Open University is not in a position to decide whether you are competent in the sense of having the requisite knowledge, experience and values. So where do K100 skills units fit? We *can* test your knowledge, through your written work on assignments and exams, but we *cannot* see whether you can use it in practice. Nor can we find out what practical skills you have learnt through experience, or watch you at work to discover whether you can uphold appropriate values. The skills units *will* help you to:

- appreciate how practice can be analysed using guidelines
- develop the skill of observing and assessing other people's practice – the sorts of skills you will need if you are to assess the competence of other people and help them improve
- record what you observe
- build up evidence of what you can do through a portfolio approach to recording 'learning from experience'.

If you want to find out how you can use K100 to contribute to a VQ which *can* testify to your competence, you will find more information in Getting a Vocational Qualification. Look at it now if VQs are your immediate goal. Otherwise, browse through it when you have time.

Key points

- K100 skills units are about applying practice skills.
- Competence requires a combination of knowledge, practical skills gained through experience, and the ability to work according to a set of values.
- All formal professional and vocational training for workers in health and social care puts maintenance of particular values at the heart of training.
- K100 can contribute to vocational qualifications, but cannot by itself offer a route to a vocational qualification.

Working with values: introducing the K100 principles of good practice

Throughout the skills units you will be asked to work with values in mind. However, values can be rather slippery to work with, so we have identified five 'principles of good practice' to help you. You will be working with these throughout the skills units, beginning with this one. The principles are:

- enable people to develop their own potential
- enable people to have a voice and be heard
- respect people's beliefs and preferences
- promote and support people's rights to appropriate services
- respect people's privacy and rights to confidentiality.

These were adapted from the principles of good practice issued by the Care Sector Consortium. At the time the course was first written this was the body responsible for developing Vocational Qualifications in care (Care Sector Consortium, 1997).

In this unit you will practice working with all of these principles. In subsequent skills units you will be focusing on each one in turn.

Working with values: taking account of the context

One criticism that can be made of working with such guidelines is that they have the potential to individualise and isolate the skills an individual possesses, taking them out of context, so that any praise or blame takes account only of the individual's performance. However well intentioned an individual might be, there are often very real constraints. These may be due to legislation, to organisational factors, to shortage of resources, or to the values of the wider society which undervalue certain groups.

Examples of such constraints can be found throughout Block 1.

- **Legal constraints**. The Carers (Recognition and Services) Act 1995 only recognises carers who are making a substantial input, and would probably exclude someone like Lynne; the principles of the Children Act 1989 and the NHS and Community Care Act 1990 place more responsibility for care with families.

- **Organisational constraints**. Good practice in nursing is often constrained by ward routines (the dinner trays arriving just when a depressed patient is ready to talk); clients of home care agencies cannot choose for themselves who their home carer is or when she visits, because lots of other people's needs have to be considered.

- **Resource constraints**. Care managers carrying out assessments have to be mindful of the overall budget, and confine themselves to 'essential needs'. Private care agencies and their employees can provide only as much home care as the purchaser will pay for, regardless of their own assessment of an individual's needs.

- **Undervaluing of some groups in the wider society**. Workers from minority ethnic groups like Dev Sharma routinely experience racism; people with learning disabilities, like Lynne, are denied opportunities which most people take for granted; women are expected to take much of the responsibility for care.

The nursing auxiliaries in Geraldine Lee-Treweek's article are a particularly vivid example of the way these factors interrelate. It would be easy on the basis of the researcher's evidence to cast the auxiliaries in the role of villains or bullies. But this would not take account of the circumstances in which they work – lacking training, short staffed, expected to achieve certain results without the necessary resources. The apparent absence of any supervision or close management of their work, of codes of conduct, of inspection functions might equally be at fault, as might be the way society undervalues older people in residential care. The influence of the law is not obvious, but will indirectly play a part in determining the amount and quality of external monitoring and inspection of homes like Cedar Court.

As you work through the skills units, you will need to bear these sorts of constraint in mind.

Key points

- The K100 five principles of good practice in care were developed from the original Care Sector Consortium's principles of good practice. You will be using them throughout the skills units.

- Maintaining such principles in the face of environmental and organisational constraints can present individuals with considerable challenges.

Central themes of the unit

Having introduced the skills units broadly, it's now time to concentrate on Unit 5. The focus of Unit 5 is relationships. A lot of Block 1 has been about relationships between people in care situations. In this unit you'll be using the K100 principles of good practice as a way of evaluating the quality of care relationships. But, first of all, I am going to ask you to review what you have learnt in Block 1 about care relationships. At several points we have pointed out that relationships in care situations are not just common sense. There is more to it than that.

Activity 1   **Looking at relationships in Block 1**

Allow about 10 minutes   Think back over your work on Block 1. From each unit, select one set of relationships which show that relationships in care situations demand more than common sense.

Comment   Here are some possibilities of the many you could have chosen.

Unit 1 Lynne and Arthur. Just because Lynne was Arthur's daughter it was assumed that she would care for him; but in fact their relationship was tense and unproductive, and Lynne felt oppressed by her caring role.

Unit 2 doctors and nurses. Hierarchies of power and status, and the biomedical model, lead to communication which is often formal and one-sided.

Unit 3 home care assistants and clients. Common-sense ideas of friendship are not enough to guide home care assistants in their relationships with clients.

Unit 4 Lynne and Rita. Rita experienced role conflict in her relationship with Lynne – friend and ally, or representative of the local care services.

This activity shows that you have learnt a good deal about care relationships in Block 1.

In Unit 5 you will look at some care relationships on the skills video. You will then use the principles of good practice to analyse the relationships with a view to identifying how these principles can contribute to improving practice in care relationships.

Unit 5 video content

The skills video is composed of short scripted scenes performed by actors. Before the precise instructions about viewing, here is a brief description of what you will see in the part of the video for Unit 5.

Scene 1 'Care relationships': two sequences in which there is a brief social interaction involving a service user or users and a care worker.

Scene 2 'Bathing': two sequences about bathing a client, the first involving a worker in a residential home and the second an informal carer in a domestic setting.

Scene 3 'In the pub': a short scene in which disabled people are denied access to a pub.

If you are interested in VQs and how the work you do on Unit 5 links to them you'll find details in Getting a Vocational Qualification included with your course materials.

Key points

- The video exercises in Unit 5 are about care relationships.

- The K100 principles of good practice are a useful tool to assist in analysing practice.

- To find out how to link your work on the skills units with VQs, you will need to refer to Getting a Vocational Qualification.

Section 1
Observing care relationships

Now it is time to view the video. It's probably a good idea to view the first part (scenes 1 to 3) straight through first before tackling the activities. Once you have done that, be prepared to watch each scene in detail, rewinding and viewing again as and when you need to for the activities.

1.1 Video scene 1 'Care relationships'

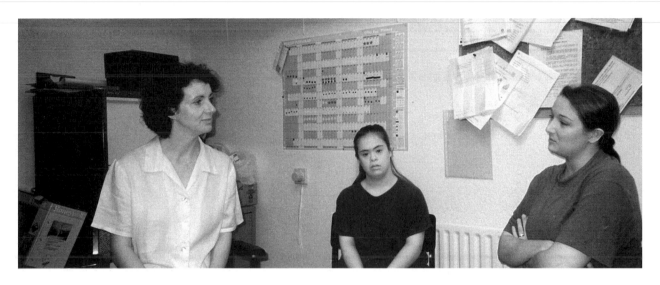

Activity 2 **Observing relationships 1**

Allow about 15 minutes This activity is in two parts.

(a) Play scene 1(a). Then make notes on your observations of the relationship between Julie, the 14-year-old, and Sue, her key worker (on the right).

(b) Now play the sequence again, and use the K100 guidelines to analyse what was good and what was bad about the relationship between Julie and Sue. Do this by completing the grid overleaf. Note down evidence of where Sue upholds the five principles (I'll call this good practice for short) in column 2 and where she doesn't uphold them (poor practice) in column 3.

Sue's relationship with Julie	Evidence of good practice	Evidence of poor practice
Enables Julie to develop own potential		
Enables Julie to have a voice and be heard		
Respects Julie's beliefs and preferences		
Promotes and supports Julie's rights to appropriate services		
Respects Julie's privacy and rights to confidentiality		

Comment   (a)   My immediate response to this sequence was that Sue seemed to know Julie well, for example she confidently answered questions about medication and physical difficulties. On the other hand, she seemed to take over and did not allow Julie to speak for herself.

(b)   I have completed the table opposite. On reflection, and using the guidelines, I could analyse what was going on more objectively.

The relationship	Evidence of good practice	Evidence of poor practice
Enables Julie to develop own potential	Opportunity for Julie to try something new	Missed opportunity for Julie to have an input into arrangements
Enables Julie to have a voice and be heard	No evidence	Julie gets little opportunity to speak
Respects Julie's beliefs and preferences	Good that young disabled people get the chance to go on activity weekends	BUT is it what Julie wants? Would she prefer a weekend in London, for example? No chance for Julie to, for example, choose her own boots
Promotes and supports Julie's rights to appropriate services	This interview is supporting Julie's access to the trip	No evidence
Respects Julie's privacy and rights to confidentiality	No evidence	Rather humiliating for a young woman to have menstruation discussed in public in this way

A manager wanting to give feedback to Sue would find it useful to be able to point to a list as you did in part (b) of the activity, rather than offer feedback which relied on his or her own subjective judgement of what's good and what's bad about a given relationship (as you did in part (a) of the activity).

Activity 3 **Observing relationships 2**

Allow about 10 minutes

Now play scene 1(b). This time jot down your initial comments on the relationships between:

(a) Val and Mrs Brown

(b) Val and Mrs Patel

(c) Mrs Brown and Mrs Patel.

Comment   (a) Val and Mrs Brown seem to know each other quite well. They appear to have an alliance based on their shared culture. Notice their body language. Val appears to be giving Mrs Brown a lead in approaching Mrs Patel.

(b) Val and Mrs Patel are superficially friendly. However, I noticed that Mrs Patel is treated as an exotic object rather than an equal human being. Val peers at the sari, and doesn't listen when Mrs Patel corrects her misapprehension that the sari is complicated to put on.

(c) This is apparently not a close relationship. Mrs Brown has been pulled in by Val to engage in a conversation with Mrs Patel. It seems unlikely she would have done so without Val. I wondered if there would have been any kind of relationship had Val not intervened.

Activity 4   *Observing relationships 3*

Allow about 10 minutes   Now use the guidelines to focus on Val's relationship with Mrs Patel, evaluating her skill in upholding the five principles. Use the grid below.

Val's relationship with Mrs Patel	Evidence of good practice	Evidence of poor practice
Enables Mrs Patel to develop own potential		
Enables Mrs Patel to have a voice and be heard		
Respects Mrs Patel's beliefs and preferences		
Promotes and supports Mrs Patel's rights to appropriate services		
Respects Mrs Patel's privacy and rights to confidentiality		

Comment Our course testers reacted very differently to this activity. For that reason, I have included two examples in the comment.

Example 1: From a white tester with little direct experience of working with people from ethnic minorities

Val's relationship with Mrs Patel	Evidence of good practice	Evidence of poor practice
Enables Mrs Patel to develop own potential	None	Mrs Patel gets no chance to put her point of view
Enables Mrs Patel to have a voice and be heard	Mrs Patel is included	Mrs Patel is not invited to talk about the intricacies of saris
Respects Mrs Patel's beliefs and preferences	Some valuing of Mrs Patel's right to dress differently	Little respect for Mrs Patel as a person
Promotes and supports Mrs Patel's rights to appropriate services	Tries to make Mrs Patel feel at home in the Day Centre	Needs to consider whether this is the most effective way of doing so
Respects Mrs Patel's privacy and rights to confidentiality	No evidence	Rather intrusive comments on matters of a personal nature

Example 2: From a black manager in a residential home

Val's relationship with Mrs Patel	Evidence of good practice	Evidence of poor practice
Enables Mrs Patel to develop own potential	None	Sees her only as a bearer of an exotic culture. No consideration of her as a person
Enables Mrs Patel to have a voice and be heard	None	No one listens to Mrs Patel. She is excluded because she is Asian
Respects Mrs Patel's beliefs and preferences	None	Val is being racist and sexist. Mrs Patel is an object, one who gets dirty and does housework, classic negative stereotyping of an Asian woman
Promotes and supports Mrs Patel's rights to appropriate services	None	Val's actions are more likely to drive Mrs Patel away
Respects Mrs Patel's privacy and rights to confidentiality	None	Very intrusive about matters which are private and personal

These two different reactions from course testers are enough to demonstrate that using guidelines is not a guarantee of consensus. Knowledge, experience and a thorough grounding in value-based work make a difference. The first tester was willing to give Val the benefit of the doubt, imagining she may have good intentions. The second tester, far more experienced and knowledgeable about anti-racism, had no hesitation in condemning this as outright racism. Both did agree, however, that the sequence shows little evidence of good practice. Which of the two analyses was closer to yours? And did the examples influence your views?

Val's manager would have a difficult task in giving feedback to Val on her performance. Now is your chance to think how you would do it.

Activity 5   **Giving feedback**

Allow about 10 minutes   Choose either example 1 or example 2, or use your own answers, and make some notes on the feedback you would give Val in the light of the analysis you chose.

Comment   I chose to use example 2 as I was convinced by the view that Val was being racist. But this made it quite difficult to think where to start. To tell Val she is a racist may be correct, but it is unlikely to encourage her to change. I'd rather start by asking Val what she was trying to achieve by talking to Mrs Patel and if, as I expect, she said she was trying to welcome Mrs Patel, I'd give her approval for that but work through the guidelines with her to show that what she did was not the best way to go about it. Some training which involves role play might be appropriate, to help Val get some insight into how it feels to be the subject of that sort of attention.

I would also encourage Val to consider her relationship with Mrs Brown. Mrs Brown is unlikely to have found the interaction damaging personally; but she and other clients may take a cue from Val in thinking that people from ethnic minorities appreciate being treated as exotic specimens, rather than fellow human beings. I'd want Val to appreciate that she is in a position to give a lead in setting a tone which could be more welcoming to clients from ethnic minorities.

Section 2
Considering the context

You have now had some practice in using the guidelines as you observe care relationships and also as a tool for managers in giving feedback. I kept the task fairly straightforward by focusing on the interpersonal relationships. Scene 2 shifts the focus from individual interactions to the significance of the context.

2.1 Video scene 2 'Bathing'

Take your time in watching the video as often as you need to, replaying as you wish, before tackling the activity.

Activity 6   **The bath in a residential home**

Allow about 5 minutes

After you have watched scene 2(a) jot down your observations of the relationship between Mrs McDonald and Marjorie, bearing in mind the five principles of good practice.

Comment   I noticed that Marjorie failed to listen to Mrs McDonald. This meant she did not respect Mrs McDonald's preferences – she didn't even wait for an answer to her own question. Nor did she enable her to 'have a voice'. She did not promote Mrs McDonald's potential by allowing her to untie her own shoelaces. She did not seem to have much time for privacy either – 'want to go to the lavvie first?' And I wonder what Mrs McDonald made of Mrs Dawson's 'accident'. Maybe she asked herself whether her own lapses might not be the subject of Marjorie's conversation with others – another violation of privacy.

Although the use of terms like 'dear' gives the appearance of a friendly enough interaction, the scene is not evidence of good practice in the light of the guidelines.

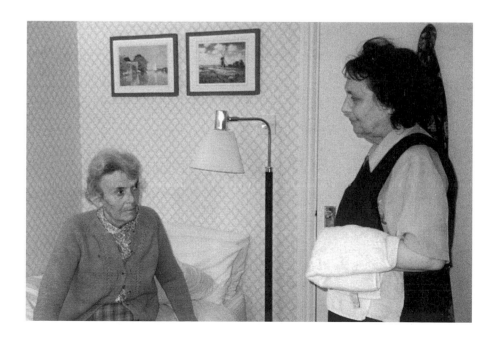

Activity 7   Valuing Marjorie?

Allow about 5 minutes   Now look at it from Marjorie's point of view. Look for evidence that her practice is constrained by the context in which she works. Note down any pointers you find.

Comment   I noted two areas of constraint.

1   Her work routine. Marjorie makes it clear that she is very pushed for time. Her work plan does not seem to allow for 'accidents' like Mrs Dawson's. She did not have time for coffee. She may be unable to afford to wait for Mrs McDonald to fumble with her clothing if she is not to be late for everyone else on her list. It's probably quicker to do it herself. Does she have any time to be listened to herself? Is that why she regales Mrs McDonald with tales of her hectic morning?

2   The awkwardness of intimate body work in care. This was the focus of detailed discussion in Unit 4. It is possible that Marjorie behaves as she does because she wants to normalise a potentially embarrassing situation in which she is clothed and Mrs McDonald naked. Does her matter-of-fact approach mask a sense of awkwardness?

In Block 2 you will be exploring ways in which practice between workers and clients in residential care can be supported through care planning. But, in introducing the whole idea of focusing on the competence of individual workers, I noted the criticism that it may take too little account of the context in which people work. As we look for evidence of poor practice by workers it is also important to ask whether the workplace is conducive to good practice. Workers need to be treated in a way which values them. You could say that the workplace itself needs to be competent if workers are to be able to demonstrate competence to the high standard that users of services should be able to expect.

Activity 8   The bath at home

Allow about 10 minutes   Now play scene 2(b). This is also about a bath, but this time in the home setting. As you watch, make notes on:

(a)   how you react to the scene, your feelings

(b)   what Neil did well

(c)   what Neil did badly.

In answering parts (b) and (c) you might find it helpful to compare Neil's approach with Marjorie's in scene 2(a).

Comment   (a)   Feelings

As a woman in my forties with a teenage son, I have more in common with Sheila and I was more immediately inclined to consider how she might feel. Embarrassment, dismay, yet impressed that my son cared enough to help. I tried to empathise with Neil, too, and thought that he probably shared the feelings of embarrassment and dismay, but that he also felt a strange mixture of love and duty – a wish to express that he cares by being prepared to act.

(b)   What did Neil do well?

•   He acted with certainty, expressed no hesitation.

- He made it clear that he had the time (unlike Marjorie).
- He made it very matter of fact: 'I've got homework to do later' (like Marjorie).
- He used humour to diffuse some of the embarrassment: 'can't have you stinking the place out for a week'.
- He asked Sheila to tell him what to do (unlike Marjorie).

(c) What did Neil do badly?

- He didn't listen to Sheila's protests.
- He tried, like Marjorie, to take over – but unlike Marjorie he learnt from his first mistake.

You were not asked to use the guidelines on this scene. How appropriate do you think it is to impose guidelines devised to assess practice by paid workers (or sometimes volunteers) to relationships between relatives? After all, Neil is unlikely to be giving his mum a bath very often. On the other hand, Neil seems to have instinctively applied some of the five principles here. He manages the situation in a way which gives Sheila some control over how things are done, and maximises her potential to control the way she is undressed.

2.2 Video scene 3 'In the pub'

The next sequence is rather different in that the failure to adhere to the sorts of principle we have been examining is quite blatant. Your task here is to consider how you might act in a situation such as this in a way which upholds the principles of good practice.

Activity 9   **The pub scene**

Allow about 10 minutes   (a) Watch scene 3. Then play it again, putting yourself in the role of the person accompanying the group of people with learning difficulties, and note down your feelings.

(b) Jot down your possible course of action in response to the barman.

(c) Then, using the good practice guidelines, make a note of how they might guide your decision.

Comment (a)   I felt furiously angry. How dare he treat my clients in such a blatantly discriminatory way.

(b)   I noted two possible courses of action:
  (i)   I could act on my feelings to confront the barman immediately, telling him what I thought of him
  (ii) I could try to suppress my feelings, go away and discuss the incident with my group to decide what to do.

(c)   Using the guidelines suggests that going away and discussing possible courses of action is definitely the thing to do. Before I can act, I need to take soundings from people, away from the scene of the incident. If I am to respect my group's choices and preferences, then I need to give them a chance to express them. I will also be fortified if I can ascertain whether the barman has contravened the Disability Discrimination Act 1996. If I can tell the group that what the barman did was illegal, it will strengthen any action we decide to take.

Through the video activities you have been able to explore how guidelines give a yardstick by which to judge the quality of care relationships, and can also be used as a guide to action. You have also begun to consider how the context in which people work influences and constrains what they can do as individuals. What you learnt in Units 1 to 4 has been brought to bear on the skills work you have been doing. This is an important point to remember when considering how relevant to practice is the work you have done as a student of K100: although we have labelled certain units as skills units, the knowledge about theories, policy and practice in the rest of the course is very relevant to what goes on in the real world, and can be used in practice.

Section 3
Acknowledging, reflecting upon and describing your skills

You have now had some practice in using guidelines to evaluate the quality of care relationships. You have also seen the limitations of an approach which focuses solely on an individual's skills without taking into account the wider context in which individuals work.

Now it's time to address the question of how you might use what you have learnt so far in the course to demonstrate what you can do. It's easy to underestimate your own skills. The next few activities encourage you to reflect on your own skills, and describe them in a way which emphasises their transferability to a range of situations.

Activity 10

Identify the job

Allow about 5 minutes

To illustrate the significance of reflecting on what you can do in order to identify your transferable skills, I include a mock job advert in the box below. Read it and then decide what job is being described.

Situation vacant

We require:

A MANAGER

to be responsible for the overall well-being and development of a team of four lively individuals.

The post demands a self-motivated person with drive, ability to cope well under pressure, without supervision, often in a busy and noisy environment for long periods of time.

The successful applicant will be required to:

- perform and co-ordinate, often simultaneously, the duties of supervisor, chef, launderer, secretary and driver
- direct and co-ordinate the activities of the team
- control and allocate its limited budget.

Decision-making and crisis-handling skills are necessary, as is an ability to communicate effectively with external agencies (including tradespeople, and education, medical and public service professionals). Sensitive negotiating skills will be required to ensure harmony within the team.

Comment

This is a job description for a housewife or househusband. The use of terms such as 'negotiating skills', 'supervisor', 'manager' lends an air of competence to what are usually regarded as mundane, everyday things almost anyone does. It shows that there is a knack to describing skills in a way which emphasises their transferability.

As the mock advert shows, how you *describe* skills is significant. In the next box is another set of guidelines on making the most of your transferable skills. These are designed to help you describe your skills in a way which emphasises their transferability to a range of situations.

Making the most of your transferable skills

- Be proud of what you do. Don't say 'I just' or 'I only'.

- Be specific about what you do. Don't use broad terms.

- Describe your skills, not your personality.

- Include the extras.

Activity 11 **Making the most of your transferable skills**

Allow about 10 minutes Now try putting this to use on yourself. Use your role as a K100 student and tick the boxes which apply to you so far in your K100 student role.

Be proud of what you do:
- ❏   I am an undergraduate student on a challenging course which brings together theory and practice in health and social care.

Be specific:
- ❏   I plan my time so that I allocate 12 hours a week to private study in a busy life.
- ❏   I draw on my own experience of health and social care to compare with the course materials.
- ❏   I read and make notes on articles and text.
- ❏   I can take the initiative in seeking out information.
- ❏   I can sort out my ideas on paper and make a strong argument based on evidence.
- ❏   I keep a filing system which I can access for revision purposes.
- ❏   I meet deadlines.

Describe your skills, not your personality:
- ❏   I stay calm when faced with competing demands on my time.
- ❏   I prioritise.
- ❏   I draw upon my knowledge/experience to solve problems.

Include the extras:
- ❏   I take part in group work at the tutorials.
- ❏   I have initiated a self-help arrangement with another student.

Comment How many of these did you think applied to you? Learning how to identify your skills in this way is important for self-esteem as well as for progression in a job or a career. Both our examples, the housewife/husband and your role as a student, illustrate how language can be used to assert a particular view.

So one of the skills we want you to develop is the skill of acknowledging what you can do *and* describing it in language which will be comprehensible to someone who is unfamiliar with you and your experience. If you can confidently say, 'I can sort out my ideas on paper, and make a strong argument based on evidence', you are on the way to developing a skill that is applicable to a huge range of work situations, as well as study. Putting it in this way emphasises its *transferability* to other situations. If you only said, 'I write essays and answer activities', it would be much more confined to the context of study. You'll have a chance to practise this in the next section.

Key points

- Everyone has skills whatever their life and work experience.
- To acknowledge your skills it is important to reflect upon what you can do.
- Skills can be described in ways which emphasise their *transferability* to a wide range of situations.

Section 4
Learning from experience

Now it's time to turn your attention to recording what you have learnt so far from K100 in a form which emphasises your transferable skills. This involves developing a structured approach to analysing what you have learnt from experience.

It's helpful to view learning from experience as a set of stages, as listed in the box. You'll see the emphasis on reflection as in Section 3, but this takes the process further.

Five stages in learning from experience

1   Reflecting on your experiences.

2   Reviewing what you have learnt from your experiences.

3   Identifying your competences.

4   Providing evidence of what you can do.

5   Identifying further learning needs.

(Adapted from Redman, 1994)

You can use this structure to try your hand at recording your own learning from experience in your study diary. Next to each of the stages in the table below is a column containing the imagined responses of one of our video characters, Sue (from scene 1(a)), reflecting on what she learnt from viewing the video of herself at work, with her manager. After they had watched the video and discussed it, Sue's manager pointed out the importance of learning to evaluate your work, and asked Sue to record what she had learnt in a 'reflective diary'.

Sue's reflective diary

Learning from experience stage	
1 **Reflecting on your experiences**	I was so pleased to have arranged the weekend for Julie that I forgot to include her in the planning. I noticed how I talked for Julie, didn't allow her to express any views.
2 **Reviewing what you have learnt from your experiences**	It is not enough to arrange nice things for people, it's the way it's done that's equally important. Maybe it's better to think of planning with them, rather than for them.
3 **Identifying your competences**	Well, I suppose I did do some things well. The session on video was about planning, and that's important. Despite what I did, Julie and I have got a good relationship. She trusts me.

4 Providing evidence of what you can do	There is already evidence of what I can do on the video. When she got back, Julie wrote me a little note to say how much she'd enjoyed herself. That might count as evidence. I'd like a video of myself again, now I've had feedback.
5 Identifying further learning needs	I think it's important to go on a disability awareness course, so I can have a real go at understanding how things done with the best of intentions can actually undermine people's confidence.

Activity 12 Writing a reflective diary

Allow about 20 minutes Now try this exercise on yourself. Choose an experience you have had, either as a K100 student or in your own work in a care setting, and try writing a reflective diary account of what you learnt from it, using the five stages. If you are stuck for ideas, you might try a study skill such as 'skills in reading' or 'getting organised'. Remember that, while you are asked to evaluate yourself honestly, as Sue did, you should also make the most of your skills by describing them in a way to emphasise their transferability.

The following examples might give you some ideas.

Example 1: Learning from Unit 5

Learning from experience stage	
1 Reflecting on your experiences	Observed a number of video scenes of relationships in a care setting.
2 Reviewing what you have learnt from your experiences	Learnt that I need to go beyond my own immediate impressions if I am going to be able to evaluate quality of relationships.
3 Identifying your competences	I practised the following skills: • observation • analysis using guidelines • giving feedback.
4 Providing evidence of what you can do	Notes of activity answers. Assignment marked by tutor.
5 Identifying further learning needs	Look for opportunities to think about upholding these sorts of principles in my relationships with playgroup mums, friends, even family! Find ways of evaluating any progress.

Example 2: K100 study skills

Learning from experience stage	
1 Reflecting on your experiences	I chose note taking from articles. I found this extremely hard at first. I didn't know what I was meant to do, and copied out long chunks.
2 Reviewing what you have learnt from your experiences	I learnt that I needed to read and follow the instructions in the study skills boxes, and take things slowly. I got better at it.
3 Identifying your competences	I can now: • read a chapter and pick out the main points • use a dictionary • ask for help if I need it. I've got a phone link with another student, and that's really useful. I've also got quicker at reading work documents.
4 Providing evidence of what you can do	No problem. I have a file full of notes, and I've got evidence in my study diary of how long it's taken me.
5 Identifying further learning needs	More practice. Re-read *The Good Study Guide* when I get stuck. See how well my work holds up when my first essay comes back.

Now try your own reflective diary account.

> **Key point**
> • Learning from experience involves developing a structured way of reflecting on your skills and describing them.

Section 5
Expanding your horizons: introducing portfolios

This unit has given you some practice at using reflection to identify your skills and describe them in a way to maximise their transferability to a wide variety of situations. I now suggest that you consider developing a portfolio approach to recording and storing your work on K100.

Portfolio

A portfolio is a collection of work that demonstrates an individual's ability and achievements. It can help learners gain accreditation for learning achieved in previous employment and unpaid work as well as from formal training and education.

(The Open University, 1996, p. 45)

Put simply, a portfolio is a collection of documents, video or audio tapes recording individual experiences, ability and achievement. As a result of studying K100 you will be in a position to build a portfolio to show the work you have done on the course. The portfolio could include:

- your tutor-marked assignments

- written responses to activities, such as the last piece of work you will do in this unit, on working with numbers

- your study diary

- your personal file

- your course credit, once you have successfully passed the course, as we trust you will.

However, one of the arts of portfolio building is to make a portfolio work for you. A portfolio containing your written work on K100 will show someone else that you have undertaken the course, but if that person is unfamiliar with K100 you will need to do some additional work to show the *transferability* of your skills. An employer, in contrast to your tutor, is unlikely to want to read all your assignments, but will be interested in your skills and analytic ability. The example of how the imaginary K100 student in Activity 12 analysed his experience of learning how to take notes is relevant here, because in doing so he highlighted two key communication skills – picking out key points from written text, and knowing where to go for help.

What I have suggested here is just to get you started in thinking constructively about building a portfolio. It's important to emphasise that if you are planning to use your portfolio for a particular purpose you will need to take advice on how to present it. For example, if you are working towards a Vocational Qualification, you will need to structure your portfolio with VQ requirements in mind.

However, I do not suggest anything more at this stage than making sure you store your work safely and consider what you have done in the light of your work on transferability of skills.

If and when you are ready to think seriously about using your K100 work for VQs, you will find advice on making use of your portfolio for that purpose in Getting a Vocational Qualification which accompanies your course materials.

Key points

- A portfolio is simply a collection of work that demonstrates an individual's ability and achievements.

- Portfolios can help people gain credit for learning achieved in previous employment and unpaid work as well as from formal training and education.

- If portfolios are to be used for a specific purpose, such as Vocational Qualifications, they need to be structured to meet VQ requirements.

- If you wish, you can consider using your work on K100 for the purpose of Vocational Qualifications now, by turning to Getting a Vocational Qualification. Otherwise, just make sure you store all your work from K100 in a place where it can be easily located.

Section 6
Study skills

6.1 Working with numbers

Units 1 to 3 have introduced you to some basic skills in reading charts and tables. In this section you will consolidate these skills.

Study skills: Reading bar charts

In your studies of caring you will often come across numbers presented in the form of charts of various kinds. In Unit 1 you did an exercise with some pie charts about families. Then in Unit 3 there was a bar chart, but this time with no exercise to help you read it. Did you make yourself stop and read it anyway? If so, were you able to work out what it was telling you? Just in case the answer to either of these questions is no, the next activity is a retrospective exercise to make sure you have a basic grasp of reading a bar chart.

Activity 13   **Reading bar charts**

Allow about 10 minutes   Look back to Figure 1 in Unit 3 and then answer the questions below.

(a)   Is it true that in 1994 less than 2% of the population were 85 years old or over?

(b)   Is it true that in 1994 four million people in the UK were 75 years old or over?

(c)   Is it true that the projected figure for people over 84 halfway through the twenty-first century is over two and a half million?

(d)   Is it true that by the middle of the twenty-first century it is expected that 15% of the population will be 75 or over?

Comment   (a)   If you look at the first bar on the left you will see that it is shaded light blue. The key above tells us that light blue bars show numbers of people 85 or over. At the bottom you can see that this bar is for 1994. So it shows the number of people 85 or over in 1994. Up the side of the chart you can see it says 'percentages'. There are lines ruled across the chart at 2%, 4% and so on. The bar you are looking at on the left reaches to just under the 2% line. So just under 2% of the population were 85 or over in 1994. The answer to question (a) is therefore 'yes'.

(b)   Now you need to look at the other bar for 1994, in other words the darker one next to the one you have just been looking at. This time you are looking for the number instead of the percentage. The figure at the top of the bar is 3,965, but if you look at the bottom of the chart you will see that the numbers shown are 'thousands', so that figure is 3,965,000. In words this is three million, nine hundred and sixty-five thousand. This is not quite four million. So strictly the answer to question (b) is 'no'. But it's very close to four million and if you were giving a rough figure, four million is a suitable approximation (just as £3.95 can be conveniently thought of as £4.00). So a reasonable answer to question (b) would be 'yes'.

(c)   For halfway through the twenty-first century the bars we want are the ones for 2051 on the right. But the question says 84 instead of 85. That's all right – over 84 means the same as 85+. (Think about it.) If you look at the light bar, you will see that the figure at the top is 2,768 thousand, that is, 2,768,000. Is this over two and a half million? Yes, it's two and three-quarter million. So the answer is 'yes'.

(d)   Now look at the dark bar for 2051. It reaches nearly to 14%. So 14% would be a fair estimate for the proportion of the population aged 75 or over. The answer to question (d) is 'no' (but it's not far off).

You will get some more practice in reading charts in Unit 6. Now we switch to reading tables.

Study skills: Reading tables

In Unit 2 you did an exercise with a table of numbers about people's perceptions of health. Shortly you will build on that work by looking at two more tables and then completing the number work section of your Block 1 assignment. But first this is a good point at which to get some ideas on table reading from *The Good Study Guide*. Read Sections 8.1 to 8.4 of Chapter 8 now (pp. 191–207). When you have done that and worked through the following activities, you will be able to tackle Part 3 of TMA 01.

Unit 1 made brief mention of children who are taken into state care. But how many children does this involve? And are the figures changing? Without getting too bogged down in numbers, we can get an idea by looking at some statistics for one part of the UK – in this case we'll take Northern Ireland.

Table 1   Number of children in care of health and social services boards in Northern Ireland

	1986	1989	1992	1995
Boarded out	1,313	1,540	1,621	1,660
In statutory homes	333	312	261	206
In voluntary homes	144	123	124	111
In other accommodation	787	808	654	647
All children	2,577	2,783	2,660	2,624

(Source: adapted from Northern Ireland Statistics and Research Agency, 1997, Table 3.18)

Activity 14 Reading tables 1

Allow about 10 minutes

(a) What years does Table 1 cover?

(b) Find the figure 1,313 at the top left of the main table. Try writing a sentence to say what it tells us.

(c) Taking the most recent year, roughly how many children in Northern Ireland were in care?

(d) Looking at the changes over the years, is the total number of children in care rising or falling?

(e) Do most children in care live in state-run homes?

Comment

(a) If you look at the top of the first column you will see 1986. And at the top of the last column you see 1995. So the table covers the years 1986 to 1995. The gaps between columns are three years.

(b) If you look above 1,313 you can see that this figure is for the year 1986. If you look to the left you can see it is the figure for children boarded out. So my sentence is: 'In Northern Ireland in 1986, one thousand, three hundred and thirteen children were boarded out.'

(c) The most recent year is 1995 – the column on the right. To find the number of children in care you need to look at the row for 'All children' – the bottom row. The bottom figure in the right-hand column is 2,624. But the question said 'roughly how many'. So instead of 'two thousand, six hundred and twenty-four', we could say: 'About 2,600 children were in care in Northern Ireland in 1995'.

(d) You can see that the figure rose from 2,577 in 1986 to 2,783 in 1989. But since then it has fallen back to 2,660 and then 2,624, which is not much above the 1986 figure. So, if we only had the first and the last figure to go on we might say that the number of children in care has risen slightly. However, we know from the other figures that there was a rise in the middle of the period.

(e) No, only about 200 were in state run homes in 1995, out of a total of about 2,600 children in care. (If you divide both figures by 200, you can see that about 1 in every 13 children in care was in a statutory home.)

But is 2,600 a large proportion of the children in Northern Ireland? To find out we can look at population figures for Northern Ireland.

Table 2 Population of Northern Ireland

	1981	1991	1995
Under 20 years	558,400	513,000	514,600
Total population	1,532,200	1,577,800	1,649,000

(Source: Northern Ireland Statistics and Research Agency, 1997, Table 1.2)

Activity 15 Reading tables 2

Allow about 5 minutes

(a) Roughly how many under-20s were there in Northern Ireland in 1995?

(b) What roughly was the population of Northern Ireland in 1981?

(c) Is the population rising?

(d) Is the number of children rising?

Comment

(a) Looking along the row for the under-20s, until you reach 1995, you find 514,600. I would say that in 1995 there were a little over five hundred thousand under-20s – or about half a million.

(b) The figure for the total population in 1981 is 1,532,200. This is just over one million five hundred thousand. I would say the population of Northern Ireland in 1981 was about one and a half million (roughly one million over 20 and half a million under 20).

(c) Yes. You can see a steady increase in the total population from around 1.53 million to 1.65 million. (I rounded 1.532 down to 1.53 and I rounded 1.649 up to 1.65.)

(d) No. Although the population is rising, the number of under-20s has gone down from about 558,000 to about 515,000.

Comparing the two tables, you can see that in 1995 the total number of children in care in Northern Ireland was about two and a half thousand – out of a total of about five hundred thousand under 20s. (If you divide out the thousands you get about two and a half children in every five hundred. If you double both those figures you can see that about 5 children in every 1,000 are in care.)

I hope you can follow all this work with numbers. If you take it slowly and, where necessary, go back over things again, you should be able to cope with it. If not, try asking someone you know to help you through it. If that doesn't work, your tutor will be able to help. You should now be able to do Part 3 of TMA 01 quite easily.

6.2 Writing assignments

The course assignments are much more than an exercise at the end of each block to check what you have learnt (although they do serve that purpose). Essays in particular are probably the part of the course where you *learn* most intensively.

Study skills: Learning through writing

Writing essays makes you bring new ideas and information together in your head in a such a way as to make some kind of sense to you. And by putting these thoughts into words you make the new ideas your own – not just something you have 'memorised' to pass a test, but knowledge you can *use* for your own purposes. At the same time you learn to 'speak the language' of the subject area.

At the end of a course, and indeed some years later, the essays you have written often turn out to be what you remember best. They make a lasting impression on your ways of thinking about the world.

Study skills: The challenge of writing

Because you learn so much through the writing, essays present quite a challenge. So if you find them difficult, don't worry that there's something wrong. Thinking deeply and finding the right words are both hard work, but they are also the essence of learning. So treat the assignments with respect by building yourself up towards them. Yet don't let yourself get weighed down by them. Start your thinking early by looking at the assignment a week or two ahead. Expect the preparation and planning to take at least as long as the actual writing. Be sure to allow enough writing time to do yourself justice. And try to arrange matters so that you do not have to write the whole essay in one session. The quality will improve if you can come back and rework what you have written. The assignments are far more than a last-minute chore. Think of them as a key learning opportunity, deserving of serious time and energy.

Finally, do be sure to get assignments off to your tutor by the deadlines. Don't wait to get them perfect. Few people think they have done very well at the moment of finishing an assignment. You just have to do your best in the time available and then let it go. Often you will find you have done better than you think. But in any case it is important to be able put it behind you and move on to the next block of work.

You will be given plenty of advice on how to tackle essays in the Assignment Book and in *The Good Study Guide*. Also, your tutor will try to help you with your writing as much as with your understanding of the course. In fact, one of the major objectives of this course is that you should consider yourself to be a much better assignment writer by the end (and that is regardless of how strong or weak you may feel now). Looking back, you may feel that the writing aspect was the part of the course from which you gained most.

Study skills: What makes a good essay?

You will be writing an essay every four weeks. But are you clear what you should be aiming for in your essays? Your tutor's comments on your practice assignment provide one source of insight. Another source is Chapter 10 of *The Good Study Guide*, 'Writing the way "they" want'. Read Sections 10.1 to 10.3 now (pp. 245–262). It will be excellent preparation for working on Part 1 of your assignment. (It should take about an hour.)

6.3 Open learning

You have reached the end of the first K100 block. You have been studying as an independent student working from an open-learning text. How have you found it?

Courses based on open-learning texts are becoming increasingly popular. Instead of listening to lectures – struggling to keep your attention focused and to take down all the relevant points – you move forward at your own pace, staying with each new idea until you have hold of it and are ready to move on to the next. What is more, you can come back as often as you want, to check points again. And you don't have to take mountains of illegible notes; you just write your own ideas on to the texts as you read. Also, a course planned in detail in advance can be tightly structured, so that you don't waste time and effort. You can be given all the information you need, but only what you need. Texts, audio cassettes, videos and activities are carefully co-ordinated, to give consistent and coherent development of ideas and information.

Healthcare connections

K100 is very relevant to the work of all healthcare professionals. Already in Block 1 you have been introduced to important themes relating to healthcare which continue throughout the course.

Values

The five K100 principles of good practice express values that underpin healthcare work. They provide a benchmark against which to deliver clients' needs. You can also use them as a tool to aid reflective practice.

Perceptions and meanings

Unit 2 focuses on healthcare and discusses differing concepts of health. Understanding how perceptions of health and healthcare may vary provides insight into the experiences of your patients, their priorities, hopes and fears, and also ways in which their needs can be met (see also Reader Chapter 6 and Chapter 30).

The biomedical model: the medicalisation of care

Unit 2 discusses how the biomedical model focuses on diagnosis, treatment and cure. Within this model the roles of professionals tend to be sharply defined: e.g. the doctor as 'The Great I Am', as illustrated in the audio cassette 'A Day in the Life of a Hospital Ward'.

Where there is no cure, healthcare workers can support people in managing a chronic condition (Reader Chapter 13) by adopting a more social and holistic model of care, focusing on the patient's needs within the social setting.

Doyal's chapter, The New Obstetrics (Reader Chapter 14), introduces a theme relevant to all healthcare professionals – the tension between the needs of patients and the needs of workers.

Roles and relationships

Unit 3 describes how care within the community has been transformed, shifting the boundaries between healthcare and social care and the roles of healthcare workers. The new emphasis on market forces and management affects both patients and ways of working within the healthcare team.

In Unit 4 Goffman's model of relationships, based on 'roles' and 'scripts', helps to explain the inequalities of power that can arise between healthcare workers and between workers and clients.

Lawler's chapter (Reader 26) shows how the roles of healthcare workers require them to step outside social norms such as when washing naked bodies.

Unit 4 also discusses the emotional labour required in playing healthcare roles.

Portfolios and transferable skills

Unit 5 gives guidance on how to compile a portfolio. Healthcare workers can use portfolios to present evidence of transferable skills, for example, observation skills, or oral and written communication skills.

Social work connections

K100 explores various themes that are central to social work.

Values

In Block 1 you were introduced to the five K100 principles of good practice, which express the values underpinning ethical and anti-oppressive practice in health and social care. These are very similar to the values of social work. As the five K100 principles of good practice are discussed throughout the course, think how they relate to the Value Requirements of the DipSW.

The family

In Unit 1 it becomes clear that most care takes place within the family. You also saw how the nature of families is changing. Social workers often work with families and, as the example of Dev Sharma illustrates, this can mean managing complex situations, sometimes involving competing rights and interests.

Attachment theory

Unit 1 looks at attachment theory as originally developed by John Bowlby. Although his earlier ideas were criticised and later significantly revised, his theory is now very influential in social work in helping to understand the behaviour of both children and adults and the relationships between them.

Biomedical model

Social work has a long history of working in multi-disciplinary settings, but in recent times the boundary between health and social care has become more diffuse. It is important that social workers understand the biomedical model of care, as it is still very influential in health settings and is to some extent at odds with the social model that social work promotes.

Community care

The changes associated with the shift towards community care have had a huge impact on both the work and the role of social workers. Much of the task for social workers with adults is now supporting people with high care needs so that they can remain in the community. Social workers are often care managers, purchasing care rather than delivering it directly.

Boundaries

A recurring theme throughout Block 1 is the need for professional boundaries. Residential social workers can be involved in providing intimate care, while field social workers often have to enter the private home world of the individual and the family. It is therefore very important that social workers understand the importance of professional boundaries and how to maintain them in often difficult circumstances, such as you saw in the skills video. Erving Goffman's model understood relationships and boundaries in terms of the scripts and roles that can be played out. This is a useful framework for social workers to help make sense of these complex issues.

Children and young people: connections

Care and the family

Unit 1 introduces key debates about the nature of care and about the close connection between families and care roles and responsibilities. You saw how the involvement of families in the care of children is both a private and a public matter. You also saw that children, such as Katrina, can themselves be carers within families. Because young carers tend to be invisible at the public level, they are more common than is generally realised, raising issues about the nature of 'childhood' and whether taking on a major carer identity compromises a young person's status as a 'child'.

Bowlby and attachment theory

Some theories have had a profound impact on the ways we see children and families and on the services provided for them. Bowlby's 1950s writing and Rutter's modifications of Bowlby in the 1970s and 1980s continue to resonate as the meaning and implications of 'attachment theory' are propounded and challenged by parents, carers, service providers and policy makers.

Family diversity and change

Unit 1 looks at how families have changed over the years and at the diversity of the modern family. It also shows how the meaning of 'family' changes over time, as do ideas about what a 'normal family' looks like. And as these images of 'normality' shift some families can find themselves positioned as inadequate or even unhealthy.

Care standards

Unit 3 discusses the 2001 establishment of the General Social Care Council and the introduction of the first nationally agreed standards in the form of a code of conduct for social care staff. This will have major implications for social work with children and young people.

Goffman

The complex negotiation of meaning in care contexts is something everyone working with children and young people needs to be aware of and Goffman's model of social interactions offers key insights. It also helps us understand how dominant definitions of what it means to be disabled, to be gay, or to be a child are 'socially constructed'. This understanding is crucial to the development of policies and practices that shape the lives of children and young people.

References

Care Sector Consortium (1992) *Care Awards*, Local Government Management Board, London.

Care Sector Consortium (1997) *Review of the Care Sector Awards: Values and Principles of Good Practice and their Implementation*, CCS, London.

Northern Ireland Statistics and Research Agency (1997) *Northern Ireland Annual Abstract of Statistics*, No. 15, HMSO, London.

The Open University (1996) K503 *Learning Disability: Working as Equal People, Building Your Portfolio*, The Open University, Milton Keynes.

Redman, W. (1994) *Portfolio for Development: A Guide for Trainers and Managers*, Kogan Page, London.